Teachers' Perceptions, Experience and Learning

Teachers' Perceptions, Experience and Learning offers insightful views on the understanding of the role of teachers and the impact of their thinking and practice. The articles presented in this book illustrate the influence of teachers on student learning, school culture and their own professional identity and growth as well as highlighting challenges and constraints in pre- and in-service teacher education programmes that can impact teachers' own learning.

The first article examined teacher experiences in the use of "design thinking" by Retna. Next, Hong's and Youngs' article looks into contradictory effects of the new national curriculum in South Korea. Lu, Wang, Ma, Clarke and Collins explored Chinese teachers' commitment to being a cooperating teacher for rural practicum placements. Kainzbauer and Hunt investigate foreign university teachers' experiences and perceptions in teaching graduate schools in Thailand. On inclusive education in Singapore, Yeo, Chong, Neihart and Huan examined teachers' first-hand experiences with inclusion; while Poon, Ng, Wong and Kaur study teachers' perceptions of factors associated with inclusive education. The book ends with two articles on teacher preparation by Hardman, Stoff, Aung and Elliott who examined the pedagogical practices of mathematics teaching in primary schools in Myanmar, and Zein who focuses on teacher learning by examining the adequacy of pre-service education in Indonesia for preparing primary school English teachers.

The contributing authors' rich perspectives in different educational, geographical and socio-cultural contexts would serve as a valuable resource for policy makers, educational leaders, individual researchers and practitioners who are involved in teacher education research and policy.

This book was originally published as a special issue of the *Asia Pacific Journal of Education*.

Woon Chia Liu, PhD is Associate Professor with the Psychological Studies Academic Group at the National Institute of Education (NIE), Nanyang Technological University (NTU), Singapore, and a founding member of NIE's Motivation in Educational Research Laboratory. She holds a concurrent appointment as Dean of Teacher Education and is involved in Singapore's preservice teacher preparation programmes. She is currently the co-editor of the *Asia Pacific Journal of Education* and *Pedagogies: An International Journal.*

Christine C. M. Goh, PhD, is Professor of Linguistics and Language Education at the National Institute of Education, Nanyang Technological University (NTU), Singapore. She is a qualified secondary school English teacher, a teacher educator, and a researcher with a strong interest in the interface between linguistic theories and language education. She holds a concurrent appointment as Dean of Graduate Studies and Professional Learning and she is involved in the strategic initiatives for teacher continuing education in Singapore. She was an elected member of the NTU Senate and is currently a member of the NTU Advisory Board. She is currently the co-editor of the *Asia Pacific Journal of Education* and *Pedagogies: An International Journal.*

Teachers' Perceptions, Experience and Learning

Edited by
Woon Chia Liu and Christine C. M. Goh

LONDON AND NEW YORK

First published 2018
by Routledge
2 Park Square, Milton Park, Abingdon, Oxon, OX14 4RN, UK

and by Routledge
711 Third Avenue, New York, NY 10017, USA

Routledge is an imprint of the Taylor & Francis Group, an informa business

© 2018 National Institute of Education, Singapore

All rights reserved. No part of this book may be reprinted or reproduced
or utilised in any form or by any electronic, mechanical, or other means,
now known or hereafter invented, including photocopying and recording,
or in any information storage or retrieval system, without permission in
writing from the publishers.

Trademark notice: Product or corporate names may be trademarks or
registered trademarks, and are used only for identification and
explanation without intent to infringe.

British Library Cataloguing in Publication Data
A catalogue record for this book is available from the British Library

ISBN 13: 978-0-8153-8728-2

Typeset in Times New Roman
by RefineCatch Limited, Bungay, Suffolk

Publisher's Note
The publisher accepts responsibility for any inconsistencies that may have
arisen during the conversion of this book from journal articles to book chapters,
namely the possible inclusion of journal terminology.

Disclaimer
Every effort has been made to contact copyright holders for their permission to
reprint material in this book. The publishers would be grateful to hear from any
copyright holder who is not here acknowledged and will undertake to rectify
any errors or omissions in future editions of this book.

Contents

Citation Information	vii
Notes on Contributors	ix

Introduction: Teachers' perceptions, experience, and learning   1
Woon Chia Liu and Christine C. M. Goh

1. Thinking about "design thinking": a study of teacher experiences   4
Kala S. Retna

2. Why are teachers afraid of curricular autonomy? Contradictory effects of
the new national curriculum in South Korea   19
Won-Pyo Hong and Peter Youngs

3. Exploring Chinese teachers' commitment to being a cooperating teacher
in a university-government-school initiative for rural practicum placements   33
Lijie Lu, Fang Wang, Yunpeng Ma, Anthony Clarke and John Collins

4. Meeting the challenges of teaching in a different cultural environment –
evidence from graduate management schools in Thailand   55
Astrid Kainzbauer and Brian Hunt

5. Teachers' experience with inclusive education in Singapore   68
Lay See Yeo, Wan Har Chong, Maureen F. Neihart and Vivien S. Huan

6. Factors associated with staff perceptions towards inclusive education in
Singapore   83
Kenneth K. Poon, Zijia Ng, Meng Ee Wong and Sarinajit Kaur

7. Developing pedagogical practices in Myanmar primary schools: possibilities
and constraints   97
Frank Hardman, Christian Stoff, Wan Aung and Louise Elliott

8. Pre-service education for primary school English teachers in Indonesia:
policy implications   118
Subhan Zein

Index   135

Citation Information

The chapters in this book were originally published in the *Asia Pacific Journal of Education*, volume 36, issue S1 (May 2016). When citing this material, please use the original page numbering for each article, as follows:

Editorial
Teachers' perceptions, experience, and learning
Liu Woon Chia and Christine C. M. Goh
Asia Pacific Journal of Education, volume 36, issue S1 (May 2016), pp. 1–4

Chapter 1
Thinking about "design thinking": a study of teacher experiences
Kala S. Retna
Asia Pacific Journal of Education, volume 36, issue S1 (May 2016), pp. 5–19

Chapter 2
Why are teachers afraid of curricular autonomy? Contradictory effects of the new national curriculum in South Korea
Won-Pyo Hong and Peter Youngs
Asia Pacific Journal of Education, volume 36, issue S1 (May 2016), pp. 20–33

Chapter 3
Exploring Chinese teachers' commitment to being a cooperating teacher in a university-government-school initiative for rural practicum placements
Lu Lijie, Wang Fang, Ma Yunpeng, Anthony Clarke and John Collins
Asia Pacific Journal of Education, volume 36, issue S1 (May 2016), pp. 34–55

Chapter 4
Meeting the challenges of teaching in a different cultural environment – evidence from graduate management schools in Thailand
Astrid Kainzbauer and Brian Hunt
Asia Pacific Journal of Education, volume 36, issue S1 (May 2016), pp. 56–68

Chapter 5
Teachers' experience with inclusive education in Singapore
Lay See Yeo, Wan Har Chong, Maureen F. Neihart and Vivien S. Huan
Asia Pacific Journal of Education, volume 36, issue S1 (May 2016), pp. 69–83

CITATION INFORMATION

Chapter 6
Factors associated with staff perceptions towards inclusive education in Singapore
Kenneth K. Poon, Zijia Ng, Meng Ee Wong and Sarinajit Kaur
Asia Pacific Journal of Education, volume 36, issue S1 (May 2016), pp. 84–97

Chapter 7
Developing pedagogical practices in Myanmar primary schools: possibilities and constraints
Frank Hardman, Christian Stoff, Wan Aung and Louise Elliott
Asia Pacific Journal of Education, volume 36, issue S1 (May 2016), pp. 98–118

Chapter 8
Pre-service education for primary school English teachers in Indonesia: policy implications
Subhan Zein
Asia Pacific Journal of Education, volume 36, issue S1 (May 2016), pp. 119–134

For any permission-related enquiries please visit:
http://www.tandfonline.com/page/help/permissions

Notes on Contributors

Wan Aung works with UNICEF in Myanmar.

Woon Chia Liu, PhD is Associate Professor with the Psychological Studies Academic Group at the National Institute of Education, Nanyang Technological University, Singapore.

Wan Har Chong is Associate Professor at the National Institute of Education, Nanyang Technological University, Singapore.

Anthony Clarke is Professor at the Faculty of Education, University of British Columbia, Canada.

John Collins was Adjunct Professor in the Faculty of Education, University of British Columbia, Canada.

Louise Elliott is based at the Institute for Effective Education, University of York, UK.

Christine C. M. Goh, PhD, is Professor of Linguistics and Language Education at the National Institute of Education, Nanyang Technological University, Singapore.

Frank Hardman is based at the Institute for Effective Education, University of York, UK.

Won-Pyo Hong is based at the College of Sciences in Education, Yonsei University, Seoul, Korea.

Vivien S. Huan is Associate Professor at the National Institute of Education, Nanyang Technological University, Singapore.

Brian Hunt is based at the College of Management, Mahidol University, Bangkok, Thailand.

Astrid Kainzbauer is Assistant Professor at the College of Management, Mahidol University, Bangkok, Thailand.

Sarinajit Kaur is a Teaching Fellow at the National Institute of Education, Nanyang Technological University, Singapore.

Lijie Lu is based at the Faculty of Education, Northeast Normal University, China.

Yunpeng Ma is based at the Faculty of Education, Northeast Normal University, China.

Maureen F. Neihart is Associate Professor at the National Institute of Education, Nanyang Technological University, Singapore.

NOTES ON CONTRIBUTORS

Zijia Ng is based at the National Institute of Education, Nanyang Technological University, Singapore.

Kenneth K. Poon is Associate Professor at the National Institute of Education, Nanyang Technological University, Singapore.

Kala S. Retna is Senior Lecturer at the School of Management, Victoria University of Wellington, Wellington, New Zealand.

Christian Stoff works for UNICEF in Myanmar.

Fang Wang is based at the Faculty of Foreign Languages, Northeast Normal University, China.

Meng Ee Wong is Associate Professor at the National Institute of Education, Nanyang Technological University, Singapore.

Lay See Yeo is Associate Professor at the National Institute of Education, Nanyang Technological University, Singapore.

Peter Youngs is Professor at the CISE Department/Curry School of Education, University of Virginia, USA.

Subhan Zein is based at the School of Language Studies, The Australian National University, Canberra, Australia.

INTRODUCTION

Teachers' perceptions, experience, and learning

Woon Chia Liu and Christine C. M. Goh

Much has been said about the need for individuals to cultivate various competencies in order to succeed in the new century. These include cognitive competencies (such as critical thinking, reasoning and argumentation, decision making and creative thinking), intrapersonal competencies (such as intellectual openness with an appreciation for diversity, and metacognitive skills such as planning and self-reflection), as well as interpersonal competencies (such as leadership, empathy and the ability to collaborate and work in teams) (see Pellegrino & Hilton, 2012). To deal with different facets of challenges in increasingly complex environments, individuals also need other twenty-first century competencies that include new forms of thinking: big picture, inter-disciplinary, simulation, design, and computational forms of reasoning. In developing these competencies, teachers play a critical role. They have to embed these educational goals into the curricula they teach, and to do their job well, teachers need to be aware of their own perceptions and beliefs, feel that they are supported to carry out their plans and goals, and have the motivation to develop new pedagogies to improve their practice (e.g., Liu & Tan, 2015; Tan, 2003).

What and how teachers think about their work and the programmes that support their learning can have powerful implications for the system they work in, as the collection of 8 articles in this issue demonstrates. These articles centre on the theme of teachers' perceptions, experience, and learning. Although different in educational, geographical, and socio-cultural contexts, these articles collectively illustrate the influence of teachers on student learning, school culture, and their own professional identity and growth, as well as highlighting challenges and constraints in pre- and in-service teacher education programmes that can impact teachers' own learning.

The first article by Retna examined teachers' perceptions, experiences, and challenges in the use of design thinking in a Singapore school. The findings showed that teachers perceived design thinking to have the potential for helping students develop important twenty-first century skills. For it to be implemented successfully, however, teachers would need to address a number of challenges arising from their own ability to change the way they have been teaching and thinking about the goals of student learning. They would also need resources and time to carry out this initiative well. Related to this issue of teachers implementing change and innovations, Hong and Youngs examined the effects of a new national curriculum in South Korea that was intended to grant more autonomy to individual schools and teachers. Contrary to the general belief that teachers welcomed greater autonomy and flexibility in customizing curricula to meet students' needs, the participating teachers did not take positively to their new-found curricular autonomy and were even doubtful that such efforts would diversify the school curriculum. Factors contributing to such perceptions were identified and discussed. In another study of teacher perceptions in the context of innovations, Lu, Wang, Ma, Clarke and Collins investigated Chinese teachers' commitment to being a cooperating teacher for rural practicum placements under a University-Government-School (UGS) initiative. The results in this study were also compared with the responses of supervising teachers in three other countries. The researchers found that the Chinese teachers were more highly motivated as a result of positive perceptions of what the scheme enabled them to do in learning from the students as well as enhancing the quality of their supervision.

Teacher experiences and perceptions were examined from a cultural angle in a study in Thailand by Kainzbauer and Hunt. They gathered information about the efforts of foreign university teachers in learning about and demonstrating cultural sensitivity in graduate management schools. The authors identified five aspects of Thai culture which the teachers felt they needed in order to expand or adapt their existing repertoires. Although these aspects are specific to Thai culture, the discussion of cultural intelligence will find resonance in teacher experiences in other countries and for those interested in inter-cultural communication.

Two articles on inclusive education in Singapore are also featured in this issue. In the first article by Yeo, Chong, Neihart, and Huan, teachers' first-hand experiences with inclusion were examined. The authors documented two broad clusters of teachers' positive and negative experiences. Specifically, the most salient positive experiences were satisfaction with pupils' progress and new learning for teachers, while the most dominant negative experience was stress experienced from challenging behaviours and instructional activities for catering adequately for the diverse needs within a classroom. In the other article, Poon, Ng, Wong, and Kaur, collected information using an instrument that measured teachers' perceptions of factors associated with inclusive education. They reported that teachers had neutral attitudes and that inclusive perceptions were predicted by teachers' confidence in teaching, while other factors, such as experience and level of training special educational needs support, accounted for a large proportion of the variance in ratings of inclusive perceptions. The findings from both articles affirmed the importance of teacher preparation and support for their role.

The final two articles in this collection focus on wider issues of teacher preparation in different areas and contexts. Hardman, Stoff, Aung, and Elliott examined the pedagogical practices of Mathematics teaching in primary schools in Myanmar. They reported the use of a transmission model of teaching where information and content ("recipe knowledge") was transmitted to pupils for recall. The authors applied insights from the study to propose reforms to the designs of teacher education programmes in order to improve the quality of teaching and learning in the country. Likewise, Zein focused on teacher learning by examining the adequacy of pre-service education in Indonesia for preparing primary school English teachers to meet the demands of English learning in an age of globalization. He further focused on factors contributing to the efficacy or the lack thereof in such programmes and offers insights for improvements.

The articles in this collection provide interesting cases for a more detailed understanding of the role of teachers and the impact of their thinking and practice. Generally, scholars agree that one way of strengthening professionalism in teaching is to prepare teachers well, give them the tools and time to do their job, and support and empower them to carry out their responsibilities well (Liu & Tan, 2015; Weingarten, 2010). This entails quality teacher education and a high level of professional standard. Amongst other things, teachers need to undergo rigorous preparation so that they have good content mastery, and develop a deep understanding of their learners along with a strong understanding of and skills for teaching (e.g., Darling-Hammond & Bransford, 2005). They also need to develop the values, knowledge, and skills to nurture every learner they interact with (Tan, Liu, & Low, 2012). In addition, teachers need to feel supported and empowered within the school system to believe that they can make a difference. They also need to have the autonomy to make decisions about teaching and learning in the classroom (Adedoyin, 2012; Muijs & Harris, 2003).

It is also important that teachers see themselves embodying new roles beyond the traditional one of transmitters of information or authoritative conveyors of knowledge. Education scholars have suggested that teachers play multiple roles: facilitators, architects, guides, tutors, counsellors, instructors, and models. Similarly, new learning environments require students themselves to wear a whole range of "hats": searchers, partners, designers, explorers, investigators, thinkers, clients, subjects, memorizers, and trainees (Cheng, 2012). This wider range of roles and dynamics provide space for higher order learning, where students become less passive and more initiated as teachers choose to play less didactic and more facilitative roles in the learning process.

It is our hope that the selected articles for this themed issue of "Teachers' Perceptions, Experience, and Learning" will offer powerful reflections of many of these ideas and that the constraints and challenges discussed by the authors will also serve as a much needed reminder that for good ideas to take root and grow, realities experienced on the ground have to be anticipated and addressed.

References

Adedoyin, O. (2012). The significance of teacher empowerment as related to teaching effectiveness within the school system: Perceptions of pre-service teachers in Botswana. *National Teacher Education Journal, 5*(4), 95–100.

Cheng, Y. C. (2012). Teachers for new learning: Reform and paradigm shift for the future. In O. S. Tan (Ed.), *Teacher education frontiers: International perspectives on policy and practice for building new teacher competencies* (pp. 93–121). Singapore: Cengage Learning Asia.

Darling-Hammond, L., & Bransford, J. (Eds.). (2005). *Preparing teachers for a changing world: What teachers should learn and be able to do*. San Francisco, CA: Jossey-Bass.

Liu, W. C., & Tan, O. S. (2015). Teacher effectiveness: Beyond results and accountability. In O. S. Tan & W. C. Liu (Eds.), *Teacher effectiveness: Capacity building in a complex learning era* (pp. 335–345). Singapore: Cengage Learning Asia.

Muijs, D., & Harris, A. (2003). Teacher leadership – improvement through empowerment: An overview of the literature. *Educational Management Administration Leadership, 31*(4), 437–448.

Pellegrino, J. W., & Hilton, M. (Eds.). (2012). *Education for life and work: Developing transferable knowledge and skills in the 21st century*. Washington, DC: The National Academies Press.

Tan, O. S. (2003). *Problem-based learniing innovation*. Singapore: Thomson.

Tan, O. S., Liu, W. C., & Low, E. L. (2012). Educational reforms and teacher education innovations in Singapore. In O. S. Tan (Ed.), *Teacher education frontiers: International perspectives on policy and practice for building new teacher competencies* (pp. 71–91). Singapore: Cengage Learning Asia.

Weingarten, R. (2010). A new path forward: Four approaches to quality teaching and better schools. *American Educator, Spring*, 36–39.

Thinking about "design thinking": a study of teacher experiences

Kala S. Retna

Schools are continuously looking for new ways of enhancing student learning to equip students with skills that would enable them to cope with twenty-first century demands. One promising approach focuses on design thinking. This study examines teacher's perceptions, experiences and challenges faced in adopting design thinking. There is a lack of empirical research on the adoption and implementation of the design thinking process in educational context from the teachers' point of view. This paper fills this gap and also provides insight on a recent initiative adopted in Singapore schools. Qualitative case study research was carried out in a school using teacher narratives. Data includes in-depth face-to-face interviews and participant observation. The findings show that teachers perceive that design thinking holds the potential for enhancing skills such as creativity, problem solving, communication and team work as well as empower students to develop empathy for others within and beyond the community. The research also highlighted several challenges such as inadequate resources, time constraints, fear of poor grades and the difficulty of shifting to a new way of teaching and learning that differs vastly from the traditional approach. The findings reveal that a piecemeal approach towards curriculum redesign for adopting design thinking may not provide the desired outcomes.

Introduction

Over the years, organizations have proactively sought and embraced strategies and techniques that put them in a good stead to compete in the changing, globalizing, digitalized world (Fraser, 2007; Stegall, 2006). "Design thinking" is considered as one of the most promising ways of transforming organizations and businesses in a competitive environment (Gloppen, 2009). Though design thinking has a long history in the fields of architecture and engineering, over the last two decades several organizations outside the field of design, such as those in education and information technology, have attempted to understand how designers think and work and, as a result, have understood its value (Bell, 2008; Brown, 2009; Kimbell, 2011; Martin, 2009). Using a case study of a public school in Singapore, this research seeks to understand the perception that teachers have of design thinking and its implementation. Singapore provides an excellent context to study the implementation of design thinking since its educational system is centrally-structured and coherent. Singapore is also an early adopter of new initiatives, so this case study can provide useful insights into the practical implementation of design thinking. Last but not least, Singapore shares attributes and challenges with a wide range of countries, but its differences are readily identifiable. Accordingly, it provides a microcosm from which lessons can be drawn.

Different types of design practice have spawned across various sectors and it is now considered an effective way for organizations to provide excellent products and services (for example see, Parker & Heapy, 2006; Verganti, 2009). In focusing on the educational context, several studies have been interested in the educational benefits for students when schools adopt design thinking (Philloton & Miller, 2011). Yet, there has been less examination of teachers' experience and perspectives in implementing design thinking, whether in a specific subject or in the overall curriculum. Teachers are key players in education as they are directly involved in adopting and implementing the process of design thinking in the classroom. Accordingly, this study examines to understand the perceptions that teachers have of design thinking including its benefits and challenges in Singapore's context. The findings show that teachers perceive that design thinking holds the potential for enhancing skills such as creativity, problem solving, communication and team work as well as empower students to develop empathy for others within and beyond the community.

The paper is structured as follows. First an overview of the literature on design thinking and its application in non-design organizations is provided. This is followed by a discussion of design thinking in schools, specifically the literature on its benefits for students. Subsequently, the paper outlines the methodology followed by the findings. Altogether, the study demonstrates that the implementation of design thinking in schools has both its benefits and its challenges.

Literature on design thinking and organization

The interest in design thinking for non-design organizations can be attributed to researchers (Rittle & Webber, 1973; Simon, 1973) who identified strategies used in design to address "ill-structured" problems. Particularly, design strategies that helped detect ill-structured problems were used to initiate changes in organizations. Designs that permeated through the nineteenth and twentieth century was based on enhancing material environment. However, the twenty-first century saw a paradigm shift from material to human aspects (user experiences and relationships). This shift of mindset to understand and interact with various stakeholders in the process of creating products or service was evident in various sectors such as law, health and education. The on-going interaction between end users (customers) and those involved in the production of goods and services underlies the essence of design thinking. Argyris and Schon (1978) claim that all actions by people is design. Related to this note, it is evident that design thinking is not a new concept (Lockwood, 2009; Wong, 2011). It has been around from the time design was used by engineers and architects. However, it was David Kelly, the founder of IDEO and Stanford's "d.school", who popularized design thinking in the business and education context (McCullagh, 2010; Gloppen, 2009).

The development of design thinking has been attributed to management publications such as the *The Art of Innovation, The Tipping Point, A Whole New Mind and Creative Confidence*. These books have served as stepping stones for understanding the basic principles and application of design thinking. Yet, why is there a resurgence of interest in design thinking even though it has been in existence for many decades? It is evident from the literature that the important theme in the emerging interest in design thinking is its claim of being a new way of thinking that is underpinned by the humanistic approach towards generating new ideas, services and products. This is because, historically, designers' involvement was very much directed towards packaging, that is, they did not have much engagement or contribution towards the creation of products. Nevertheless, design played a crucial role in market growth, especially in the electronics and consumer packaged industries. Not only did design make new products attractive through advertisement and communication, it was considered to be a competitive asset by businesses. However, this situation changed towards the later part of the twentieth century when the role of design changed from one that made developed products attractive to one that created new ideas for products and services. It required a fundamental shift from seeing design as just "styling" to one of the core "activity", crucial across all sectors and to the economy (Lee, 2011). One of the key aspects in this change-over was that of paying specific attention to human needs, the need of users of products or services. In order to do this, several theorists (for example, Martin, 2009) have put some processes in place that focus on customer needs.

Defining design thinking

Design thinking is interpreted by theorists in various ways. Lockwood (2009) refers to design thinking as an application of using designers' sensibility and methods on problem solving. He has emphasized that design thinking must be viewed as a methodology and not a substitute for the professional craft of designing (2009, p. xi). Moreover, it is a way to explore the unmet needs of customers and to come up with new solutions. According to Liedtka (2011), design thinking is a process that requires continuous redesigning of a business, taking customers' views and insights into consideration. It is basically an approach in examining the process and the business model of innovation (p. 13). Simon (1996) defined design thinking as the changing of existing conditions to preferred ones. This is explained as using designers' way of thinking and methods to create new ideas or alternatives to meet the stakeholders' needs. Here the essence of design thinking is considered to be abductive reasoning, not deductive or inductive alone. Moreover, he distinguishes traditional management thinking from design thinking in that the latter needs specifically three skills: cognitive, affective, and interpersonal. Furthermore, the main argument against traditional management thinking is the attitude of treating "constraints" as a barrier for implementation. He does caution users of design thinking that it is a rigorous process but a good pathway for approaching problems (Simon, 1996). According to Pink (2005), design thinking is a frame of mind for problem solving that is essential for the "conceptual age" where creativity and innovation are key contributors to higher productivity. Last but not least, Martin (2012) defines design thinking as one that involves both analytical and intuitive thinking.

The definitions above show that design thinking requires a distinct way of approaching and solving problems that entails a systematic process in order to achieve the desired outcomes. Understanding and meeting the users' needs, a different way of thinking and innovation are the perceived outcomes of design thinking. Based on these definitions, innovation can take place in many forms such as service, product, behavioural and organizational culture through the practice of design thinking. Altogether, design thinking can be regarded as a thoughtful process and organizations could benefit from using design thinking to stay ahead in a competitive environment (Clark & Smith, 2008).

Design thinking in schools

Schools are continually looking for new ways of enhancing student learning and equipping students with skills that would enable them to cope with twenty-first century demands. One particularly promising approach is to utilize design thinking. Proponents argue that students must be nurtured to think like designers (particularly those who are involved in doing project-based work in schools), as it will enhance creativity among students and help them understand the process of innovation (Brown, 2008; Martin, 2009).

Clearly few pedagogical ideas are completely new or unique, and many aspects of design thinking echo concepts that have been advocated over the past century, particularly in the constructivist perspective. Maria Montessori, with her emphasis on student-centred discovery of knowledge, would have recognized an affinity with this approach. For instance, the Urban Montessori Charter School in Oakland, California, explicitly utilizes design thinking (http://www.urbanmontessori.org/design_thinking). There are also similarities with the problem-solving approach that was espoused by the educational theorist John Dewey (1910). According to Dewey, students learned most effectively by doing and the concept of experience plays an important role in learning (Dewey, 1938). Dewey's concept of problem-solving is still popular and is used in schools in project work. However, Dewey's work has been critiqued for abstractness of its recommendations on assessing performance. Design thinking surmounts the abstractness problem by being a human-centred process that offers opportunities for concrete recommendations for complex problems (Scheer, Noweski, & Meinel, 2012). It promotes the learning of social skills and solving problems to meet the "needs" of people. The focus is on people, and their articulated problems requiring solutions, rather than on abstract problems that exist independently of the social milieu.

According to Anderson (2012), design thinking skills are important for future workplaces in terms of innovative contributions. Increasingly, schools are adopting design thinking into their curricula and therefore understanding the distinct experiences of teachers becomes important. Research has shown that using design thinking as the basis for a pedagogical framework in schools is reaping positive benefits. Barseghian (2010) reported such work in North Carolina and stated that design thinking offers an "antidote" to the traditional method of teaching that is practised in most district schools. The practice of design thinking has achieved significant improvements in terms of overall students qualifying for state standards (Philloton & Miller, 2011). In another example, Krieger (2010) has successfully introduced design thinking in schools in India and Mexico. Some schools have used design thinking in specific subjects like science (Kolodner et al., 2003), mathematics (Goldman, Knudsen, & Latvala, 1998), technology (Kafai & Resnick, 1996) and religious studies (Tan & Wong, 2012). These studies have indicated that design thinking has the potential to enhance skills such as creativity and problem solving which also help students to build on their cognitive and social skills (Todd, 1999). These studies have reported on the educational benefits for students, but there has been less examination of teachers' experiences and perspectives in implementing design thinking. This study seeks to understand the perceptions of teachers in understanding design thinking and its benefits and challenges in the educational context.

Method

The main aim of this study was to understand teachers' perceptions of using design thinking as an approach to teaching. For teachers in this study, design thinking was a new concept or a new teaching strategy aimed at enhancing creativity among students. Since detailed experiences in a particular context were important for understanding teachers' perceptions and the challenges they faced, a case study approach was undertaken. Case study research is viewed as an important form of qualitative inquiry in qualitative research (Cassell & Symon, 1994) that enables thick description and interpretation (Denzin &

Lincoln, 2000; Stake, 1995). According to Eisenhardt (1989) a case study should be used when little is known about the phenomenon. This approach allowed for multiple sources of information such as interviews, observations and documents for data collection and analysis (Creswell, 2007). Stake (2000, p. 448) aptly summarized "the purpose of a case report is not to represent the world, but to represent the case". Hence, the truth claims are limited to generating new insights.

A Singapore school provides an interesting and internationally relevant case study of the implementation of design thinking because Singapore in general is an early adopter of organizational developments (Retna & Ng, 2006). Moreover, education is highly prized and schools are very competitive (Luo, Luo, Paris, & Hogan, 2011). This means that schools in Singapore are more liable than those in most other countries to seize upon new initiatives and implement them vigorously in order to differentiate themselves from the competition. The case organization in this research is a public secondary school in Singapore that has implemented design thinking for two years. The students are in secondary one and two classes, and are aged between 13 and 14 years.

Semi-structured interviews were the primary source of data collection in this study which aimed to explore the perceptions, views and opinions in a "natural language" (Easterby-Smith, Thorpe, & Jackson, 2007, p. 142). Furthermore, qualitative interviews enable one to not only gain an understanding of participants' perspectives but also to explore the reasons or rationales for their specific viewpoints on particular issues (King, 2004). Face-to-face interviews lasting approximately an hour each were conducted with 16 teachers at the school. The interviews allowed reflection on participants' experiences of being trained in the design process and how it shaped their teaching in the classroom. An interview guide derived from the literature and from the objectives of the study was used to gather information about their viewpoints on three key areas. Firstly, they were asked about their understanding of the design thinking initiative and the importance of it in schools. For example, questions included: What do you understand of Design Thinking? Why is it important to integrate it in your teaching? This was followed by questions of their involvement in the initiative and the types of processes that were introduced in the school. The final question asked about the benefits and challenges faced in using design thinking for teaching and learning.

All interviews were recorded and transcribed. Besides these interviews, I also attended students' presentations on projects that involved design thinking. These sessions added more insights to the inquiry. Audio visual material that captured the school's vision and design thinking initiatives were made available by the school and they contributed to the analysis. The transcripts were read closely and the main themes were identified. This was followed by the coding process: categorizing, sorting data, separating, labelling and also adding the notes taken during the interviews, student informal conversations and school brochures/audio visual material on design thinking in the school. The data from the various sources were analysed using Constas' (1992) category process development approach which focuses on the combination of views from literature and the study.

Findings and discussions

In the following sections a number of issues are discussed. These include teachers' perceptions and understanding of design thinking, and their experience in integrating it into some subjects. In addition, the benefits, such as creativity and developing empathy within and beyond the community, are explored as are some of the challenges, such as resource and time constraints, and the difficulty in shifting from the traditional to a new way of teaching and learning.

Educators' interpretation of design thinking

Since design thinking originated in traditional design, it has gained currency among different professional disciplines as an approach to deal with problems (Brooks, 2010). So, it is important to clarify what it means when it is adopted in a discipline that differs from its origination. This is because different professions are inclined to view or interpret things according to how they make sense of it (Goodwin, 1994). As such, it was important to identify in this research how educators define design thinking in a school context. The discussion on their understanding of design thinking indicated a general understanding by all the participants. Design thinking was characterized as a process that enables students to solve problems, generate creative ideas and come up with solutions that meet the needs of people. The core message they communicated was that design thinking was a humanistic approach of solving problems. Though their responses did not carry a cohesive definition, they included the core elements of design thinking and its process. This does not come as a surprise as there is yet no consensus among academics and business writers on a clear definition (Lawson, 2006; Lockwood, 2009; Martin, 2009). Overall, the findings suggest that the majority of the teachers had some formal knowledge of design thinking before they used it in the classroom, having been trained by design thinking experts at Stanford University. Subsequently, they attended several in-house training sessions that enabled them to integrate design thinking into their curriculum and teaching. However, there were strong indications from all participants throughout the interviews that design thinking is a "unique" and a "different" approach compared to the usual teaching practices. The following quote is an example of a typical interpretation of design thinking from a participant:

> Design thinking is a process that helps us to be more mindful of people's needs and to come up with solutions that really help to meet their needs. It is a powerful process because it teaches us to understand peoples' feeling about things they need and value.

Other teachers expressed their thoughts on design thinking in a way that resonates with the emphasis on needs and feelings in the above comment:

> It is a process. It involves five phases: empathy, define, ideate, prototype and test. I like the 'empathy' part of the process because it teaches us to link to other peoples' needs and realities. It is good for our students because it makes them think about what other people need.

> Basically it has a lot to do with phases. It is not a text book kind of approach. It connects students to 'real' people. Students learn the true meaning of understanding other peoples' needs through the empathy phase.

Most of the participants in this research emphasized and repeated the word "empathy" throughout the interviews as they felt that students in general have been nurtured to think for themselves. Though "empathy" is only one of the steps involved in the design thinking process, teachers and students found this specific aspect very beneficial for the development of skills that is important for personal growth. This is supported by key proponents; for example, Anderson (2012, p. 46) claims that design thinking helps to foster empathy and a "deeper understanding" of others (Brown, 2008; McDonagh & Thomas, 2010). Along this line of thought, there were strong statements by some participants who expressed their concern that students in this "generation" represent an "'I' thinking culture", "it is always me first" and "everything is about me". This suggests that one of the reasons behind teachers' attraction to "empathy" is the intention to effect behavioural changes among students.

Design thinking versus traditional thinking

Design thinking requires integrative thinking (Martin, 2009). This includes both mindset and specific techniques and skills that nurture creative thinking. The driver behind introducing design thinking in the school was summed up by a participant as "to change our students' mindset of traditional thinking". A number of participants pointed out that the twenty-first century needs different ways of thinking and skills for students to cope with future demands, and so the school wanted to address the challenge through design thinking, as explained by one of the senior teachers:

> Design thinking offers skills for our students to meet twenty-first century skills. I think it is good that my school is trying design thinking. From my experience, design thinking is very powerful in getting our students to think differently. It makes them think a lot to come up with new ideas.

While all participants approved integrating design thinking into project work and other academic subjects like biology, the majority of them felt that design thinking was a "real" challenge because of the profile of the students. Some participants commented that design thinking could be more effectively introduced in top-achieving schools. One participant explicitly said:

> If design thinking is introduced in Raffles Institution, it will work wonders. The students there are 'high grade' students. It will fit them well. Our school is so different but maybe the 'higher end' classes should be involved rather than doing it [design thinking] with everyone in the school.

These quotes and other comments (for example, "we are only a neighbourhood school" and "our students are from the normal stream") suggest that the teachers consider design thinking more appropriate for students with high academic excellence. This conflicts with some research that claims that design thinking can be applied across schools irrespective of scholastic status (Razzouk & Shute, 2012). The teachers in this school were vocal proponents of design thinking and this may suggest that they have thought that their students are "not good enough" for this approach. Nevertheless, they acknowledged that design thinking had the potential to nurture creative and critical thinking in their students. This ambivalence may be a reflection of the realities faced by practising teachers (with limited time and resources), in utilizing a system which places greater demands on students, and hence on them as teachers, than more conventional methods. They felt that it was not an easy task and some reasons for the difficulty surfaced during the interviews:

> I gave my students very little [brief] information about the project and expected them to do the research and come up with ideas and questions. Some questioned me and said that it is not the same type of learning and wasted a lot of their time to search for information before they can start the project.

Another teacher also expressed her concern:

> Even though we have conducted seminar for the students on design thinking and have given them a demonstration, they still prefer the old style of learning. Most of my students like design thinking but they say that they cannot afford the time. They prefer to spend more time on studying other subjects than researching and doing activities that is required in the process.

A specific concern that came up repeatedly throughout the interviews was the fear of not getting good grades when using the design thinking approach. For example:

Most of the students asked two main questions during the process: is this going to come out in the examination? Is this important for examination? Their focus is learning for examination. I have to assure them and tell them not to worry throughout the process. This mindset has to change.

The participants' concern seems legitimate in that teacher and students are concerned with the final outcome that is the academic result, which is of top priority in Singapore. This concern is prevalent in Singapore schools where results play an important role in ranking the students and schools. According to participants, at that stage, they were not able to make students see the connection between design thinking, learning and results. Despite this fear and inhibitions, the majority of the participants claimed to have a moderate success among students who employed design thinking in their project work. Furthermore, they were positive and contended that the students have picked up skills such as interviewing and analysing information from adopting the process. However, several of the participants made the point that the process was excessively time-consuming and that this affected students' preparation for examinations. This conflict between the ideals of "real education" and the demands of measurement (i.e., examinations) is a common one, not confined to design thinking, or to Singapore. It can be argued that the realization of the gap between what is espoused in design thinking process and what happens in practice can enable teachers to let go of rigid teaching methods. In doing so, they realize one of the challenges for students and themselves. Nevertheless, the tension between academic results, as measured by examinations and the idea that design thinking is a time-consuming process must be acknowledged. Singapore's education system is well known for its focus for "academic results" (Hogan, 2010, p. 2; Ng, 2008, p. 13). Any new approach, such as design thinking, will be subject to the culture that strives to achieve high examination results. It is interesting to note that participants recognize this constraint, yet are motivated to experiment and learn new pedagogy for enhancing student learning. It also raises the issue of whether the examinations themselves need to be reformed so that they more accurately measure the outputs the new pedagogies are trying to achieve.

Altogether, it is not merely a matter of modifying the process but also requires a major shift in the thinking of teachers and stakeholders. Design thinking along with advanced pedagogical ideas in general, also presents a challenge to education policy makers in Singapore. The current system is examination-oriented and privileges the acquisition and display of conventional information. Design thinking, with its emphasis on creativity, is somewhat subversive in this context. Educational policy needs to address this contradiction.

Integration of design thinking with course content

The literature shows that design thinking could be employed across disciplines and in schools. Brown (2009, p. 37) claims that design thinking has become important, necessary for continuous improvement and innovation, and is not for designers only. Design thinking methods and processes can also be applicable to managing change (Dunne & Martin, 2006; Liedtka, 2000). Some researchers (for example see, Bourdieu, Accardo, Balazs, Beaud, & Bonvin, 1999) claim that design has a distinct way of thinking and practice and can be transferred to any other professional domain. In this research, the question of how design thinking was applied in teaching and learning was responded to with enthusiasm. For example, a teacher explained that a project was given to the students whereby they were required to solve a community issue related to elderly people. Students had to use the five steps: empathy, define, ideate, prototype and test. As this was the first project that involved the design thinking process, the participants were equally as excited as the students. Despite such enthusiasm and excitement, two learning constraints were consistently identified: student inexperience with real life problems and with research. One teacher stated:

> My secondary one students are not used to dealing with 'real' issues. They come from a system of finding correct answers. So, when they had to go out to the community to speak to people, they were afraid whether the answers they get from people are right or wrong.

Other participants described their experiences:

> Doing research and getting a lot of information is part of the design thinking process. My students did not know what is relevant because there is so much of information they find in Google. Each time I meet the group they will ask me whether their information is right or wrong for the project. A lot of time was required in coaching them.

> Students are good at gathering information through various websites for their research. They spent a lot of time but not sure about what is important or relevant for their project. Because of this, I have to put in lots of time in guiding them.

While the teachers acknowledged the demands made by the students in facilitating the process, most of the participants were empathetic by commenting that as students moved from primary to secondary schools, it was difficult for them to shift from books to research and interaction with people to learn about the needs of the community. Furthermore, some participants emphasized that though students struggled with some of the steps, they appreciated the experience of understanding issues at a deeper level. A few of the participants also stated that as a result of students' exposure to the real world issues, they were able to come up with various ideas and view the issue at hand from different perspectives. This was further elaborated by a teacher:

> I can see the change in my students. They showed empathy for people. This made them think more and more for ideas that can meet people's needs.

The comments on students discomfort with brain-storming were also relevant:

> They dislike thinking, brainstorming or going back and forth about ideas. Sometimes, they could not think of anything. Worse still, they come up with the same set of solutions that they have come up with earlier. This is a challenge I think for teachers who use design thinking.

Two themes emerged. On the one hand, the findings point towards the development of creative ideas, confidence and empathy for end users. This aligns with some studies (for example, Brown, 2008) that suggest the design thinking process helps students to develop creative ideas and confidence. Furthermore, design thinking is a humanistic approach and its strength lies in understanding the end users' needs (Martin, 2009). On the other hand, findings showed the difficulties teachers undergo to nurture a culture of creative thinking in a school. This cannot be achieved solely by a design thinking approach. It appears that participants are using the stages as prescribed or taught during their training on design thinking but they need to go beyond that mechanical application. It is essential for educators to create activities that teach or promote the fundamental mindset for creative thinking.

Another feature of the design thinking process that teachers' perceived to be very useful is prototyping. Prototyping is a process where one gets an opportunity to convey an idea through simple models, sketches or cardboards. The majority of the participants indicated that prototyping has been very well-received by students as it allowed them to experiment and fail at an early stage and then recover from that. The realization that they will not be punished if the prototype did not turn out as expected acts as a form of encouragement to further improve and learn from the mistakes. According to some teachers prototyping is a good way to expose students to experimentation. For example:

> It is fun and interesting for my students. They do mistakes but they don't worry. They are not scared if they fail. In prototyping they become confident about the project and the solutions and look forward to test it out.

> Students thought design thinking is pretty fun. They like the interaction and chit-chats during prototyping. They feel excited in testing it out.

Overall, based on the interpretations, it can be assumed that the practice of design thinking involves a major shift in the teaching and learning process and it poses challenges for teachers during its implementation.

Challenges perceived by teachers

Introducing a new model, concept or approach to educational practice raises issues that affect teachers, students and all stakeholders who contribute to teaching and learning in schools. In this research, several challenges were identified. First, changing the mindset of students was considered to be the most difficult challenge among the majority of participants. This is because there is a difference between design thinking and the traditional approach of teaching and learning. Participants expressed their views as follows:

> Currently our students expect us to know everything and have answers to questions. At each stage, they want straight-forward answers. They are used to depending on teachers for answers. But the design thinking process wants them to think and come up with an answer.

> Design thinking is an experimental approach. It is a way of approach allowing students to explore new things on their own. This is difficult for our students because they are used to getting the right answer from teacher.

Design thinking requires students to think and consider a problem from different perspectives. Also, in design thinking there are no right or wrong answers but a solution that meets the users' needs. It was evident from the findings that the traditional mindset of students put a demand on teachers to drive the process of design thinking.

Second, another challenge faced by participants is the issue of team work among students. Fostering collaboration is an essential part of the process. However, several participants were concerned that students were not being able to collaborate and work as a team. The general feeling among the teachers was captured by a teacher:

> The biggest challenge was for them to work with people whom they do not know. This is particularly true for secondary one [first year] students. When they get members whom they don't like, they complain and we have to do a lot of de-conflicting. It is not the actual work itself but de-conflicting that makes the whole thing difficult for students to move on.

This quote shows the importance of team dynamics and the problems associated in handling members working as a team. The conflict among students could be understood from the point that the students in the first year of secondary education are new to the school, classmates and school culture. In effect, they are in a transition from primary to secondary education. Though some teachers empathized with the situation, they claimed that design thinking seeks to promote collaborative and cooperative behaviour and skills and therefore it is important for students to understand the value of teamwork.

Third, the issue of class size was another point of challenge for the participants. Class size is an important indicator for teaching and learning effectiveness. Several researches

TEACHERS' PERCEPTIONS, EXPERIENCE AND LEARNING

assert that a small size classroom is effective for promoting interactive learning. The size in the school is 40 students with two teachers. Most of the participants found two teachers insufficient and argued for more staff. As explained by a participant:

> It would be good if we can have four teachers so that the groups can be broken down to 10. It will be so much easier to facilitate. It will allow us to be a good guide and facilitator at individual and group level. But now with manpower shortage it would be pretty hard but the perfect scenario for students to learn the process properly would be four teachers in a class.

The above quote and comments such as "design thinking is a guided process", "it is very student oriented", "a process that needs close supervision", and "students need more guidance and feedback" indicate that classroom size matters, especially when it differs from the traditional method of doing project work. Most of participants strongly felt that more resources (teachers) must be involved if design thinking is to be effectively integrated into their daily teaching practices.

Fourth, all participants claimed that design thinking was not possible or useful across all subjects and disciplines. Some participants expressed that from their own and other teachers' experiences, design thinking to some extent has proven to be useful for project work, design and technology and co-curricular activities projects. Others reported that they had used it in only one topic (e.g., in biology or geography). In contrast, two other participants said that they had tried but could not apply the approach of design thinking. For example:

> I teach Maths. It is very difficult to use design thinking. In Maths – A plus A is just 2A. There is nothing about design thinking that changes that. I am not forced to do it but encouraged to think and try design thinking in my subject [Mathematics].

Given this reaction to the application of design thinking, on one hand we find mixed messages and feelings as "good technique", "good for problem solving", "useful to generate great ideas", and on the another hand we find, "it is only for some subjects", "of limited use for certain subjects", and "difficult to change the whole curriculum". This suggests that participants were receptive to the design thinking process and understand its benefits but strongly felt that the integration of design thinking into the entire curriculum was near impossible.

The final challenge that emerged in this research was the physical resources in terms of a room that is conducive for the design thinking process. It was clear from the findings that a room was allocated specifically for design thinking in the initial stage of implementation. However, in the following year this room was not available because of shortage of rooms for other teaching purposes. Most of the participants felt that it would be good to have facilities and resources that promote learning. This is summarized in the following statements:

> We need a room like the one we saw when we attended our training in Stanford. The design thinking rooms they have and the resources, equipment does create the kind of environment we need for design thinking. After we came back we all became excited and was hoping to have a room like that. Until now we have not materialized it.

> We do have a room for design thinking – a project room. But it is hard to do project work for students like the way we saw in Stanford. The school must provide proper facilities to teachers and students to do design thinking like the way they do in Stanford.

The above quotes and other discussions on resources suggest that participants were disappointed that they could not have facilities similar to those available in Stanford. They were impressed by the facility and expected something similar in the school. One participant commented that "there was no budget constraint" and expressed their hope for an improved version of the current classroom in future. This signals the importance of providing a conducive environment for adopting design thinking process. However, a point to note is that design thinking originates from designers and they perform their work in studios. Thus, ideas on modification of facilities need to be carefully considered.

Conclusion

Design thinking is a process that promotes teaching and learning of important skills that are required for the twenty-first century. Although the principles of design thinking have been recognized in the educational context, teachers' experience and perspectives in implementing design thinking has been overlooked. To address this issue, this paper aimed at understanding the perceptions of teachers of design thinking and its benefits. This paper found that most participants considered design thinking to be a "unique" and "different" approach relative to traditional teaching methods. The need to develop empathy as a key skill in design thinking resonated with both teachers and students. Participants perceived the implementation of design thinking to be very advanced for most students, and believed that it would work best in top-achieving schools. They often found their students lacked the necessary experience to engage with the real life problems posed by design thinking, and that a culture of creative thinking needed to be nurtured. To this end, they found the prototyping aspect of design thinking was well-received by students as it allowed them to experiment and fail at an early stage, and thus learn from recoverable mistakes.

This paper also examined the challenges of implementing design thinking in a school and the complexity of its practice. It found that the most significant challenge was students' reluctance to change their mindsets to the new way of thinking. As Singaporean schools and their students are highly geared toward maximizing examination results, participants struggled to convince their students that design thinking, with its creative emphasis, would not distract from the traditional focus on acquiring the information needed to gain good grades. Indeed, despite being proponents of design thinking, participants often found it too time-consuming as it undermined students' preparation for their examinations. This study also found that the teamwork aspect of design thinking posed another challenge for students, and that participants spent a lot of time "de-conflicting". Another challenge reported by participants was an insufficient teacher-to-student ratio in implementing what is an intensive, guided process, and thus they argued for more resourcing in the form of teachers. Furthermore, it was also found that design thinking was not considered by participants to be universally applicable to all aspects of the curriculum, and that participants felt the need for more physical resources in the form of rooms that were conducive to the design thinking process.

This paper concludes that to implement design thinking, and to realize the benefits it can bring, education policy makers must give thorough consideration to curriculum redesign and the modification of the process according to subjects and disciplines. It is important to fully understand how design thinking can benefit students and how the integration of design thinking into various subjects can help students develop thinking skills for the future. But for this to happen, adequate resources must be provided and that includes time for teachers and students to develop the appropriate mindset needed for design thinking. The findings of this study could be beneficial to those schools that are implementing design thinking or proposing to do so. The study adds to both the literature on design thinking and that of educational management. The paper therefore concludes that transporting a concept from the field of design to education calls for a radical change, not only in curricula and pedagogy but also through a major shift in the modes of thinking and behaviour of teachers and students and this has resource implications which must be addressed. The cultural context of the educational system must be also considered in the implementation. The principles of design thinking offer considerable benefits to an education system seeking to equip students with the skills they need now and into the future, but addressing the issues of implementation are crucial if these benefits are to be realized.

The study has its limitations. Though it intended to include every teacher who was involved in using design thinking in their subjects, this was not possible as the research took place during the national examinations period (and thus only 80% of the teachers who were involved participated). The study was exploratory and its purpose was to focus on teachers' perceptions and their challenges they faced in implementing design thinking. Thus, the research does not claim to address the nuances of the design thinking process. Nevertheless, the study shows that design thinking could prove beneficial for students and teachers taking into consideration the challenges discussed. Future research could focus on students' experiences of design thinking. Also, the research could expand to explore teachers' and students' perceptions across various schools and compare national contexts.

References

Anderson, N. (2012). Design thinking: Employing an effective multidisciplinary pedagogical framework to foster creativity and innovation in rural and remote education. *Australian and International Journal of Rural Education*, 22(2), 43–52.

Argyris, C., & Schon, D. (1978). *Organizational learning: A theory of action perspective*. Reading, MA: Addison-Wesley.

Barseghian, E. (2010). *Design thinking sparks learning in rural North Carolina*. Retrieved from http://blogs.kqed.org/mindshift/2010/11/design-thinking-sparks-learning-in-rural-n-carolina/

Bell, J. S. (2008). Design. *American Libraries*, 39(1/2), 44–49.

Brooks, F. P. (2010). *The design of design-essays from a computer scientist*. Boston, MA: Pearson Education.

Brown, T. (2008). Design thinking. *Harvard Business Review*, 86(6), 84–92.

Brown, T. (2009). *Change by design*. New York, NY: Harper Collins.

Bourdieu, P., Accardo, A., Balazs, G., Beaud, S., & Bonvin, F. E. (1999). *The weight of the world*. Cambridge, England: Polity Press.

Cassell, C., & Symon, G. (1994). *Qualitative methods in organizational research: A practical guide*. London: Sage.

Clark, K., & Smith, R. (2008). Unleashing the power of design thinking. *Design Management Review*, 19(3), 8–15.

Constas, M. A. (1992). Qualitative analysis as a public event: The documentation of category development procedures. *American Educational Research Journal*, 2(2), 253–266.

Creswell, J. W. (2007). *Qualitative inquiry and research design: Choosing among five traditions* (2nd ed.). Thousand Oaks, CA: Sage.

Denzin, N., & Lincoln, Y. (2000). *Handbook of qualitative research* (2nd ed.). Thousand Oaks, CA: Sage.

Dewey, J. (1910). *How we think*. Boston, MA: D.C Heath.

Dewey, J. (1938). *Experience and education*. New York, NY: Kappa Delta Pi.

Dunne, D., & Martin, R. (2006). Design thinking and how it will change management education: An interview and discussion. *Academy of Management Learning and Education*, 5(4), 512–523.

Easterby-Smith, M., Thorpe, R., & Jackson, P. R. (2007). *Management research*. London: Sage.

Eisenhardt, K. M. (1989). Building theories from case study research. *Academy of Management Review*, 14(4), 532–550.

Fraser, H. (2007). The practice of breakthrough strategies by design. *Journal of Business Strategy*, 28(4), 66–74.

Gloppen, J. (2009). Perspectives on design leadership and design thinking and how they relate to European service industries. *Design Management Journal*, 14(1), 33–35.

Goldman, S., Knudsen, J., & Latvala, M. (1998). Engaging middle schoolers in and through real world mathematics. In L. Leutzinger (Ed.), *Mathematics in the middle* (pp. 129–140). Reston, VA: National Council of Teachers of Mathematics.

Goodwin, C. (1994). Professional vision. *American anthropologist, 96*(3), 606–633.

Hogan, D. (2010, November 2). *Current and future pedagogies in Singapore.* Presentation at TE21 Summit, NIE, Singapore. Retrieved from http://www.nie.edu.sg/about-nie/teacher-education-21

Kafai, Y., & Resnick, M. (1996). *Constructionism in practice: Design thinking, and learning in a digital world.* Mahwah, NJ: Lawrence Erlbaum.

Kimbell, L. (2011). Manifesto for MBA in design better futures. In R. Cooper, S. Jungiginger, & T. Lockwood (Eds.), *Handbook of design management.* Oxford: Berg.

King, N. (2004). Using templates in the thematic analysis of text. In C. Cassell & G. Symon (Eds.), *Essential guide to qualitative methods* (2nd ed., pp. 118–134). London: Sage.

Kolodner, J. L., Camp, P. J., Crismond, D., Fasse, B., Gray, J., Holbrook, J., & Ryan, M. (2003). Promoting deep science learning through case-based reasoning: Rituals and practices in learning by design classrooms. In N. M. Steel (Ed.), *Instructional design: International perspectives* (pp. 89–114). Mahwah, NJ: Lawrence Erlbaum.

Krieger, M. (2010). *Introduction to design thinking.* Retrieved from http://www.slideshare.net/mileyk/intro-to-design-thinking

Lawson, B. (2006). *How designers think: The design process demystified* (4th ed.). Amsterdam: Elsevier.

Lee, K. (2011). Beyond blueprints and basics: A service design conference report. *Design Issues, 27*(4), 95–100.

Liedtka, J. (2000). In defense of strategy as design. *California Management Review, 42*(3), 80.

Liedtka, J. (2011). Learning to use design thinking tools for successful innovation. *Strategy & Leadership, 39*(5), 13–19.

Lockwood, T. (Ed.), (2009). *Design thinking: Integrating innovation, customer experience, and brand value.* New York, NY: Design Management Institute/Allworth Press.

Luo, W., Luo, Z., Paris, S. G., & Hogan, D. (2011). Do performance goals promote learning? A pattern analysis of Singapore students' achievement goals. *Contemporary Educational Psychology, 36*(2), 165–176.

Martin, R. L. (2009). *The design of business: Why design thinking is the next competitive advantage.* Boston, MA: Harvard Business Press.

Martin, R. (2012). Design thinking: An interview with Martin Roger. *Research Technology Management, May–June* (pp. 10–14).

McCullagh, K. (2010). Stepping up: Design thinking has uncovered real opportunities. *Design Management Review,* (3), 36–39.

McDonagh, D., & Thomas, J. (2010). Rethinking design thinking: Empathy supporting innovation. *Australasian Medical Journal, 3*(8), 458–464.

Ng, P. T. (2008). Educational reform in Singapore: Quantity to quality. *Educational Research for Policy and Practice, 7*(1), 5–15.

Parker, S., & Heapy, J. (2006). *The journey to the interface: How public service design can connect users to reform.* London: Demos.

Philloton, E., & Miller, M. (2011). *Design, build, transform.* Retrieved from http://www.studio-h.org/about

Pink, D. H. (2005). *A whole new mind: Why right-brainers will rule the future.* New York: Riverhead.

Razzouk, R., & Shute, V. (2012). What is design thinking and why is it important? *Review of Educational Research, 82*(3), 330–348. doi:10.3102/0034654312457429

Retna, K. S., & Ng, P. T. (2006). The challenges of adopting the learning organization philosophy in a Singapore school. *International Journal of Educational Management, 20*(2), 140–152.

Rittle, H. W., & Webber, M. M. (1973). Dilemmas in general theory of planning. *Policy Sciences, 4*(2), 155–169.

Scheer, A., Noweski, C., & Meinel, C. (2012). Transforming constructivist learning into action: Design thinking in education. *Design and Technology Education: An international Journal, 7*(3), 819.

Simon, H. A. (1973). The structure of ill-defined problems. *Artificial Intelligence, 4*(3), 181–201.

Simon, H. A. (1996). *The sciences of the artificial* (3rd ed.). Cambridge, MA: The MIT Press.

Stake, R. E. (1995). *The art of case study research.* London: Sage.

Stake, R. E. (2000). Case studies. In N. K. Denzin & Y. Lincoln (Eds.), *Handbook of qualitative research*. Thousand Oaks, CA: Sage.

Stegall, N. (2006). Designing for sustainability: A philosophy for ecologically intentional design. *Design Issues, 12*(2), 56–63.

Tan, C., & Wong, Y. (2012). Promoting spiritual ideals through design thinking in public schools. *International Journal of Children's Spirituality, 17*(1), 25–37.

Todd, R. (1999). Design and technology yields a new paradigm for elementary schooling. *Journal of Technology Studies, 25*(2), 26–33.

Verganti, R. (2009). *Design-driven innovation: Changing the rules by radically innovating what things mean.* Cambridge, MA: Harvard Business Press.

Wong, Y. L. (2011). Developing opposable minds: Why design thinking should become an integral part of the core curriculum in 21st century education. In W. Choy & C. Tan (Eds.), *Education reform in Singapore: Critical perspectives* (pp. 127–144). Singapore: Prentice Hall.

Why are teachers afraid of curricular autonomy? Contradictory effects of the new national curriculum in South Korea

Won-Pyo Hong and Peter Youngs

> Using interview data from secondary teachers, this study examines conflicting perspectives on the effects of the new national curriculum in South Korea, which was intended to grant more autonomy to individual schools and teachers. Contrary to the general belief that teachers want more autonomy to customize their curricula to meet students' needs, this study found that the participating teachers did not welcome the enhanced curricular autonomy nor did they believe it would diversify the school curriculum. The primary causes of this contradiction are the gap between the desired and the granted autonomy, the new national curriculum's negative impact on the relationships among teachers and their job security, and the prevalent credential culture in South Korea. Based on these findings, this study suggests wider implications for curriculum scholars and policymakers in other contexts concerning the nature and effects of teacher autonomy in curriculum development.

Introduction

South Korea (referred to as Korea throughout) has maintained a highly standardized and centralized curriculum since it first adopted a national curriculum after the Korean War in the mid-1950s (H.-J. Kim, 2004; Seth, 2002). The central education agency in Korea has determined nearly all of the significant aspects of curriculum, specifying subject areas, content knowledge, and instructional hours for every stage of public education. Through this centralized curriculum, Korean schools have contributed to the country's rapid economic development and social cohesion, by providing a resource of qualified humans with similar beliefs and work ethics (Hanson, 2008; H-J. Kim, 2004; Seth, 2002; Sorenson, 1994).

Recently however, there has been growing attention to the need to reform Korea's centralized and uniform curriculum. Scholars have argued that students are overwhelmed by a severe burden of learning, taking a variety of subjects packed with heavy content knowledge (Hong & Kim, 2008; B.-J. Kim, 2009; Park, 2008). They have also pointed out that Korean teachers lack the flexibility necessary for modifying their curricula to meet students' needs and the changing social environment. As a response to this social demand, a critical measure was taken in 2009, when a new national curriculum was adopted. The 2009 National Curriculum was designed to target two major goals: reducing students' academic workload and enhancing school-based curricular autonomy (Ministry of Education, Science and Technology [MEST], 2009a).

In spite of these goals, the new national curriculum has created heated controversies between teachers and policymakers, which provide a useful opportunity to rethink the nature and role of teacher autonomy in curriculum development. It has been contended that teachers prefer more curricular autonomy, whereas central education authorities are likely to maintain their control over curriculum (Jackson, 1990; Lortie, 1975). Interestingly, this position is reversed in Korea because teachers have reservations about the enhanced curricular autonomy whereas policymakers intend to give them more autonomy. Scholars have also argued that curricular autonomy encourages teachers to connect their curricula to students' interests and local conditions and, therefore, to diversify and customize their curricula (Kauffman, 2005; Skilbeck, 2005; Vieira, 2007). Contrary to this general belief, Korean teachers are concerned that the enhanced curricular autonomy would instead make their curricula more uniform and imbalanced.

To examine these unexpected outcomes of the new national curriculum, this study pursues the following questions: (1) How do teachers respond to the new national curriculum which appears to give them more autonomy? (2) How does enhanced curricular autonomy affect the school curriculum in practice? (3) Is it achieving the targeted goals? And if not, why not? (4) What general implications can be drawn from the Korean case of teacher autonomy in curriculum development?

The following section presents a review of the literature on the significance and effects of teacher autonomy in curriculum development. In the third section, we describe the Korean context and the main features of the 2009 National Curriculum. Using interview data from secondary school teachers, we then present the major findings of this study, which are followed by discussion of wider implications that can be drawn from the Korean case concerning the nature and effects of teacher autonomy in curriculum development.

Significance and effects of teachers' curricular autonomy

Education scholars and practitioners have underscored the significance of teacher autonomy in making decisions over educational matters (Jackson, 1990; Johnson, 1990; LaCoe, 2006; Skilbeck, 2005). They argue that teacher autonomy has a great value in education, since it is closely connected to a teacher's professional status (Pearson & Moomaw, 2005). This is because external agencies cannot meet the unique needs of individual students and local communities. Therefore, to better help students in unique contexts, teachers should be empowered to make their own professional decisions instead of being forced to follow externally-imposed decisions (LaCoe, 2006; Vieira, 2007). Research findings have supported this contention by showing that the more autonomy teachers have, the more likely they are to feel empowered and professional (Ingersoll, 1997; Pearson & Moomaw, 2005; Skinner, 2008).

Attending to the complicated and uncertain nature of curricular issues, scholars have also underscored the significance of teacher autonomy in curriculum development and implementation (Ben-Peretz, 1980; Kennedy, 1992). This is mainly because there are an infinite number of variables associated with students, content knowledge in subjects, and ways to connect the two (Shulman, 1987). For this reason, curricular autonomy has been defined as having the right to make professional decisions in selecting curricular materials and teaching methods and in organizing instructional plans and sequences (Ben-Peretz, 1980; LaCoe, 2006; Pearson & Moomaw, 2005). Curriculum scholars have argued that curriculum materials given by external agencies have only limited value in practice, whereas teachers feel a stronger commitment to implementation when they have curricular autonomy (Garrett, 1990; Kennedy, 1992).

In particular, in the curriculum field, teachers' professional autonomy has been advocated in the name of school-based curriculum development (SBCD) (Bolstad, 2004; Garrett, 1990; Kennedy, 1992; Skilbeck, 2005). Even though SBCD can vary in practice, its proponents support the shift in curriculum decision-making power and authority from central agencies to local schools (Bolstad, 2004). They argue that schools should take more active and creative roles in constructing curricula and organizing learning experiences for their students (Skilbeck, 2005). Unlike the traditional notion of teacher autonomy, which tends to be individualistic, SBCD emphasizes collective efforts among teachers within a school to develop and revise their curriculum (Bolstad, 2004). This results from teachers working together to synchronize the scope and sequence of the school-wide curriculum, which requires communication and collaboration among them. In this sense, curricular autonomy is crucial for teachers' individual and collective efforts to envision and implement a curriculum that best serves their children's interests (Nelson & Miron, 2005): by making use of autonomy, they can work with other teachers to develop a school-wide curriculum while making curricular choices for their own students.

Empirical studies, however, have demonstrated that teachers may not welcome more curricular autonomy, and that enhanced autonomy may not produce desirable consequences in practice. Prideaux (1985), for instance, reported that most of the teachers he interviewed preferred to use a centralized curriculum, pointing out the difficulty of building consensus with other teachers on curriculum issues. Kennedy (1992) also argues that SBCD requires time, skills, and support and, thus, will not foster positive changes simply because teachers have more curricular autonomy. Other researchers (Marks & Louis, 1997; Nelson & Miron, 2005) find that enhanced teacher autonomy tends to increase teachers' non-academic duties and, therefore, distract them from instruction. It has also been argued that external control over curriculum has little influence on teachers' perceived or actual autonomy (Archbald & Porter, 1994; Kauffman, 2005; LaCoe, 2006).

The above arguments support the notion that, as Shulman (2004, p. 151) points out, teacher autonomy is both "resolution and problem". That is, one cannot simply assume that teachers prefer more curricular autonomy and would use it to develop localized, student-centred curriculum. Rather, seemingly enhanced autonomy could lead to complicated, often unexpected, results in practice. Accordingly, it is necessary to examine how teachers respond to enhanced curricular autonomy, how it interacts with environmental factors inside and outside schools, and its consequences.

The Korean context

Even though Korean students are globally well known for high academic achievement, they suffer from a severe burden of learning. Korean secondary students spend approximately 50 hours a week doing schoolwork, the most among Organization for Economic Cooperation and Development (OECD) countries (Korean Youth Policy Institute, 2010). Most students go to private institutions for tutoring until late at night after the regular school day is over. This heavy burden of learning and the competitive school culture has overwhelmed many Korean students with stress, and they show the highest rates of depression and suicide among students from OECD countries (Korean Youth Policy Institute, 2009). Also, there is a growing concern that, although Korean students seem to perform well on standardized tests, many of them are not interested, or lack confidence with regard to learning. In fact, Korean students rank near the bottom in international tests in terms of confidence in and level of enjoyment with regard to studying maths and science (Mullis, Martin, & Foy, 2008).

Many educators and policymakers in Korea believe that the centralized curriculum, which features demanding academic knowledge and is not based on students' concerns, is one of the main causes of these problems. To resolve this problem, Korea has attempted to localize school curricula by granting some discretion to individual schools since the late-1980s. Early efforts however, did not produce substantial changes in the way school curricula were developed or managed. The central agency was reluctant to yield its control over curriculum, while local schools considered curricular autonomy as more of a token than a serious change (Park, 2008). As a result, until recently, most Korean schools were still using a uniform curriculum.

Significant measures were taken in 2009, when the central education agency, the Ministry of Education, Science and Technology (MEST)[1], declared a "plan for enhancing school autonomy". According to the plan, a new national curriculum was enacted to give more autonomy to individual schools so that they could develop more engaging curricula, while reducing students' burden of learning (MEST, 2009a, p. 7). More specifically, whereas the annual hours to be devoted to each subject used to be centrally determined, the new curriculum only specifies the total number of instructional hours for a given secondary school subject (MEST, 2009b). Also, the number of subjects that a school can offer was reduced to eight or fewer in a semester, whereas students used to take more than 10 subjects at a time. To meet this new requirement, schools were encouraged to offer intensive courses. That is, if a school had previously offered both music and visual arts for an hour per week throughout the year, it now had to make them semester-long course subjects and offer only one of them per semester. This change was expected to reduce students' workload and thus, make learning more engaging and in-depth.

Another unprecedented measure is that individual schools were allowed to reduce or increase the number of instructional hours of each subject up to 20% in general schools and 35% in self-managing schools designated by provincial authorities. This was regarded by teachers as quite innovative, as it was the first time trade-offs became possible across subjects (Korean Institute for Curriculum and Evaluation [KICE], 2010; B.-J. Kim, 2009). For instance, a school can teach more of certain subjects as long as it maintains the total number of instructional hours by reducing those assigned to others. Therefore, teachers in a school have to work together to determine how to adjust instructional hours across subjects considering the local context and students' needs.

Policymakers insist that this enhanced autonomy by the 2009 National Curriculum would free schools from central controls and encourage them to develop varied curricula according to local conditions. They also contend that the new curriculum would reduce students' burden of learning, as schools are now to provide fewer, but more engaging courses in a semester. Teachers however, have raised concerns about the effects of the new national curriculum (KICE, 2010; B.-J. Kim, 2009). They contend that not only does it fail to decrease students' burdens of learning, but more significantly, that it further simplifies the existing school curriculum.

Teachers were also wary of the political intent underlying the new national curriculum. As a matter of fact, the national curriculum had been revised in 2007, and was supposed to be adopted in schools beginning in 2009. However, the conservative government, which was inaugurated in 2008, determined to change the 2007 National Curriculum even before it was implemented. Some curriculum scholars and teachers believe that even though the policymakers insist that they intended to give more autonomy to teachers, the conservative ideology of the new government, which emphasizes deregulation and privatization of public sectors, was inherent in the 2009 National Curriculum (C.-G. Kim, 2012; J.-W. Kim, 2011).

As a result, there have been controversies among teachers, policymakers, and scholars with regard to the impact of the new national curriculum on schools. Focusing on these controversies, this study investigates how the new national curriculum is perceived by teachers, whether it produces the intended results in schools, and if not, why not. By investigating the Korean case, this study draws wider implications for the nature and role of teacher autonomy in curriculum development.

Method

Data collection

To achieve the above goals, this study uses interview data from 12 secondary teachers in Seoul, Korea and its metropolitan area. Secondary teachers were selected because the 2009 National Curriculum has caused great controversies in secondary schools, especially in high schools, where the primary concern is to send as many students as possible to prestigious universities. In selecting participants, this study used purposeful sampling. According to Patton (1990), purposeful sampling is effective when a researcher looks for participants who are likely to give in-depth information necessary for addressing his/her research questions. Following this parameter, the first author identified experienced teachers who were or previously had been in charge of coordinating school-wide curriculum frameworks in secondary schools. Through these experiences, they were expected to understand how the 2009 National Curriculum affects school curricula in practice.

Through contact with a teacher association that addresses curriculum issues, three middle school teachers and nine high school teachers were selected considering their specialties, experiences, and locations. One was a principal, seven were vice-principals and the remaining four were curriculum coordinators in their schools.[2] Except for one teacher who had 18 years of teaching experience, all of the interviewees had more than 20 years of teaching experience at the time of the study, and all had been involved in leadership roles in organizing school curricula.[3] See Appendix 1 for a brief profile of the participating teachers.

Teacher interviews were conducted in the winter and spring of 2011. Referring to the literature on teachers' curricular autonomy and the Korean context mentioned above, we drew upon the interview data to examine how teachers responded to the 2009 National Curriculum and how the latter affects school curricula in practice. The first author then visited each school and carried out a semi-structured interview with each participant (Fontana & Frey, 2000); although a consent letter and a common interview protocol were emailed to the teachers prior to interviews, the specific content and length of each interview were adjusted according to the context. Follow-up contact was made by telephone and email to supplement the interview data. In addition to conducting the interviews, the first author also obtained curriculum materials, such as handbooks, curriculum guidelines, and frameworks, in order to better understand changes in school curricula after the new national curriculum was adopted.

Data analysis and validation

In analysing the collected data, we followed a three-step interpretivist approach (Miles & Huberman, 1995). The first step involved reading through the entire set of interviews in light of the research questions, and determining emerging patterns and themes which could become codes to identify phrases or ideas that represent patterns. Sample codes included "teachers' indifference", "increased instructional hours to major subject areas", "the existing teaching staff", "college entrance exam", and "erosion of job security". Second, we compared initial findings from the interview data with curricular documents from participating teachers' schools and national data to check the relevancy of the sample codes. Third, we revised the original codes and created meta-matrices that allowed us to make contrasts and comparisons, and to note patterns, quotes, and themes (Miles & Huberman, 1995).

To enhance the validity of our interpretation, we triangulated multiple sources of data and obtained feedback from the participating teachers (Hatch, 2002; Patton, 1990). The interview data were cross-checked with external data such as nation-wide surveys on Korean teachers' perceptions of curricular autonomy and actual changes in school curricula generated by the 2009 National Curriculum (Baek, Han, & Min, 2011; KICE, 2010). As discussed later, we found that our findings generally corresponded to external data, while more fully revealing the voices of the participating teachers than survey research. In addition, we organized and reported our initial findings in Korean and sent a draft paper to the interviewed teachers for feedback. Most of them agreed with the main findings in the draft but a few corrected misinformation and proposed minor changes. The current manuscript was revised and developed based on their feedback.

Results

This section presents the results of our study. It reveals how the participating teachers responded to the seemingly enhanced autonomy granted by the 2009 National Curriculum; why it was hard for the teachers to implement the new national curriculum in practice; how the flexibility in organizing school curricula affected Korean teachers' job security; and how the credential culture in Korea affected the way schools made use of the granted curricular autonomy.

Gap between the desired autonomy, the granted autonomy, and the majority of teachers' indifference

Korean teachers have aspired to more curriculum autonomy beyond the centrally-controlled, standardized curriculum. In a nationwide survey (B.-J. Kim, 2009) for example, more than 70% of high school teachers indicated that they want more curricular autonomy. The national curriculum guidelines which specify detailed aspects of school curriculum have been considered as a major hurdle in developing locally relevant, student-centred curriculum (KICE, 2010). As a result, in the Korean context, curriculum autonomy has meant reducing regulations in the national curriculum and empowering teachers and schools to customize their curriculum according to local contexts and students' needs (Park, 2008).

The teachers in this study agreed that Korean teachers need to obtain more autonomy in making decisions over their curricula. Five of them explicitly insisted that, if the curriculum so far has been decided by central agencies, teachers should take a more active role in designing varied curricula. Mr Kim[4] for example, stated, "I think autonomy is the ultimate goal. I am one of those who believe schools should have autonomy rather than the government controlling the curriculum." Another teacher, Ms Ann, concurred: "I agree that developing enriched, customized instructional programmes is becoming more and more significant to Korean teachers."

However, the curricular autonomy desired by the teachers seemed to differ from that promoted by the 2009 National Curriculum. According to Mr Kim, for instance:

> Teachers believe that, if they have more discretion in determining what and when to teach, they are more likely to cater to their students' needs by customizing their curriculum. I think this is a bit different from what policymakers have in their minds. As you know, the national curriculum has specified content knowledge to be addressed in each subject in detail, which constrains teachers' autonomy. As long as this constraint remains, trading instructional hours across subjects would not affect teachers' perception of autonomy in making their curricula.

As he contends, the 2009 National Curriculum has little to do with allowing teachers to determine the content and sequence of their own curriculum, since subject area content standards still exist and teachers are required to follow them. Rather, it grants individual schools the right to determine which subjects to offer and when, and to partially modify instructional hours assigned to the subjects. Even though this could potentially affect what and how individual teachers teach, its impact will be limited since teachers still should address externally-developed content standards.

According to the interviewed teachers, the gap between the desired and the granted autonomy has made teachers in their schools uninterested in the new national curriculum. As Mr Jeon stated, "except for curriculum leaders or the principals who are in charge of handling curriculum, the majority of teachers do not take the national curriculum seriously". Mr Hong further explains the situation in his high school:

> Teachers tend to think that if their instructional hours are determined, school-wide curriculum issues are not their business anymore. Even department chairs don't care, as long as hours for their subject areas are secured. The school-wide curriculum framework is a secondary concern to them. Some young teachers may be interested in these matters, but most are not.

In fact, most participating teachers reported that a few faculty members have to obtain consent from the majority of their fellow staff members to adjust instructional hours and reorganize the curriculum framework according to the new national curriculum. According to them, this process is often very difficult. As implied above, secondary teachers tend to adhere to the instructional hours of their subjects, as this is closely related to their status in schools. As a result, changing the existing curriculum often causes conflicts among teachers teaching different subjects, because some benefit from the change while others are marginalized. These conflicts seemed to lead teachers to believe that the newly-granted autonomy has worsened the situation in their schools. For instance, Mr Hong states, "I do not see any positive effects yet. It was quite troublesome to reconcile conflicting voices. It was a big nuisance to adjust our curriculum according to the new national curriculum."

Constraints of the regulated autonomy

Survey data supports the above responses; only 20% of secondary teachers agreed that the 2009 National Curriculum gave them more autonomy (KICE, 2010), while as aforementioned, the majority of Korean teachers desire more curricular autonomy. Teacher informants traced the origin of this gap to the very nature of the autonomy described in the 2009 National Curriculum. In Mr Park's words,

> We rarely feel like we came to have more autonomy through the new curriculum. In fact, we did not demand it, but the central agency handed it to us. Now, when we attempt to apply the new autonomy to our school, there are too many constraints, no less than those in the previous national curriculum. So, we don't feel like we have more autonomy.

As this implies, many teachers appeared to regard the new curricular autonomy more as something Skott (2004, p. 227) once referred to as "forced autonomy", because it was given by the central agency regardless of their demands. The more serious problem is that the autonomy is quite limited and, as Mr Park explained, places significant constraints on teachers when they attempt to apply the given autonomy to their curricula. Mr Shin also concurred: "schools are not free because we are regulated to offer eight or less subjects in a semester and modify instructional hours less than 20%. Whereas the government insists that schools now have more discretion, we feel like we are stuck because of the regulations".

This is true considering the fact that most schools have to offer at least one course in English, maths, Korean, science, and social studies, which already totals five of the eight subjects permitted by the national guidelines. In addition to these nearly fixed areas, they also have to provide courses in music, visual arts, and physical education. As this makes eight subjects, it is hardly possible for schools to create new courses relevant for their students. Therefore, there seems to be little space for schools to localize and diversify their curricula.

Despite the restriction, it is still true that secondary schools were granted more curricular autonomy through the 2009 National Curriculum. They can modify instructional hours across subjects up to 20%, or 35% if they apply to be a self-managing school. This is not a minor change, as this can strengthen certain subjects by giving them more instructional hours while diminishing the hours of others. Also, a few participating teachers admitted that students had midterms and final tests in fewer subjects than previously since the adoption of the 2009 National Curriculum. Furthermore, by teaching fewer subjects more intensively, as Ms Yin points out, "it has become possible for teachers to employ more enriched and student-centred instructional methods". Mr Jeon agreed:

> If teachers teach visual arts three hours a week instead of an hour, they have to revise teaching methods to be more relevant for the increased instructional hours. They can't keep using previous teaching methods. Also, if instructional hours of sciences are increased, teachers are more likely to make use of diverse, student-centred instruction such as block scheduling or experiments.

In fact, this was one of the main goals targeted by the 2009 National Curriculum: reducing students' burden of learning and making learning more engaging and in-depth. According to participating teachers however, there are structural and socio-cultural factors that limit such changes. In particular, they explained that the existing teaching staff and the social pressure on secondary schools make it hard for schools to utilize curricular autonomy in a fruitful way.

Inflexibility in restructuring the existing teaching staff

Most of the interviewed teachers, even those who believe the new national curriculum could generate positive results, indicated that the inflexibility in repositioning teachers hinders schools from reforming their curricula. That is, even though they want to redesign the school curriculum, the existing teacher population obstructs such changes. Mr Kim, for example, talked about the situation in his high school:

> If we want to reduce the instructional hours of a subject, we have to wait until the teacher teaching that subject moves to another school. If the teacher has been teaching in our school for just a year, we have to wait for a few more years. Different teachers have a different number of years of teaching in our school. If we want to send some of them to other schools earlier than is due, they would not accept it. So, this is the biggest difficulty in restructuring our curriculum.

This inflexibility originates from the unique teacher employment system in Korea. Teachers in public schools are hired and paid by the central government, even though they are assigned to schools by provincial education authorities. Once hired, Korean teachers in public schools move from one school to another in the same province every four to five years. This is to equalize the quality of teachers across public schools so that students receive a similar quality of education regardless of their location.

According to the interviewed teachers, schools lack flexibility when it comes to changing their curricula because of this employment structure. As Mr Kim explained above, if a school has a new curriculum plan, it often takes a few years for the school to retain a teaching staff that conforms to the plan. Thus, without changing the teacher employment system, schools are not likely to have the flexibility required to reform their curricula. Even though such changes are unlikely in the near future, it seems to cause teachers worry because from their point of view, curricular autonomy could threaten their job security. They seem to be afraid that schools will hire more non-tenured, contracted teachers instead of tenured teachers, which could destabilize job stability. Mr Hong further explained:

> I already heard that a school hired a large number of term-based instructors instead of tenured teachers. As you know, teachers have been proud of their jobs because even though it is demanding and tough, [teaching] is secure. If teachers lose this advantage, they will fear for their position because they can lose their job at any time.

The worry over job security is especially serious among teachers teaching non-major subjects such as visual arts, music, and social studies. Many informants said that these teachers are already concerned with the shrinking job openings in their subject areas. At times, teachers seemed to be frustrated because, in their view, the new national curriculum could impede the basic ideal of public education: a balanced development of the learners. Ms Ann, for example, contended that "the new national curriculum has caused schools only to focus on a few selected subjects while marginalizing others in the school curriculum. It made it harder for teachers to pursue holistic education". Unfortunately, this outcome seems increasingly likely because of the social pressure on Korean secondary schools.

Social pressure on secondary schools and the imbalanced school curriculum

As noted earlier, Korean secondary students are well-known for working hard. The first and foremost reason for this excessive work is to gain entrance into prestigious universities. As aforementioned, a significant rationale for writing the 2009 National Curriculum was to reduce students' heavy burden of learning by limiting the number of subjects in a semester to eight or fewer. The underlying assumption was that, if the number of subjects was reduced, the students' burden of learning would be as well. However, teachers, especially high school teachers in this study, insisted that the lowered number of subjects has little to do with students' burden of learning. Mr Choi insists, for example,

> Policymakers tend to believe that students' workload would diminish if they take a smaller number of subjects in a semester. However, the latter has little to do with the former. Regardless of the number of subjects, students still spend most of their time doing Korean, English and math.

This is because student performances in Korean, English and maths carry the most weight in the college admission process, thus, becoming the primary concerns for parents and students. Therefore, students' heavy burden of learning is not caused by the number of subjects in the regular curriculum, but by the competition to enter prestigious universities. As Mr Chin notes, "As long as the competition to enter top-tier universities remains, high schools have no choice but to focus on Korean, English, and math."

Teachers were also afraid that the enhanced autonomy in the 2009 National Curriculum would further narrow and simplify their school curricula. They worried that schools would abuse the given autonomy to teach the major subjects more often while further marginalizing the other subjects. As a matter of fact, according to survey data (Baek et al., 2011), more than 80% of high schools were planning to allocate more hours to English and maths while reducing those allocated to home sciences, practical arts, music, and visual arts. Curriculum documents from participating teachers' schools also revealed similar patterns. In Mr Hong's high school for example, Korean, English and maths took 60% of the total instruction hours that a student learns, an increase of 6% compared to the previous year. This is inevitable, according to Mr Choi, because "the most important thing that a high school needs to consider is the number of students that enter prestigious universities". Mr Yoon, an English teacher, further described the situation in his high school:

> Even teachers of the major subject areas are concerned with the newly increased instructional hours given to their subjects. Our students now take English nine hours a week, which I feel is too many. Also, such changes are compensated by taking away hours from the social studies. I am afraid that this will cause students to be provided with an imbalanced and one-sided curriculum, which will ultimately not be helpful for the students because they will be going to major diverse areas in college.

In fact, Mr Yoon reveals another contradictory consequence of curricular autonomy in Korea. That is, local autonomy is forcing a narrowing of the curriculum instead of enriching and diversifying it. As Mr Yoon lamented, "The new discretion given to high schools only allows them to strengthen a few college-track courses. It only makes high school curriculum further uniform."

Discussion

The above results are consistent with the existing literature on the nature and effects of teachers' curricular autonomy. Despite its professional significance, researchers have demonstrated that teachers may not welcome more curricular autonomy, since it requires teachers to make their own decisions regarding complicated issues instead of following external guidelines (Archbald & Porter, 1994; Kennedy, 1992; Nelson & Miron, 2005). They have also shown that school-based curriculum development may not promote positive changes in practice, since it tends to increase teaches' non-academic duties (Kauffman, 2005; LaCoe, 2006; Prideaux, 1985; Skilbeck, 2005). Similarly, this study also demonstrates that Korean teachers do not like the new autonomy granted by the 2009 National Curriculum. It also reveals that the new national curriculum disturbs the relationships among teachers within a school, which can obstruct collaborative efforts among teachers to re-organize school-wide curriculum frameworks.

This study also presents findings regarding some apparent effects of the new national curriculum due to the distinctive teacher employment system and credential culture in Korea. It indicates that the enhanced flexibility in organizing school curricula has negative impacts on Korean teachers' job satisfaction and commitment. This seems to contradict the assumption that teacher autonomy and professional commitment are positively related (Garrett, 1990; Kennedy, 1992; Vieira, 2007). This study supports that the growing number of contracted teachers and the further marginalization of teachers teaching non-major subjects are the main causes of this contradiction. Another contradictory result is the fact that the enhanced curricular autonomy is likely to make school curricula further imbalanced and simplified instead of diversifying them. The participating teachers contend that the credential culture and the college entrance system in Korea lead secondary schools, especially high schools, to abuse the newly granted autonomy.

Based on the above findings, we propose the following suggestions for those who are interested in teacher autonomy in curriculum development.

First, curriculum scholars need to examine more closely when and how teachers' curricular autonomy promotes positive results in practice. This study reveals that Korean teachers did not feel more empowered by the artificial autonomy given by the 2009 National Curriculum. Rather, they were worried about its negative effects. As a matter of fact, the Korean government announced a new secondary curriculum in 2012, which partly modified the 2009 National Curriculum (MEST, 2012). The main change was allowing schools to offer more than eight courses in a semester by lessening the original regulation. Also, schools were prohibited from reducing instructional hours assigned to music, visuals arts, or physical education. This early retreat from the 2009 National Curriculum affirms that it has created turmoil in practice rather than producing intended changes. In fact, there is little research on the conditions under which teachers' curricular autonomy produces positive changes in reality. Curriculum scholars tend to assume the necessity of curricular autonomy instead of elucidating its complicated nature. If this situation continues, curricular autonomy could be manipulated by curriculum policies, which in fact have little to do with teachers' autonomy, as the Korean case illustrates. Therefore, curriculum scholars need to further investigate when and how teachers' curricular autonomy contributes to developing a student-centred, engaging curriculum.

Second, with regard to this issue, this study suggests that the aligned change between general guidelines and subject area content standards is a condition for successful implementation of curricular autonomy. The participating teachers in this study pointed out that the 2009 National Curriculum rarely gave them more autonomy since the subject area content standards remained unchanged. In fact, content standards in Korean secondary schools are known to consist of heavy content knowledge which is often too advanced for students' intellectual development (Park, 2008). Therefore, for curricular autonomy to produce positive results in practice, changes not only in structural aspects but also in the substance of school curricula need to be made accordingly. The emphasis on content knowledge in curriculum standards needs to be reduced so that teachers exert more professional autonomy in designing their teaching programmes. Also, subject area content standards should be rewritten to be more relevant for students' intellectual development to lessen their burden of learning.

Third, a more consistent and predictable approach is necessary in managing the national curriculum. As mentioned earlier, the Korean national curriculum was already revised in 2007 and was supposed to be implemented from 2009. However, the newly elected government disregarded this schedule and determined to change the national curriculum once again. This unpredicted change has caused confusion in schools and as the participating teachers have expressed, many teachers felt that they were not ready to execute its changes. Therefore, curriculum revision must take a more stable and consistent approach, one which is more free from political influence, to be better accepted by teachers.

Fourth, to diversify high school curricula, policymakers need to assure teachers that offering varied and enriched courses would be beneficial for students' efforts regarding college entrance. As a matter of fact, Korean policymakers have encouraged higher education institutions to count more diverse aspects of applicants' potential in the admission process. Accordingly, a growing number of universities have hired admission officers; they have also introduced early admission processes that consider applicants' overall academic records and experiences instead of just focusing on their scores on a standardized test (Korean Council for University Education, 2012). Despite these changes, teachers in this study still believed that they had to prepare students to achieve high scores in the college entrance examination. They seemed to be unsure that students' performances in diverse courses actually matter in the college admission process. Therefore, policymakers need to continue reforming the college admission process, convincing teachers that universities will consider whether applicants have involved in various learning experiences in high schools.

Lastly, despite its potential contribution to deepening our understanding of teacher autonomy in curriculum development, this study is limited in nature. It is based on interview data from a limited number of teachers in a selected area. The major findings of this study, therefore, cannot be generalized to all Korean teachers (or to teachers outside Korea) but, rather, should be considered as exploratory and suggestive. We expect curriculum scholars in other national contexts to further examine under what conditions teachers' curricular autonomy contributes to developing and implementing school-based curricula catering to local conditions and student needs.

Notes

1. This name was changed to the Ministry of Education by a new government in 2012.
2. In Korea, a curriculum coordinator is selected among experienced teachers in a school to organize and manage the school-wide curriculum framework. Thus, he or she is still a teacher, not an administrator.
3. In Korea, the track to becoming vice-principal or principal is not specialized. Experienced classroom teachers are thus promoted to these positions, usually after 25 or 30 years of teaching experiences.
4. All the names in this study are pseudonyms presented through last names.

References

Archbald, D. A., & Porter, A. C. (1994). Curriculum control and teachers' perceptions of autonomy and satisfaction. *Educational Evaluation and Policy Analysis, 16*, 21–39.
Baek, K.-S., Han, H.-J., & Min, Y.-S. (2011). A study on the present practice of organizing and implementing the 2009 revised high school curriculum. *The Korean Journal of Learner-Centered Curriculum and Instruction, 11*, 123–148.
Ben-Peretz, M. (1980). Teachers' role in curriculum development: An alternative approach. *Canadian Journal of Education, 5*, 52–62.
Bolstad, R. (2004, November 24–26). *School-based curriculum development: Redefining the term for New Zealand schools today and tomorrow*. Paper presented at the conference of the New Zealand Association of Research in Education (NZARE), Wellington, New Zealand.
Fontana, A., & Frey, H. J. (2000). The interview: From structured questions to negotiated text. In N. Denzin & Y. Lincoln (Eds.), *Handbook of qualitative research* (pp. 645–672). Thousand Oaks, CA: Sage.
Garrett, R. M. (1990). The introduction of school-based curriculum development in a centralized education system: A possible tactic. *International Journal of Educational Development, 10*, 303–309.
Hanson, M. (2008). *Economic development, education, and transnational corporations*. New York, NY: Routledge.
Hatch, A. (2002). *Doing qualitative research in educational settings*. Albany: State University of New York Press.
Hong, H.-J., & Kim, D.-S. (2008). Inquiry of the optimal number of courses within one semester and one school day. *The Korean Journal of Curriculum Studies, 26*, 73–101.
Ingersoll, R. M. (1997). *The status of teaching as a profession: 1990–1991 (NCES 97–104)*. Washington, DC: U.S. Department of Education, National Centre for Education Statistics.
Jackson, P. W. (1990). *Life in classrooms* (2nd ed.). New York, NY: Teachers College Press.

Johnson, S. M. (1990). *Teachers at work*. New York, NY: Basic Books.

Kauffman, D. (2005). *Curriculum prescription and curriculum constraint: Second-year teachers' perceptions* PNGT Working Paper. Cambridge, MA: Project on the Next Generation of Teachers. Retrieved from http://www.gse.harvard.edu/~ngt

Kennedy, K. (1992). School-based curriculum development as a policy option for the 1990s: An Australian perspective. *Journal of Curriculum and Supervision, 7*, 180–195.

KICE (Korean Institute for Curriculum and Evaluation). (2010). *A study for supporting schools' autonomous curriculum organization and implementation*. Seoul, Korea: Author.

Kim, B.-J. (2009). Analytical study on teachers' conception on the actual condition of school autonomy. *The Korean Journal of Politics of Education, 16*, 103–123.

Kim, C.-G. (2012). The process and characteristics of neoliberalization of Korean education. *The Korean Journal of Education Research, 10*, 119–149.

Kim, J.-W. (2011). An analysis of school autonomy policy implementation by the MB government: Focusing on curriculum autonomy at school level. *The Korean Journal of Politics of Education, 18*, 61–85.

Kim, H.-J. (2004). National identity in Korean curriculum. *Canadian Social Studies, 38*, Retrieved from http://www.quasar.ualberta.ca/css

Korean Council for University Education. (2012). *Plan for 2014 college admission process*. Seoul, Korea: Author.

Korean Youth Policy Institute. (2009). *2009 Survey on high school students' school lives*. Seoul, Korea: Author.

Korean Youth Policy Institute. (2010). *Brief statistics on youth's life*. Seoul, Korea: Author.

LaCoe, C. S. (2006). *Decomposing teacher autonomy: A study investigating types of teacher autonomy and how current public school climate affects teacher autonomy*. (Unpublished doctoral dissertation). PA: University of Pennsylvania.

Lortie, D. C. (1975). *School teacher*. Chicago, IL: University of Chicago Press.

Marks, H. M., & Louis, K. S. (1997). Does teacher empowerment affect the classroom? The implications of teacher empowerment for instructional practice and student academic performance. *Educational Evaluation and Policy Analysis, 19*, 245–275.

MEST (Ministry of Education, Science and Technology). (2009a). *Press material for the 2009 national curriculum*. Seoul, Korea: Author.

MEST. (2009b). *General guidelines for the 2009 national curriculum*. Seoul, Korea: Author.

MEST. (2012). *General guidelines for the elementary and secondary education*. Seoul, Korea: Author.

Miles, M., & Huberman, M. (1995). *Qualitative data analysis: An expanded sourcebook*. Thousand Oaks, CA: Sage.

Mullis, I. V. S., Martin, M. O., & Foy, P. (2008). *TIMSS 2007 International mathematics report: Findings from IEA's trends in international mathematics and science study at the fourth and eighth Grades*. Boston, MA: TIMSS & PIRLS International Study Centre, Boston College.

Nelson, C., & Miron, G. (2005). *Exploring the correlates of academic success in Pennsylvania charter schools*. New York, NY: National Centre for the Study of Privatization in Education.

Park, S.-K. (2008). A beginning discussion on searching for the starting point and direction of curriculum decentralization in Korea. *Korean Journal of Curriculum Studies, 26*, 87–106.

Patton, M. Q. (1990). *Qualitative evaluation and research methods*. Thousand Oaks, CA: Sage.

Pearson, L. C., & Moomaw, W. (2005). The relationship between teacher autonomy and stress, work satisfaction, empowerment, and professionalism. *Educational Research Quarterly, 29*, 38–54.

Prideaux, D. (1985). School-based curriculum decision making in South Australia: Change of policy or change of action. *Curriculum Perspectives.* 5(October), 7–10.

Seth, J. M. (2002). *Education fever: Society, politics, and the pursuit of schooling in South Korea*. Honolulu: University of Hawaii Press.

Shulman, L. (1987). Knowledge and teaching: Foundations of the new reform. *Harvard Education Review, 57*(1), 1–21.

Shulman, L. (2004). *The wisdom of practice*. San Francisco, CA: Jossey-Bass.

Skilbeck, M. (2005). School-based curriculum development. In A. Lieberman (Ed.), *The roots of educational change* (pp. 109–132). Dordrecht, The Netherlands: Springer.

Skinner, R. (2008). *Autonomy, working conditions, and teacher satisfaction: Does the public charter school bargain make a difference?*. (Unpublished doctoral dissertation). Washington, DC: The George Washington University.

Skott, J. (2004). The forced autonomy of mathematics teachers. *Educational Studies in Mathematics,* *55,* 227–257.

Sorenson, W. C. (1994). Success and education in South Korea. *Comparative Education Review,* *38,* 10–35.

Vieira, F. (2007). Teacher autonomy: Why should we care? *Independence, 41,* 20–28.

Appendix 1. Teachers profile.

Name	School	Teaching Career	Position
Mr Kim	High school	23 years	Vice-principal
Mr Choi	High school	28 years	Vice-principal
Mr Hong	Self-managing high school	27 years	Vice-principal
Mr Park	High school	30 years	Principal
Mr Shin	High school	24 years	Curriculum coordinator
Mr Chin	High school	28 years	Vice-principal
Mr Yoon	Self-managing high school	22 years	Curriculum coordinator
Mr Woo	Self-managing high school	18 years	English department chair
Mr Lim	High school	22 years	Vice-principal
Mr Jeon	Middle school	26 years	Vice-principal
Ms Ann	Middle school	25 years	Vice-principal
Ms Yin	Middle school	23 years	Curriculum coordinator

Exploring Chinese teachers' commitment to being a cooperating teacher in a university-government-school initiative for rural practicum placements

Lijie Lu, Fang Wang, Yunpeng Ma, Anthony Clarke and John Collins

Faced with urban schools' reluctance to host student teachers on practicum because "student teachers disturb their teaching order", Northeast Normal University in Changchun, China, collaborated with four rural provinces to develop a University-Government-School (UGS) initiative for rural practicum placements. To understand the teachers' commitment to this alternative approach to practicum placements, we posed the question: What motivates and challenges teacher participation in the UGS initiative? To provide answers, we drew on the recently developed Mentoring Profile Inventory – a 62-item inventory that captures teachers' motivations and challenges in supervising student teachers on practicum. Further, by comparing the UGS results with those of supervising teachers from three other countries, we were able to discern aspects of the UGS teachers' commitment that were particularly distinctive to the Chinese context. For example, UGS supervisors are significantly more motivated than their international counterparts to participate in the practicum because student teachers: act as a *Reminder about Career Development;* enable supervisors to have *Time-Out to Monitor Pupil Learning;* and they *Promote Pupil Engagement.* These results provide important baseline data for making sense of the UGS teachers' commitment to the practicum, for situating their responses within current educational reform efforts, and for determining their professional development needs.

Introduction

This paper explores teachers' commitment to supervise student teachers on practicum within the context of Northeast Normal University's recent University-Government-School initiative for rural practicum placements. This initiative, currently undertaken in four northeast rural provinces in China, is a deliberate attempt to address the lack of urban practicum placements for North East Normal University's student teachers; a situation brought about by urban teachers' increasing reluctance to supervise student teachers due to, among other things, rising parental pressure for local schools to excel in the "university entrance exam competition".

North East Normal University's (NENU) University-Government-School (UGS) initiative is occurring within the context of two larger educational reforms efforts in China. The first is the 2001 School Curriculum Reform (China Ministry of Education, 2001). The second, in direct response to the first, is the 2007 Teacher Education Reform (China Ministry of Education, 2007). These two reforms seek to change student learning from passive to more active forms of engagement. In the case of the School Curriculum Reform this involves a radical shift in classroom pedagogy that stands in sharp contrast to what many supervisors experienced when they were students in schools themselves; for example, less direct instruction by teachers and more active learning by students. In the case of the Teacher Education Reform this involves a greater commitment to the practicum as a site for learning-to-teach; for example, the time-on-practicum has increased to the equivalent of one of eight semesters that typically comprise a 4-year Bachelor of Education degree in China. Both reforms have implications for securing teachers' involvement in the practicum. In the first instance, supervising teachers are expected to incorporate and model the School Curriculum Reform efforts in their classrooms. In the second instance, teachers are expected to share their classrooms with student teachers for a longer period of time than was previously expected of practicum settings.

Central to this study is the concept of commitment. Following Meyer, Becker, and Vandenberghe (2004), we define "commitment" in terms of what motivates and challenges an individual to pursue a particular course of action. As such, we draw on the recently developed Mentoring Profile Inventory (MPI) – a 62-item survey that measures teachers' motivations and challenges to supervise student teachers – to gather data on a teacher's commitment to being a cooperating teacher in the UGS initiative (Clarke, Collins, Triggs, & Nielsen, 2012). The results shed light on how rural teachers are responding to the UGS initiative within the context of the two current nation-wide educational reform efforts (School Curriculum and Teacher Education) and suggest what is working but also what needs to be addressed to ensure Chinese teachers continued commitment to the UGS initiative.

Review of the literature

Classroom teachers who supervise student teachers play a critical role in teacher education. The most common term in the literature used to refer to these teachers, and the one used in this study, is "cooperating teacher" (Clarke, Triggs, & Nielsen, 2012). It is widely reported that cooperating teachers are poorly prepared for their work with student teachers (Goodfellow, 2000). Indeed, the poor state of professional readiness of cooperating teachers has become a near constant in the teacher education literature (Kent, 2001). Further, it is well established that professional development for cooperating teachers is almost non-existent in many contexts and that, in the absence of such support, cooperating teachers draw almost exclusively on their own experiences when they were student teachers to guide their current advisory practices (Hobson, Ashby, Malderez, & Tomlinson, 2009; Knowles & Cole, 1996; Wang & Odell, 2002). Research has consistently shown that unarticulated and tacitly held beliefs about one's advisory practice can be detrimental to learning in these contexts (Crasborn, Hennissen, Brouwer, Korthagen, & Bergen, 2008; Zeichner, Liston, Mahlios, & Gomez, 1987). In contexts where professional development does exist, the opportunity for cooperating teachers to engage in a dialogue about their advisory practice is deemed essential. However, not just any dialogue is sufficient (Borko, 2004; Bullough & Draper, 2004; Loucks-Horsley, 2003). In attempting to problematize one's own practice, it is important to make explicit one's underlying commitments to that practice. The literature shows that commitment to being a cooperating teacher arises from at least three sources:

- a commitment to pupils in terms of wanting to ensure the best possible learning environment for one's students (Feiman-Nemser, 2001; Kent, 2001);
- a commitment to the profession in terms of wanting to "give back" to the profession (Kitchell & White, 2007; Sinclair, Dowson, & Thistleton-Martin, 2006); and

- a commitment to self in terms of being exposed to new ideas and strategies through one's involvement in teacher education (Clarke, 2006; Koskela & Ganser, 1998).

These commitments represent important motivators for being a cooperating teacher and represent a starting point for exploring the beliefs and assumptions that underlie their practice (Ambrose, Bridges, DiPietro, Lovett, & Norman, 2010).

In responding to these questions within the context of the UGS initiative, the current project draws on the recently developed Mentoring Profile Inventory (MPI) (Clarke et al., 2012) to capture the motivations and challenges that cooperating teachers encounter in their work with student teachers. Further, by aggregating responses for particular cohorts of cooperating teachers (e.g., a Chinese cohort, a Canadian cohort, etc.), the MPI allows for comparative analyses across cohorts. Such comparisons are important for the identification of motivations and challenges that are particularly distinctive and that might otherwise remain invisible or unrecognized from a single-context perspective (Alexander, 2001; Bray, 2007). Therefore, the results contribute to both national (i.e., providing insights to a local teacher education initiative) and the international (i.e., providing comparative analyses) teacher education literatures.

Method

This study proceeded through three phases. The first phase involved administering the MPI to a cohort of UGS cooperating teachers. The second phase involved site visits to UGS practicum schools. The third phase involved a comparative analysis of the Chinese MPI data with the MPI data from three other cohorts (Australia, Canada, and New Zealand); these additional data sets were readily available and therefore constituted "convenience samples" for comparative purposes (Gravetter & Forzano, 2009).

Mentoring profile inventory: individual and comparative analyses

Individual analysis

The MPI is a web-based inventory freely available to cooperating teachers and is currently offered in five languages: Chinese, Thai, French, Spanish, and English. The MPI was constructed in a North American context (Canada). However its development occurred in concert and direct collaboration with Chinese, Thai, Spanish, and French collaborators to ensure that as far as possible the underlying concepts were relevant, consistent, and valid beyond the North American context (Clarke, 2012). Once respondents complete the MPI, they automatically receive a single-page report depicting their results in an easy to read graphical form (Figure 1).

The core of the MPI is a 62-item survey that quantifies the important features that motivate (32 items) and challenge (30 items) cooperating teachers in their work with student teachers (Table 1, Column 1). Motivator items ask teachers to indicate the degree to which a particular statement represents a motivator for working with student teachers (e.g., "Supervising helps refine my own teaching practices and skills"). The five possible response options for motivator items are: Not a Motivator (or Does Not Apply), A Slight Motivator, A Moderate Motivator, A Significant Motivator, or A Critical Motivator. Challenge items asks teachers to indicate the degree to which a particular statement represents a challenge in working with student teachers (e.g., "Lack of clarity about supervisory responsibilities at the district or regional level for student teachers"). The five response options for the challenge items are: Not a Challenge (or Does Not Apply),

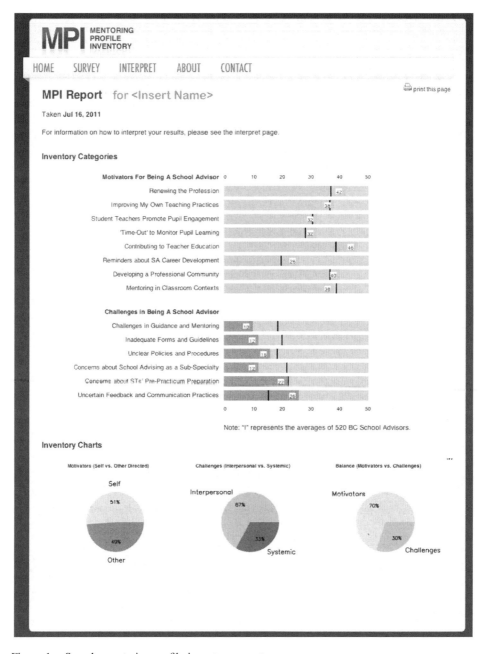

Figure 1. Sample mentoring profile inventory report.

A Slight Challenge, A Moderate Challenge, A Significant Challenge, or A Critical Challenge. Item responses are scored from zero to 4 (e.g., 0 for Not a Motivator or Not a Challenge, 1 for A Slight Motivator or A Slight Challenge, 2 for A Moderate Motivator or A Moderate Challenge, etc.). The responses to the MPI are then processed into 14 scales: eight motivator scales and six challenge scales (Table 1, Column 2). A respondent's scale scores are the linear sums of each respondent's answers to the items that comprise each of

Table 1. Mentoring profile inventory: items, scales, and balance charts.

Items: Motivator (32) and Challenge (30)	Scales: Motivator (8) and Challenge (6)	Intermediate Balance Charts: Motivator Chart and Challenge Chart	Overall Balance Chart: Motivators versus Challenges
Sample Motivator Items: • It's the 'right thing to do' to help and mentor Student Teachers • It's satisfying to know I can facilitate a Student Teacher's development • I'm making a real difference when I coach beginning teachers • Supervising helps refine my own teaching practices and skills	Renewing the Profession • Improving My Own Teaching Practices • Student Teachers Promote Pupil Engagement • "Time-Out" to Monitor Pupil Learning • Contributing to Teacher Education • Reminders about SA Career Development • Developing a Professional Community • Mentoring in Classroom Contexts	• Motivators: Self versus Other	• Motivators versus. Challenges
Sample Challenge Items: • Difficulties in outlining what Student Teachers can expect from me as a Cooperating Teacher • Difficulties in articulating the evaluation procedures at the start of the practicum • Challenges in developing a meaningful mentoring relationship with my Student Teacher	• Challenges in Guidance and Mentoring • Inadequate Forms and Guidelines • Unclear Policies and Procedures • Concerns about School Advising as a Sub-Specialty • Concerns about STs' Pre-Practicum Preparation • Uncertain Feedback and Communication Practices	• Challenges: Interpersonal versus Systemic	

the scales. For convenience, all scale scores are renormalized to a common range of zero to 50 in the final report.

Beyond the 14 scales, there are two internal MPI structures that provide an additional level of detail for understanding teacher commitment to the practicum (Clarke et al., 2012). These structures result in two intermediate balance charts: one for motivators illustrating the balance between "self" and "other" motivations; and one for challenges illustrating the balance between "interpersonal" and "systemic" challenges (Table 1, Column 3). For the motivators, the "self" score reflects personal gains from working as a cooperating teacher. The "other" score reflects gains offered to others as a result of working as a cooperating teacher. For the challenges, the "interpersonal" score reflects challenges with communication, feedback, among others, that arise from interpersonal relations when working as a cooperating teacher. The "systemic" score reflects a lack of clarity about policies, a paucity of guidelines, or unclear evaluation forms or procedures, among others, that are essentially procedural in nature and arise when working as a cooperating teacher. Calculations for the internal components of the two balance charts (self/other and interpersonal/systemic) are reported as percentages. A third and final balance chart depicts the overall balance between the 32 motivator items and the 30 challenge items of the MPI (Table 1, Column 4). Calculations for the internal components of the third balance chart (motivator/challenge) are also reported as percentages.

Finally, all respondents are invited to provide basic demographic information when completing the MPI (e.g., years of teaching experience, level of teaching, number of student teachers supervised). At the conclusion of the MPI respondents are invited to respond to one open-ended question: "What single piece of advice would you offer to other cooperating teachers?" The demographic information and the responses to the open-ended question are not reported back to participants but are used by MPI researchers to capture a broader sense of who the respondents are and what they regard as essential to their work with student teachers.

Comparative analysis

Aggregate reports can be generated for cohorts of cooperating teachers (e.g., a Chinese cohort) and used for comparative analyses between cohorts. Aggregate MPI reports are available in three forms: an Aggregate MPI Report, an Aggregate Demographic Report, and an Aggregate Open-Ended Question Report. The Aggregate MPI Report is identical in structure to an individual MPI report but displays the cohort averages for each element of the report (i.e., scales and balance charts). The Aggregate Demographic Report is generated using descriptive statistics to provide a sense of the overall background of the cohort members. The Open-Ended Question Report is a simple listing of all the cohort members' responses to the question: "What single piece of advice would you offer to other cooperating teachers?"

Statistical comparisons across cohorts using Aggregate MPI Reports are done with one-way ANOVAs for the 14 scales, where $p < .05$ Games-Howell tests for post-hoc multiple comparisons are applied to determine which specific cohort means differed from each other and by how much. In particular, the Games-Howell procedure does not assume equal variances across groups, hence corrects for unequal sample sizes while remaining sensitive to small differences between means. Throughout, we maintained a standard $p < .05$ alpha level to determine the significance of differences between means or any pairs of means. Comparisons of Aggregate Demographic Reports are done using descriptive statistics and then compared across cohorts. Finally, Open-Ended Question

TEACHERS' PERCEPTIONS, EXPERIENCE AND LEARNING

Report comparisons are generated by categorizing the participants' responses and then constructing overarching themes using the constant comparative method (Lincoln & Guba, 1985). Theme construction is an inductive process and begins with category identification. As each new category is proposed, a working definition (including key criteria for item inclusion in each category) is established. As each new item for inclusion in a category is examined, the existing categories are scrutinized and judged to be either "still robust", "subject to modification" (including the addition of a new category if necessary) or "discarded". As the categories become increasingly stable, overarching themes are constructed that represent the general tenor of the respondents' comments.

Participants

Chinese cohort

In 2011, there were approximately 500 secondary school cooperating teachers involved in the UGS practicum initiative. Of these, 240 took up the invitation to attend a two-week residential professional development programme at NENU offered as a benefit to all UGS teachers participating in the UGS initiative. The residential programme provides advanced studies in the teachers' areas of disciplinary expertise (e.g., Maths, Chinese Literature, etc.). However, it is important to note that the programme does not provide any professional development associated with their work as cooperating teachers. The 2011 residential programme provided an ideal opportunity to administer the MPI to an intact group of UGS teachers. Ninety-seven percent (n = 234) of the UGS teachers completed the MPI and constitute the Chinese cohort which is the central focus of this paper.

International cohorts

Between 2009 and 2012, three separate groups of cooperating teachers in both urban and rural contexts in Australia (n = 82, secondary teachers), Canada (n = 456, elementary and secondary teachers), and New Zealand (n = 61, secondary teachers) also completed the MPI. The response rates represent 60%, 73%, and 85% respectively of those invited to participate in each of these jurisdictions. Similar to the Chinese cohort, the cooperating teachers for the international cohorts were connected to an urban university (Monash University in Australia, the University of British Columbia in Canada, and the University of Auckland in New Zealand).

Site visits

Chinese cohort

The purpose of the site visits was for the researchers to familiarize themselves with the contexts in which the UGS initiative took place. In 2011 and 2012, two members of the research team (both co-authors of this paper, one Chinese and one North American) went to two of the four northeastern provinces (one province each year) and visited three UGS schools in each of those provinces. The researchers engaged in informal conversations with a total of 16 UGS cooperating teachers (2–3 teachers in each of the six schools) and six administrators (one associated with each of the six schools, comprising of three principals, one vice-principal, and two regional administrators). The researchers also engaged in informal conversations with 24 student teachers and observed 18 student teacher lessons evenly distributed across the six schools. Field notes were taken during all conversations and classroom observations. The field notes are used in this paper to provide contextual details enabling a broader understanding of the MPI survey responses than would otherwise be possible using the MPI data only.

Cohort contexts

The contexts of the four cohorts used in the comparative analysis differed in a number of ways (e.g., politically, culturally, professionally). For example, some of the cooperating teachers in the Chinese cohort worked with three or four student teachers during the practicum in one or two classrooms. Further, to complete the practicum, the Chinese student teachers had to successfully teach 12 full lessons over the course of their practicum. In the other contexts, cooperating teachers typically work with one or two student teachers in one or two classrooms and therefore student teachers have more teaching time within those classrooms during the practicum. Also, in other contexts student teachers were expected to successfully teach up to 36 full lessons. However, it should be noted that Chinese student teachers spent a considerable amount of their time micro-teaching their lessons in front of their peers prior to their actual classroom teaching. Additionally, in UGS schools, which are for the most part boarding schools, the pupils return to their classrooms after their evening meal to study, to do their homework, and to seek additional assistance from their teachers. As a result, it is not unusual for cooperating teachers and student teachers to spend two or three evenings a week providing additional help to their students. Finally, student enrolment in the Chinese classrooms is at least twice the size of student enrolment in classrooms in the other three countries used for the comparative analysis in this study. Therefore, the amount of time devoted to helping students plus the time required to evaluate student work is twice that for classrooms in the other contexts. Therefore, we would argue that the total time that the student teachers spend "teaching" is reasonably comparable across the four contexts in terms of eliciting the cooperating teachers' sense of their work with student teachers in the practicum setting.

Another difference across contexts is the reward structures for the cooperating teachers. In China, the UGS teachers have the opportunity to participate in a fully paid two-week residential programme at NENU based on their subject area expertise (N.B.: at the present time no part of this programme is spent addressing their work as cooperating teachers). Similarly, teachers in the three international comparative countries receive very little recognition for their work as cooperating teachers. In Australia and New Zealand, the cooperating teachers received a small stipend for supervising student teachers. In Canada, the cooperating teachers received a tuition fee waiver to take a course at the University. The MPI does not ask about compensation but it is a factor to consider when comparing contexts. However, the literature suggests that intrinsic rather than extrinsic rewards are more important in determining cooperating teacher participation in the practicum and therefore rewards such as those outlined above are likely to have less impact than might initially be anticipated (Ganser, 1996; Korinek, 1989; Sinclair et al., 2006). Finally, the length of the practicum varies from country to country: the extended practicum is 13 weeks in Canada, 12 weeks in New Zealand, 11 weeks in Australia, and 10 weeks in China.

In sum, while differences exist across contexts, we believe that the similarities are greater than the differences. As such, we contend that comparisons across the Asian, Australasian, and North American contexts in this study are reasonable and able therefore to provide useful insights that might not be possible through a single-context perspective.

Results

The analysis is presented in two parts:
Part 1. Baseline Chinese Data, including:

(a) an overview of the Chinese cohort demographics;
(b) a macro-level analysis of MPI: the three balance charts;
(c) a micro-level analysis of MPI: the fourteen scales; and
(d) the teachers' responses to the MPI open-ended question.

Part 2. International Comparative Data, including a comparison of:

(a) the three motivator scales that are significantly different for the Chinese cohort;
(b) the three challenge scales that are significantly different for the Chinese cohort;
(c) the third balance chart that is significantly different for the Chinese cohort; and
(d) the teachers' responses to the MPI open-ended question.

The first part provides baseline data for the Chinese cohort and is important for understanding how UGS cooperating teachers conceive of their work with student teachers. The second part, the comparative analysis, shifts the analysis to a higher level as it moves from a single-context to a multi-context analysis enabling the identification of statistically significant differences between the Chinese and the other three cohorts. As such, these results highlight particularly distinctive outcomes for the Chinese cohort and are therefore critical for our exploration of the UGS initiative for rural practicum placements.

Part 1. Baseline Chinese data

1 (a) An overview of the Chinese cohort demographics

The demographic information collected as part of the MPI provides general background information for the Chinese cohort. Of the respondents who completed the MPI, all 234 were secondary school teachers: 144 were female and 90 were male. All 234 had post-secondary qualifications with the majority (74%) holding bachelor's degrees in arts, science, or education (see Table 2). A large majority of cooperating teachers (79%) had six or more years of teaching experience at the time of the study (Table 3).

About three-quarters of the cooperating teachers (78%) had supervised at least one student teacher, but 18% (41 teachers) had not supervised any student teacher prior to the study (see Table 4). Of those with supervisory experience, the average number of students supervised was four. It should be noted that many teacher education institutions that are located outside the large urban centres in China (unlike NENU) do not have the resources

Table 2. Cooperating teachers' qualifications.

Educational Qualification	Males	Females	Totals
Secondary School Diploma	15	22	37
Bachelor of Arts	36	41	77
Bachelor of Science	14	41	55
Bachelor of Education	1	4	5
Other Bachelors Degree	14	22	36
Masters Degree	9	14	23
Doctoral Degree	0	0	0
Other	1	0	1
Total	90	144	234

TEACHERS' PERCEPTIONS, EXPERIENCE AND LEARNING

Table 3. Cooperating teachers' years of teaching experience.

Number of Years Teaching	Males	Females	Totals
0–5	17	31	48 (21%)
6–10	22	38	60 (26%)
11–15	18	31	49 (21%)
16–20	15	30	45 (19%)
21–25	11	13	24 (10%)
26–30	5	0	5 (2%)
31–35	2	0	2 (1%)
Not provided	–	–	1 (negligible)
Total	90	143	234 (100%)

to formally organize practicum placements for their students. Therefore, student teachers are expected to make their own arrangements for practicum by contacting individual schools or teachers themselves. After graduation, most of the graduates from these institutions take up positions in non-urban schools (often in their original home towns). As a result, even though many cooperating teachers report having supervised student teachers, few have had the opportunity to work in any organized or structured way with student teachers such as the practicum initiative offered by the UGS initiative and of the sort that is typically found in the other three countries used for the international comparison.

1 (b) Macro-level analysis of MPI: the three balance charts

The MPI balance charts show three things: the balance between self and other-directed motivators, the balance between interpersonal and systemic challenges, and the overall balance between being motivated or challenged in working with a student teacher (Figure 2). In general, the MPI shows that the Chinese cohort were motivated to work with student teachers for a number of reasons that pertained to themselves (e.g., "It's satisfying . . .") in equal proportion to what they felt they were able to offer to others (e.g., "Develop students into teachers . . .") (Figure 2, leftmost chart). This balanced proportionality of inward and outward sources of satisfaction and rewards for teachers

Table 4. Cooperating teacher supervision experience.

Number of Student Teachers Supervised	Males	Females	Totals
0	10	31	41
1	16	26	42
2	19	34	53
3	12	22	34
4	6	3	9
5	10	8	18
6	1	3	4
7	0	0	0
8	3	4	7
9	0	3	3
10	1	7	8
11–15	6	1	7
16–20	3	1	4
No response	1	1	2
Total	90	143	234

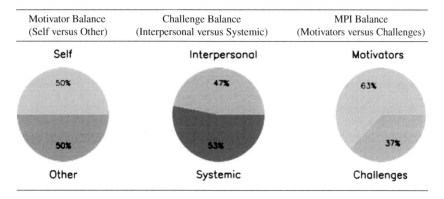

Figure 2. The three MPI balance charts for the Chinese cohort.

engaged in the UGS initiative is a positive result and indicative of a positive environment for the UGS initiative (Clarke, 2010).

The challenge chart (Figure 2, centre chart) distinguishes between interpersonal (e.g., "Communication difficulties") and systemic (e.g., "Unclear evaluation guidelines") challenges that cooperating teachers face in their work with student teachers. The analysis of the Chinese challenge chart shows that systemic issues slightly outweighed interpersonal issues by 53% to 47% indicating overall a reasonable balance between the two sectors (i.e., neither dominates in terms of the challenges inherent in cooperating teachers' work with student teachers). Again, as above, this near-balance between the sectors is a heartening outcome (Clarke, 2010).

Finally, the MPI generates an overall "balance" chart between what motivates and what challenges cooperating teachers in their work with student teachers (Figure 2, rightmost chart). The analysis of the Chinese cohort results shows that motivators for working with student teachers outweigh the challenges by 63% to 37%. This is a very encouraging result and is consistent with the willingness of the teachers in rural schools to take up the UGS opportunity.

In sum, the MPI results for the Chinese cohort show their self/other motivator sectors and interpersonal/systemic challenge sectors of the first two charts to be fairly evenly balanced and the third chart indicates that overall UGS cooperating teachers are more motivated than challenged in their work with student teachers. At a macro-level, the MPI balance charts point to a healthy future for the UGS partnership. The following micro-level analysis provides a closer examination of the 14 scales that comprise the three balance charts.

1 (c) Micro-level analysis of MPI: the fourteen scales

An analysis of the motivator scales indicates high levels of motivation across all eight scales for the Chinese cohort (in the range of 37/50–39/50, Figure 3) suggesting that the Chinese cohort are highly motivated in their work with student teachers and across a broad range of issues. Although we cannot tell if this situation existed prior to or is a result of the UGS initiative, it augurs well for the future of the partnership in which the cooperating teachers play a central role.

Further, the challenge scales indicated comparatively few serious challenges and most had numerical scores in the upper teens and low twenties (where a score of 50 would

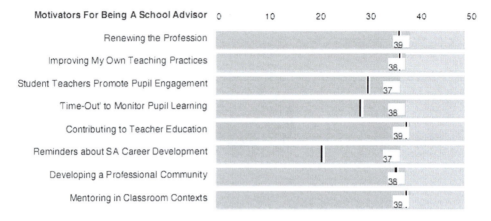

Figure 3. The eight MPI motivator scale scores for the Chinese cohort. Note: Intermediate numerical values on each bar indicate the scores for the Chinese cohorts. The black bars indicate the mean scores for the Canadian cohort, the original creator and users of the MPI.

indicate a very serious challenge). However, two of the six scales indicated moderate challenges that the cooperating teachers face in their current work with student teachers: *Inadequate Forms and Guidelines* (26/50) and *Unclear Policies and Procedures* (28/50) (Figure 4). The individual MPI items that constitute these two scales suggest particular areas that the UGS partners might wish to investigate (e.g., Evaluation forms which are sensitive, topical and relevant; Guidelines for being an effective faculty advisor).

In sum, the 14 scales for the Chinese cohort suggest that the cooperating teachers are highly motivated but two of the challenge scales warrant attention to ensure continuing support for and participation by the cooperating teachers in the UGS initiative by the Chinese cooperating teachers.

1 (d) The teachers' responses to the MPI open-ended question

The open-ended question at the end of the MPI ("What advice would you give to other cooperating teachers?") provides the opportunity for Chinese cooperating teachers to share their experience as practicum supervisors with other teachers. Fifty-seven teachers

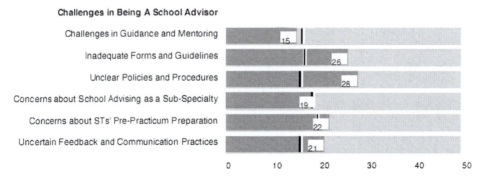

Figure 4. The six MPI challenge scales scores for the Chinese cohort. Note: Intermediate numerical values on each bar indicate the scores for the Chinese cohorts. The black bars indicate the mean scores for the Canadian cohort, the original creator and users of the MPI.

(24%) responded to this question and offered 87 suggestions. Four overarching themes emerged from the analysis of the suggestions and point to the importance that the Chinese cohort placed on: (1) practice teaching; (2) moral commitments; (3) mutual learning; and (4) practical knowledge. A brief description including the frequency of key responses within each theme follows.

Eighteen teachers mentioned that cooperating teachers should "let go of the classroom" and give their student teachers as much opportunity as possible for practice teaching. The most common support for this advice was based on the assertion that the practicum is a learning-by-observation experience as much as it is a learning-by-teaching experience. As such, the respondents to this question argued that cooperating teachers should ensure that student teachers are given ample opportunity to actually practise *teaching* during the course of the practicum.

Fourteen teachers talked about a set of *moral commitments* associated with their work as cooperating teachers, that is, "what must happen because it is the right thing to do" (Verhack, 2001). The examples that the Chinese cohort provided included:

- treat the student teachers as your own children;
- share what you know selflessly;
- be open and sincere;
- set a good example;
- be patient;
- allow them enough autonomy to develop their own teaching style; and
- learn to appreciate them for who they are (i.e., respect them as individuals).

In short, the responses revealed that the Chinese cohort consider their advisory practices as more than a set of undifferentiated skills and, in contrast, emphasized the strong moral component that underlies their work with student teachers.

Eleven teachers noted that mentoring is a *mutual learning* experience underscoring the reciprocal benefits for both the student teacher and cooperating teacher during the practicum. For example, a number of Chinese cooperating teachers indicated that they were interested in discovering what their student teachers had learned about the new School Curriculum Reform effort from their university studies, specifically the strategies that embody more active approaches to student learning.

Finally, five teachers spoke about the need to impart *practical knowledge* to their student teachers such as how to "construct clear lesson plans", "manage pupil behaviour", and "make the transition from student teacher to practising professional". These four overarching categories are not particularly surprising and are discussed in more detail in the comparative analysis section of this paper.

Part 2: international comparative data

The MPI is a relatively new instrument and has been completed by three other international cohorts of cooperating teachers to date: Australia (n = 82), New Zealand (n = 61), and Canada (n = 456). In this section we provide a comparative analysis of differences between the Chinese cohort and their international counterparts. This analysis is informed by "comparative pedagogy" (Alexander, 2001; Bray, 2007), a practice that allows us to identify distinctive differences in a particular context by comparing it with other contexts – distinctions that might otherwise remain unnoticed if only viewed from a single-context perspective. Chinese distinctiveness, as we define it, is met when the Chinese results are significantly different from all three of their international counterparts

TEACHERS' PERCEPTIONS, EXPERIENCE AND LEARNING

simultaneously for a particular scale or **simultaneously for a particular chart**. This criterion is satisfied on seven occasions in this study: for three motivator scales, for three challenge scales, and for one balance chart.

One possible explanation for these significant differences might be demographic factors. However, an examination of the demographic data for all four countries indicates there are no significant demographic differences (accounting for less than 1% of the between-country variances). This results suggests that explanations for the seven occasions in this study when the Chinese MPI results are significantly different simultaneously from all three of their international counterparts are to be found in factors other than gender, academic background, teaching experience, or supervision experience.

2 (a) The three motivator scales that are significantly different for the Chinese cohort

Of the eight MPI motivator scales that constitute the MPI, the Chinese cohort scores were significantly higher on three scales (Figure 5 and Table 5). In descending order of difference, the Chinese teachers scored significantly higher than the average of the other three countries (by the indicated amounts) on:

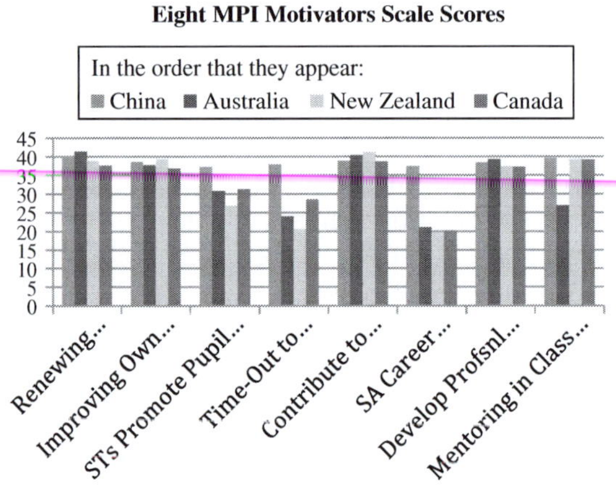

Figure 5. Comparisons of MPI motivators for four different countries.

Table 5. Significant differences in MPI motivators in China compared to other countries (shaded rows indicate significant difference simultaneous with all other countries).

Motivators Scales	Australia	New Zealand	Canada
• Renewing the Profession	ns	ns	China ↑
• Improving My Own Teaching Practices	ns	ns	ns
• Student Teachers Promote Pupil Engagement	China ↑	China ↑	China ↑
• Time-Out' to Monitor Pupil Learning	China ↑	China ↑	China ↑
• Contributing to Teacher Education	ns	ns	ns
• Reminders about Career Development	China ↑	China ↑	China ↑
• Developing a Professional Community	ns	ns	China ↑
• Mentoring in Classroom Contexts	ns	ns	ns

China ↑ = Chinese scores are significantly higher than those from the corresponding country
China ↓ = Chinese scores are significantly lower than those from the corresponding country
ns = No significant difference between Chinese scores and corresponding countries.

TEACHERS' PERCEPTIONS, EXPERIENCE AND LEARNING

- Reminders about Career Development (+17 points)
- Time-Out to Monitor Pupil Learning (+14 point)
- Student Teachers Promote Pupil Engagement (+8 point) (Figure 5 and Table 5)

Thus, compared to their international counterparts, the Chinese cohort reported more rewards and benefits: for prospects of career development, advancement, and promotion; for opportunities to monitor pupils' needs, to monitor and reflect on classroom learning, and to work one-on-one with pupils; and, finally, to take advantage of student teachers' presence in terms of enhancing pupil interest, helping raise diversity issues, and promoting pupil engagement.

2 (b) The three challenge scales that are significantly different for the Chinese cohort

Of the six MPI challenge scales that constitute the various difficulties facing cooperating teachers, the scores for Chinese cohort were significantly higher on three scales (Figure 6 and Table 6). In descending order of difference, the Chinese teachers scored significantly higher than the average of the other three countries (by the indicated amounts):

- Unclear Policies and Procedures (+10)
- Inadequate Forms and Guidelines (+8)
- Uncertain Feedback and Communication Practices (+2)

Therefore, the Chinese cooperating teachers reported being faced with more difficulties than their international counterparts in terms of: lack of clarity about roles and responsibilities, power and authority issues; lack of access to university resources; unclear evaluation guidelines for assessing student teachers, and vague feedback procedures; and communication challenges among school staff, lack of feedback from administrators, and deficient procedures for learning what is working and what is not in the practicum setting.

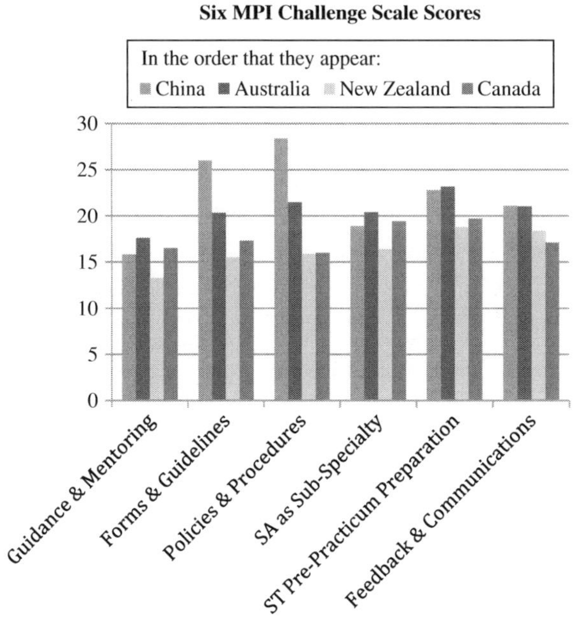

Six MPI Challenge Scale Scores

Figure 6. Comparisons of MPI challenges for four different countries.

47

Table 6. Significant difference in MPI challenges in China compared to other countries (shaded rows indicate significant difference simultaneous with all other countries).

Challenge Scales	Australia	New Zealand	Canada
• Challenges in Guidance and Mentoring	ns	ns	ns
• Inadequate Forms and Guidelines	China ↑	China ↑	China ↑
• Unclear Policies and Procedures	China ↑	China ↑	China ↑
• Concerns about School Advising as a Sub-Specialty	ns	ns	ns
• Concerns about STs' Pre-Practicum Preparation	ns	ns	China ↑
• Uncertain Feedback and Communication Practices	China ↑	China ↑	China ↑

China ↑ = Chinese scores are significantly higher than those from the corresponding country
China ↓ = Chinese scores are significantly lower than those from the corresponding country
ns = No significant difference between Chinese scores and corresponding countries.

2 (c) The balance chart that is significantly different for the Chinese cohort

Finally, the comparative analysis reveals that the third balance chart – the overall balance between the 32 motivators and 30 challenge items – shows that the size of the motivator and challenge sectors are similar for all four countries, in the ratio of approximately 3:2. However the scores for the motivator and challenge sectors for the Chinese cohort are significantly different and higher in both cases than all three other countries simultaneously but nonetheless in the ratio of 3:2.

2 (d) The teachers' responses to the MPI's open-ended question

Each of the four overarching categories identified in the Chinese cohort's response to the open-ended question – practice teaching, moral commitments, mutual learning, and practical knowledge – are consistent with the open-ended responses from the other three countries. However, conspicuous by its absence in the UGS responses compared to the other countries is any reference to "encouraging student teacher inquiry". Although we cannot establish "distinctiveness" in terms of the statistical significance (as the answers to this question rely on qualitative methods), this difference in the advice that UGS cooperating teachers offer to their peers is noteworthy in terms of both the School Curriculum Reform and Teacher Education Reform efforts in China that place an emphasis on more active forms of student engagement. This result suggests that an emphasis on inquiry is not something that the UGS teachers currently consider in their work with student teachers, even though it is an emphasis in the reform documents.

Discussion

The UGS practicum initiative situates the student teachers' practicum in locations not typically associated with large urban universities. Further, as these schools are located in relatively isolated areas, it is often harder for cooperating teachers to encounter new ideas or concepts associated with current educational practices. Working with the student teachers as part of the UGS practicum initiative is one way for the teachers to have access to these ideas and practices. As noted earlier, another advantage of the UGS initiative is that it provides a 2-week residential professional development programme for cooperating teachers which is an incentive to participate in the practicum. It is important to bear these contextual factors in mind in the discussion that follows. Further, in this discussion, we focus primarily on the six significant scale differences highlighted above and fold in the other elements (e.g., contextual details and advice offered to colleagues) as they pertain to these six results. We interpret the **three significantly different motivators** as indicators of a positive and highly supportive practicum context that augurs well for the future of the UGS initiative. We consider the **three significantly different challenges** as cautionary signals that highlight local concerns that the cooperating teachers currently encounter in their work with student teachers.

Three significantly different motivators for the Chinese cohort

Student teachers promote pupil engagement

This significantly elevated difference recorded by the Chinese cohort in comparison to their international counterparts highlights the importance that Chinese cooperating teachers place on having student teachers in their classrooms. Chinese classrooms are well known for their highly regulated approach to instruction exemplified by the extensive use of in-class lectures and "drill and practice" exercises (Gao & Watkins, 2002). This MPI outcome supports our experience in UGS schools over the past two years which suggests that in many instances UGS cooperating teachers see the arrival of a student teacher as a "breath of fresh air" (not a disruption to their teaching order) in their desire for less regulated classrooms. For example, by organizing small-group activities, using simulations, and incorporating new media, they believe their student teachers promote, not hinder, pupil learning. These new approaches to teaching are consistent with the school curriculum reform effort and the cooperating teachers regard their student teachers as more knowledgeable and better equipped in these matters than they are themselves. As such, we interpret the cooperating teachers' strong endorsement of "Student Teachers Promote Pupil Engagement" as recognition of having young professionals in their classrooms who can introduce and demonstrate new ideas and approaches to instruction that enliven their classrooms. As such, this outcome reflects one of the three central commitments to being a cooperating teacher: a commitment to pupils (Feiman-Nemser, 2001; Kent, 2001).

"Time-Out" to monitor pupil learning

The importance for UGS teachers of having time out to monitor pupil learning as a motivator, we believe, arises from the very large (even overcrowded) classrooms evident in the Chinese context and which stand in sharp contrast to classrooms in Australia, Canada, and New Zealand (OECD, 2012). For example, a typical secondary school classroom in a UGS school has 60 pupils; in each of the comparison countries the maximum size is approximately 30 pupils. Further, our experience in both East and West classrooms confirms that the 60 Chinese pupils in a Chinese classroom are accommodated in a space similar in size to that which accommodates 30 pupils in each of the three comparison countries. As such, the classroom densities (i.e., students per square foot) in China make it much more difficult to monitor pupil learning. However with a student teacher present, the Chinese cooperating teachers have a greater opportunity to pursue issues related to individual pupil learning. For example, with a student teacher present, the Chinese cooperating teachers can move around the classroom and monitor student learning in a way that they rarely get the chance to do so at any other time during the school year. We are not suggesting that these opportunities do not exist to some degree in regular Chinese classrooms, however they are greatly increased with a student teacher present. Again, this outcome reflects the cooperating teachers' commitment to pupils.

Reminders about career development

School teachers in China have heavy workloads; they work in their classroom all day long, beginning sometimes quite early in the morning and going into the early evening. As a result, there is little opportunity for them to stop and deliberately reflect on their practice. The practicum places a second adult in a classroom with whom they can share their teaching responsibilities allowing classroom teachers to have more time to pause and think about their work. This additional support represents a proportionally greater possibility for professional learning (i.e., conversations about practice, assessment of resources, etc.) in the Chinese context than might be the case in other contexts in which such flexibility already exists or is "built into" the work day (e.g., North American contexts).

Because the Chinese teachers are involved in a formal practicum partnership with a university, they are also more likely to interrogate their own teaching practice in ways that might not otherwise be the case in the course of their daily practice (Clarke, 2006). The data from this study suggests that the Chinese cohort wants to "set a good example" for the student teachers. As such, our results suggest that the UGS teachers are thinking more deeply about their educational beliefs and practices in ways that they may have taken for granted prior to entering the more formal UGS practicum initiative and as compared to their former practices with student teachers.

Why might this be significantly different for the Chinese cohort than those of their international counterparts? First, we believe that the UGS initiative provides an on-going relationship with the university that is substantially different from the ad hoc arrangements governing previous practicum arrangements in their schools. Second, we argue that the UGS initiative has come at a time of profound curriculum reform in China and has provided an unprecedented set of prompts for the cooperating teachers to reflect on their careers through: (1) energized and "knowledgeable" student teachers; (2) on-site professional interaction with a university representative; and (3) a 2-week fully-funded residential professional development programme. As a result, the reminder about career development is very much evident in their MPI results compared to their international counterparts and highlights the third of the three commitments to being a cooperating teacher reported in the literature: a commitment to self (Clarke, 2006; Koskela & Ganser, 1998).

Three significantly different challenges for the Chinese cohort

Inadequate forms and guidelines

Chinese teachers are accustomed to following instructions, especially those in schools distant from the large urban centres (where Ministry offices and universities are typically located). In short, these teachers rarely have unfettered access to the practices they are expected to enact and the curriculum that they are expected to teach. If the lines of communication are not well maintained, then these teachers are left in uncertainty and doubt about their roles and responsibilities. For example, recent studies have shown that critical thinking and creativity are not characteristics of current Chinese pedagogical practices and while these might be evident in schools in large urban centres, they are less so in rural or remote locations (Lockette, 2012). It is therefore important that the UGS initiative is well-defined and that concise guidelines for mentoring and evaluating student teachers are provided for cooperating teachers.

Also as noted earlier, many teacher education institutions outside of large urban centres in China do not typically offer organized practicum placements for student teachers. Therefore, student teachers are left to their own devices to find practicum placements. This is a practice that many UGS teachers experienced themselves when they were student teachers. This situation might come as a surprise to teacher educators from outside of China and it is not widely discussed, even if referenced, within the Chinese context (Han et al., 2007; Yao, 2012). As a result, many cooperating teachers themselves have not experienced a formalized practicum experience and therefore it is difficult for them to grasp some of the basic functions associated with mentoring a beginning teacher (e.g., modelling of classroom teaching, modelling of lesson planning, etc.). As a result, the UGS teachers are seeking very clear direction from the university. Thus, clear forms and guidelines for assessing student teachers is an important starting point for them. Even in western contexts, cooperating teachers often seek more guidance from their university partners in these matters (Clarke, 2003). Further, at the current time within the UGS initiative there are no specific mentoring programmes (workshops, seminars, or courses) for those volunteering to be cooperating teachers. As a result the cooperating teachers are heavily dependent on the university supervisor to direct their day-to-day tasks associated with working with student teachers. Of the three commitments to being a cooperating teacher – to pupils, to the profession, or to self – this result points directly to the cooperating teachers' commitment to the profession (Kitchell & White, 2007; Sinclair et al., 2006). In this instance, without adequate forms and guidelines, the UGS cooperating teachers feel that are failing to fulfil their commitment to the profession in their role as mentors to new teachers.

Unclear policies and procedures

Related to inadequate forms and guidelines but at one step higher programmatically are difficulties associated with unclear policies and procedures governing the practicum. The UGS teachers want to better understand the ways that their work is related to the broader educational imperatives upon which the UGS partnership is founded. Our experience with NENU suggests that the university has clear policies and procedures related to teacher education, however this study's results clearly suggest that either these have not been communicated to the teachers or, if so, they do not make sense to the teachers.

From our experience in UGS schools, this issue is compounded because teachers get mixed messages from the three partners in the UGS initiative indicating that the partners "may not be on the same page". One example is the regulation stipulating the minimum number of lessons that student teachers are required to teach during the practicum. The university requires at least 12 but the cooperating teachers have different interpretations depending on administrative oversight, or lack thereof, at the local level. As a result, the cooperating teachers do not know who they should listen to and, in our experience in UGS schools, the university faculty members have to constantly negotiate the student teachers' teaching loads so that there are either more opportunities to teach (for example, some teachers are reluctant to give up their senior classes) or a reduction in their workloads (for example, some teachers give over their entire junior class responsibilities to the student teachers). Thus, while the UGS initiative has been clearly welcomed by the teachers, there still is much work to be done in clearly articulating and communicating the policies and procedures upon which the UGS initiative is grounded. This outcome once again reflects the teachers' concern that they are unable to fulfil their commitment to the profession in their role as cooperating teachers.

Uncertain feedback and communication practices

Finally, the results of this study indicate that feedback and communication practices are significantly more challenging for the Chinese cooperating teachers than for their counterparts in the other three countries. In short, the Chinese cohort indicates difficulty in effectively engaging with colleagues, administrators, and university personnel around issues related to the practicum. This continues a trend evident in the two previous challenges. We interpret this further challenge as a call for greater engagement with and communication around what and how cooperating teachers are making sense of and responding to the expectations for their work as practicum supervisors. For example from our experience in UGS schools, many cooperating teachers regard the university representatives as being from "another world" and "not very approachable". In the context of teacher education reform there is still a wide gap between the two parties: the school teachers are often seen as "only focusing on daily teaching practice" and "resistant to change" while the university representatives are seen as providing "empty theories" and "unrealistic ideals". So within the context of the UGS partnership, it is important for the university representatives to reach out to cooperating teachers and invite open discussion on student teacher mentoring, teaching practice, curriculum reform, among others. Likewise, it is important for the teachers to take up that conversation in the interest of maximizing the learning opportunities for themselves and their student teachers. This result echoes the two earlier challenges in that the cooperating teachers' commitment to the profession is further threatened by uncertain feedback and communication procedures.

Conclusion

To the best of our knowledge, this study provides one of the first explorations of Chinese cooperating teachers' commitment to the practicum. The Northeast Normal University UGS initiative provides the context and the recently developed Mentoring Profile Inventory the method for this exploration. The outcome is an account of the commitments, rendered as motivations and challenges, to being a cooperating teacher within the context of the UGS initiative. The current study also provided the chance to draw on the newly developed MPI to generate baseline and comparative data within the Chinese context. In this study, the comparative analysis highlighted particularly distinctive features of the UGS cohort that might have been overlooked from a single-context perspective.

References

Alexander, R. J. (2001). Border crossings: Towards a comparative pedagogy. *Comparative Education, 37*, 507–523.

Ambrose, S., Bridges, S., DiPietro, M., Lovett, M. C., & Norman, M. K. (2010). *How learning works: Seven research-based principles for smart teaching*. San Francisco: Jossey-Bass.

Borko, H. (2004). Professional development and teacher learning: Mapping the terrain. *Educational Researcher, 33*, 3–15.

Bray, M. (2007). Actors and purposes in comparative education. In M. Bray, B. Anderson, & M. Mason (Eds.), *Comparative education research. Approaches and methods* (pp. 15–38). Hong Kong: University of Hong Kong Press, CERC & Springer.

Bullough, R. V. Jr, & Draper, R. J. (2004). Mentoring and the emotions. *Journal of Education for Teaching: International Research Pedagogy, 30*, 271–288.

China Ministry of Education. (2001). *The guidelines for curriculum reform of basic education*. Beijing: Ministry of Education.

China Ministry of Education. (2007). *The 8th press conference of the ministry of education in 2007*. Retrieved June 17, 2008, from http://www.moe.gov.cn/edoas/website18/34/info31934.htm

Clarke, A. (2003). Characteristics of cooperating teachers. *Canadian Journal of Education, 26*, 237–256.

Clarke, A. (2006). The nature and substance of cooperating teacher reflection. *Teaching and Teacher Education, 22*, 910–921.

Clarke, A. (2010). *A mentoring profile inventory for cooperating teachers.* Paper presented at the Australian Association for Research in Education, Melbourne, Australia.

Clarke, A. (2012). *Innovations in supervision: Explorations of the relationship between teacher candidate, cooperating teacher, and university supervisor.* Vancouver: Canada Symposium conducted at the annual meeting of the American Educational Research Association.

Clarke, A., Collins, J., Triggs, V., Nielsen, W., Augustine, A., Coulter, D., ... Weil, F. (2012). The mentoring profile inventory: An online professional development resource for cooperating teachers. *Teaching Education, 23*, 167–194.

Clarke, A., Triggs, V., & Nielsen, W. (2012). *A review of the cooperating teacher literature: 1948–2011.* Paper presented at the annual meeting of the American Educational Research Association. Vancouver, Canada.

Crasborn, F., Hennissen, P., Brouwer, N., Korthagen, F., & Bergen, T. (2008). Promoting versatility in mentor teachers' use of supervisory skills. *Teaching and Teacher Education, 24*, 499–514.

Feiman-Nemser, S. (2001). Helping novices learn to teach: Lessons from an exemplary support teacher. *Journal of Teacher Education, 52*, 17–30.

Ganser, T. (1996). What do mentors say about mentoring? *Journal of Staff Development, 17*, 36–39.

Gao, L., & Watkins, D. A. (2002). Conceptions of teaching held by school science teachers in P.R. China: Identification and cross-cultural comparisons. *International Journal of Science Education, 24*, 61–79.

Goodfellow, J. (2000). Knowing from the inside: reflective conversations with and through the narratives of one cooperating teacher. *Reflective Practice, 1*, 25–42.

Gravetter, F. J., & Forzano, L. B. (2009). *Research methods for the behavioral sciences* (3rd ed.). Belmont, CA: Wadsworth/Thomson.

Han, L., Yu, X., Qin, W., Liu, L., Min, H., & Qiuli, G. (2007). Investigation about teaching practice of Normal universities' and colleges' students. *Higher Education Research and Evaluation, 11*, 5–9.

Hobson, A. J., Ashby, P., Malderez, A., & Tomlinson, P. D. (2009). Mentoring beginning teachers: What we know and what we don't. *Teaching and Teacher Education, 25*, 207–216.

Kent, S. (2001). Supervision of student teachers: Practices of cooperating teachers prepared in a clinical supervision course. *Journal of Curriculum and Supervision, 16*, 228–244.

Kitchell, T., & White, C. (2007). *Barriers and benefits to the student teacher/cooperating teacher relationship.* Paper presented at the National Agricultural Education Research Conference.

Knowles, G. J., & Cole, A. L. (1996). Developing practice through field experiences. In F. B. Murray (Ed.), *The teacher educator's handbook: Building a knowledge base for the preparation of teachers* (p. xv). San Francisco: Jossey-Bass.

Korinek, L. A. (1989). Teacher preferences for training and compensation for field supervision. *Journal of Teacher Education, 40*, 46–51.

Koskela, R., & Ganser, T. (1998). The cooperating teacher role and career development. *Education, 119*, 106–125.

Lincoln, Y. S., & Guba, E. G. (1985). *Naturalistic inquiry.* Newbury Park, CA: Sage.

Lockette, K. (2012). Creativity and Chinese education reform. *International Journal of Global Education, 1*, 34–39.

Loucks-Horsley, S. (2003). *Designing professional development for teachers of science and mathematics.* Thousand Oaks, CA: Corwin Press.

Meyer, J. P., Becker, T. E., & Vandenberghe, C. (2004). Employee commitment and motivation: A conceptual analysis and integrative model. *Journal of Applied Psychology, 89*, 991–1007.

OECD. (2012). How many students are in each classroom? Education at a Glance 2012: Highlights. *OECD Publishing.* Retrieved: Dec 25, 2012. Available at: http://dx.doi.org/10.1787/eag_highlights-2012-25-en

Sinclair, C., Dowson, M., & Thistleton-Martin, J. (2006). Motivations and profiles of cooperating teachers: Who volunteers and why? *Teaching and Teacher Education, 22*, 263–279.

Verhack, I. (2001). The meaning of the moral imperative. *Ethical Perspectives: Journal of the European Ethics Network, 8*, 232–253.

Wang, J., & Odell, S. J. (2002). Mentored learning to teach according to standards-based reform: A critical review. *Review of Educational Research, 72*, 481–546.

Yao, Y. (2012). The reform of teaching practice in China. *Educational Research, 2012*, 17–32.

Zeichner, K. M., Liston, D. P., Mahlios, M., & Gomez, M. (1987, April). *The structure and goals of a student teaching program and the character and quality of supervisory discourse*. Paper presented at the annual meetings of the American Educational Research Association, Washington, DC.

Meeting the challenges of teaching in a different cultural environment – evidence from graduate management schools in Thailand

Astrid Kainzbauer and Brian Hunt

In this paper we describe the efforts of foreign university teachers in graduate schools in Thailand as they incorporate cultural knowledge into their classroom teaching styles and methodology. Through in-depth semi-structured interviews we have gathered qualitative data on the teachers' concerns, mindsets and their proposed solutions. We build up our discussion in several stages. We set the scene by discussing the importance of cultural sensitivity in settings where teacher and learners have different cultural backgrounds. We then introduce the concept of cultural intelligence and use this to help us examine the literature on cultural sensitivity in teaching from a new perspective. We then describe the cultural context of teaching in Thailand and offer empirical data from our respondents' experiences. From our research data we identified five main aspects of Thai culture where teachers felt the need to expand/adapt their existing teaching repertoires. These aspects are: fun/*sanuk*; hierarchy/*kreng jai*; authority with a kind heart/*jai dee*; collectivist group activities; and localized class content. We discuss our findings in relation to cultural adjustments that the teachers sought to make and, in conclusion, link this discussion to our earlier examination of cultural intelligence.

Introduction

This paper focuses on the efforts of foreign teachers in Thailand to utilize cultural knowledge to refine and develop their teaching styles. The specific context of our research is Thai graduate management classes. We present original research that indicates how culturally responsive international teachers attempt to shape the context of their classroom environment with students of a different cultural background. In a globalizing world, the ability to deal with people from different cultural backgrounds has become increasingly important. In the context of teaching, this has two implications. As teachers, we need to prepare our students for the global challenges and we need to be culturally intelligent ourselves in dealing with students from different cultural backgrounds (Goh, 2012). In this paper, our focus is on the latter, that is, the challenges of teaching in a different cultural environment. We take insights from two relevant literatures, namely, culturally responsive teaching (e.g., Ladson-Billings, 1995; Weinstein, Tomlinson-Clarke, & Curran, 2004; Young, 2010) and cultural intelligence (Earley & Ang, 2003; Thomas, 2006; Thomas et al., 2008).

We employ a qualitative methodology using in-depth semi-structured teacher interviews. All of our respondents have repeatedly received positive feedback from anonymous student evaluations of their teaching. Our aim in this paper is to understand how these teachers make sense of the Thai cultural environment in their classrooms and which efforts they make to teach with cultural intelligence.

Cultural sensitivity and teaching

A number of authors have explored the topic of cultural sensitivity in teaching with different labels. They attribute phrases such as culturally relevant teaching (Ladson-Billings, 1995; Young, 2010), culturally centred pedagogy (Sheets, 1995), culturally responsive teaching (Bondy, Ross, Gallingane, & Hambacher, 2007; Brown, 2007; Gay, 2002; Villegas & Lucas, 2007). However, while the terminology may differ, in essence what these authors describe is "respect for cultural differences" (Nguyen, Terlouw, & Pilot, 2006, p. 2). Gay (2002) exemplifies culturally responsive teaching as "using the cultural characteristics, experiences, and perspectives of ethnically diverse students as conduits for teaching them more effectively" (Gay, 2002, p. 106).

Culturally responsive teachers therefore make efforts to learn about the cultures of their students, in particular their cultural background and prior learning experiences (Brown, 2007; Gay, 2000; Yourn & Kirkness, 2003). This also includes an understanding of their learners' broader social, economic and political context (Weinstein et al., 2004). Such awareness brings two benefits. On the one hand, teachers can thereby create a learning environment which includes recognizable features of the learners' outside world in order to create meaningful learning content (Gay, 2000). On the other hand, they can use this knowledge to employ classroom management strategies suitable for their students (Weinstein et al., 2004).

However, the literature suggests that cultural sensitivity is not solely about developing an environment that makes students feel culturally at ease. For example, Ladson-Billings (1995) emphasizes that while it is important to be aware of cultural integrity, teachers should also focus on their students' academic achievement. Thus, cultural integrity and striving for academic excellence go hand in hand. In fact, when teaching is culturally responsive, this is suggested to result in higher levels of academic achievement (Gay, 2000; Ladson-Billings, 1995; Sternberg, 2007).

Another key component of culturally relevant pedagogy is critical consciousness. In addition to striving for academic excellence and achievement, it has been emphasized that culturally relevant pedagogy should encourage students to attain a "broader socio-political consciousness" (Ladson-Billings, 1995, p. 162) through which they will be able to critique prevailing cultural norms (see also: Gay, 2010; Young, 2010). While interesting and important, this aspect of the literature is beyond the scope of our current paper.

A common response when discussing elements of culturally sensitive teaching is "But that's just good teaching!" Indeed, Gloria Ladson-Billings chose this as the title of her 1995 article on culturally relevant pedagogy. Culturally sensitive teaching is good teaching, but it is much more than that. Culturally sensitive teaching is good teaching plus consideration of the cultural context. Examples of how teachers achieved this adaptation to new cultural environments include Bodycott and Walker (2000), Richards (2004), Aguinis and Roth (2005).

The lens of cultural intelligence

It is invariably worthwhile cross-fertilizing two related but diverse literatures. One area that seems to have potential to provide valuable insights is "cultural intelligence", which focuses on understanding what it takes to be successful in working with people from different cultural backgrounds. Insights gained from research into cultural intelligence can stimulate our thinking for creating a better understanding of what it takes for teachers to be culturally intelligent in their classrooms. The construct of cultural intelligence has only recently been introduced in an attempt to define attributes that allow people to be effective in cross-cultural interactions (Earley, 2002; Earley & Ang, 2003; Thomas & Inkson, 2004). We apply this construct to the literature on culturally responsive teaching, in order to refine our understanding. Specifically, we choose the work of Thomas (2006) who describes cultural intelligence (CQ) as consisting of three components: knowledge, mindfulness, and behaviour. He defines cultural intelligence as "the capability to deal effectively with people from different cultural backgrounds" (Thomas, 2006, p. 94). Knowledge, in this framework, means knowing what culture is and how it varies, and behaviour refers to the ability to adjust behaviour based on the situation and expectations of others who are culturally different. The third component of cultural intelligence is "mindfulness" which is the "key mediating link between knowledge and behavioural ability" (Thomas, 2006, p. 86).

Cultural intelligence is therefore multidimensional and can be seen as a system of interacting abilities. The perspective of Thomas' (2006) concept of cultural intelligence provides us with a new lens to make sense of what culturally intelligent teachers do in their classrooms. Using this as our start point, we now review the literature on culturally responsive teaching in a new light.

Knowledge

Thomas (2006) proposes the following definition of knowledge as a component of cultural intelligence: "knowledge of cultural differences and knowledge of processes through which culture influences behaviour" (p. 82). In this context, "knowledge" means knowledge about the cultural environment in which teachers find themselves as well as knowledge of processes through which culture impacts social behaviour. Here, knowledge does not refer to the content knowledge to be taught as a class subject.

In the literature on culturally responsive teaching, a number of authors give examples of knowledge related aspects. Gay (2002) suggests that culturally-sensitive teachers should be able to decipher students' cultural codes, that is, the students' mental cultural coding system or how students have learned to think (also see: Villegas & Lucas, 2007). For the culturally sensitive teacher, knowledge has a number of strands and incorporates learning about students' lives (Villegas & Lucas, 2007), students' cultural background and their wider socio-economic environment (Weinstein et al., 2004) and students' cultural values, traditions, communication and learning styles and patterns of relationship (Gay, 2002).

Another facet of cultural knowledge is the teachers' knowledge about their own culture and how it shapes their worldview. Montgomery (2001) suggests that teachers need to look at their own attitudes and practices in order to develop a culturally diverse knowledge base.

Mindfulness

Thomas (2006) defines mindfulness as a state of awareness, sensitivity, and heightened attention to the present reality. Mindfulness includes openness to unfamiliar experiences, creating new mental maps and collecting information to confirm or disconfirm those new mental maps. Mindfulness enables us to control our automatic behaviour and make appropriate adjustments according to the cultural context.

In the literature on culturally responsive teaching, authors focus mainly on the behaviours of the teacher, making an underlying assumption that the teacher has a certain mindset. Several authors however explicitly emphasize the mindset dimension as a prerequisite for culturally responsive teaching and elaborate its various aspects. Weinstein et al. (2004) advocate that culturally responsive classroom management is in essence "a frame of mind" more than a set of strategies or practices (Weinstein et al., 2004, p. 27). Therefore, recognition of one's own ethnocentrism and biases, the "inner work of culturally responsive teaching" (p. 29), is crucial. Villegas and Lucas (2002, 2007) use the term "socioculturally conscious" to describe a mindset that calls for teachers to engage in self-reflection and critical self-analysis of their own cultural background. This allows them to become aware that students' way of thinking, behaving and being is equally influenced by their respective cultural background. This also goes hand in hand with "an affirming attitude towards students from culturally diverse backgrounds" which recognizes the "validity of a plurality of ways of thinking" (Villegas & Lucas, 2002, p. 23). McAllister and Irvine (2002) focus on the role of teachers' empathy leading to a more supportive climate for learning and more learner-centred classroom activities. Montgomery (2001) encourages teachers to conduct a self-assessment to learn more about their own and others' cultures, thereby increasing their own self-awareness.

Behaviour

According to Thomas (2006), cultural intelligence encompasses the behavioural capability to function competently in a range of cultural situations. This is an end result of the application of knowledge and mindfulness. In this context, the culturally intelligent person will have developed a set of behaviours that can be called upon and applied appropriately. Part of this personal competence is the ability to judge whether to adapt to the target culture or to make a conscious choice not to adapt.

The literature on culturally responsive teaching mentions various suggestions for teachers on how to adapt their teaching and classroom management. Naturally, this will depend on whether the class composition is monocultural or multicultural. Several authors emphasize the use of culturally appropriate instructional strategies (Gay, 2002; Villegas & Lucas, 2007; Weinstein et al., 2004), for example by matching instructional techniques to the learning styles of students (Gay, 2002) and by using students' strengths as instructional starting points (Morrison, Robbins, & Rose, 2008). Another strategy for taking learners' needs into consideration is to add a multicultural dimension to the teaching content and use multicultural examples (Gay, 2002) and build on students' funds of knowledge (Morrison et al., 2008). Coleman (1987) proposes an alternative approach. He puts teachers and students into new roles with the purpose of breaking traditional behaviour patterns and thereby creating learning opportunities.

A further strand of suggestions focuses on building caring relationships in the classroom (Weinstein et al., 2004). Gay (2002) advocates creating reciprocity in the classroom whereby students and teachers become learning partners. Ideally, the teacher will demonstrate connectedness with all of the students (Ladson-Billings, 1995), establish a cooperative learning environment and feel personally committed to their students' success (Morrison et al., 2008).

The Thai context: society, values and cultural norms in education

Cultural influences from Buddhism and successive migrations from China have given Thailand a strictly hierarchical social system. That notwithstanding, Thai people manage to maintain (and value) their individuality (Komin, 1990, 1991). Thais place a high value on interpersonal relationships, and people tend to nurture their social network. The emphasis on maintaining "face" and nurturing personal networks of relationships means that Thai people are likely to "prefer conflict styles that maintain harmony more than other collectivistic cultures" (Boonsathorn, 2007, p. 202). Thai culture displays a high level of "deference to authority and strong sense of social cohesiveness" (Atmiyanandana & Lawler, 2003; also see: Hallinger & Kantamara, 2001; Holmes & Tangtongtavy, 2003). Thai culture is said to be high context and thus places a high emphasis on maintaining social harmony and encouraging pleasant (non-conflict) relationships (Knutson, Komolsevin, Chatiketu, & Smith, 2003). A fundamental attribute of Thai culture, which differentiates the culture from all its Asian neighbours, is the concept of *sanuk* (fun). In practice this means that they "look for the enjoyable and amusing side of life" (Mulder, 2000, p. 54).

Thai cultural values extend into attitudes towards education. In the various Asian countries which have welcomed Chinese migrants, Confucian traditions have established prevailing paradigms of education (Biggs, 1994; Nguyen et al., 2006; Wang & King, 2008). Examples of Confucian cultural influences on educational environments include high Power-Distance between the learner and the teacher, high levels of respect and loyalty towards the teacher, a hard-working attitude focused on educational achievement and success, and strict perseverance towards goals (see relevant discussions in: Jin & Cortazzi, 2006; Nguyen et al., 2006; Wang & King, 2008).

However, education in Thailand does not wholly comply with this Confucian model. Tenets of Buddhist philosophy and practices shape education environments and these differ from the classical Confucian models (Lui & Littlewood, 1997). While there are areas of commonality such as high respect for the teacher, Thai educational traditions differ from the Confucian heritage in other aspects. One example is the Confucian notion of perseverance, that is, a person's willingness to maintain focus until a task is achieved. In Thai culture, perseverance tends to be mitigated by the emphasis on having fun (*sanuk*).

Various research studies have described the environment and background of Thai learners (see, for example: Deveney, 2005; Monthienvichienchai, Bhibulbhanuwat, Kasemsuk, & Speece, 2002). Hallinger and Kantamara (2001) describe the Thai education system and identify key attributes of Thai culture which pervade all levels of education. These include: social hierarchy, awareness of power-distance, deference towards authority, *kreng jai* (self-effacing, respectfulness, humility) and *bunkhun* (indebtedness, especially to those who have provided a kindness). Hofstede (1991) classifies Thai culture as feminine. Values such as caring for others and their feelings, building and maintaining social relationships, expected reciprocity and obligations in personal relationships, and decision-making based in intuition rather than logic all point to a feminine-type culture (see discussions in Hallinger & Kantamara, 2001, pp. 397–398, 403).

In Thai classrooms (at all levels of education), the teacher is the authority-figure; a feature which follows Confucian traditions. Conversely, the role of the learner is to listen. Thai cultural mores proscribe criticism or even questioning of the teacher. In the context of Thailand, this attribute has implications for learning in a wider sense as Thai learners expect their teacher to take responsibility for their learning (Apfelthaler, Hansen, Ong, & Tapachai, 2006, p. 28).

To an outsider, these perspectives may seem inherently conflicting. On the one hand, teachers receive extremely high levels of esteem in Thailand (somewhat unusual in a Western educational setting), while simultaneously being allotted more than expected responsibility for students' learning success. The issue here is a matter of degree.

Thai culture is characterized by high power distance such that the teacher is held in great respect by the body of students. In Thai language, university teachers are called "*Ajarn*" which carries the admiring connotation of "master", in a similar sense to "*sensei*" in Japan. At the same time the teacher has high levels of "duty of care" (*in loco parentis*) towards the students and particularly towards their successful learning. This juxtaposition of two seemingly opposite concepts can be explained by saying that respect and responsibility are two sides of the same coin.

Research methodology

Our personal and professional experiences from teaching in Thailand and our discussions with close colleagues suggested that international faculty teaching in Thailand need to make cultural adjustments to their teaching styles and techniques.

In our investigation we used a qualitative methodology. We conducted in-depth interviews face-to-face in a semi-structured format with selected teachers. Interview respondents were for the most part foreign university instructors who had spent between three and 20 years living and teaching in Thailand. We later included in our respondent corpus Thai nationals with international teaching experience. All of the respondents teach on management courses at graduate level. The respondents were purposely selected from faculty whose classroom teaching has gained positive evaluations from learners. This seemed to indicate that the instructors were addressing (at least) some learner concerns (see Table 1).

We began our interviews with biographical details regarding our respondents' background and their subsequent experiences as educators. A second stage of our interviews could be designated as a series of critical incidents. In the third stage of our

Table 1.   Profiles of interview respondents.

Profiles of the Interview Respondents

	Respondent	Nationality	Years of teaching	Years of teaching in Thailand
1	A	American	13	13
2	B	Australian	30	10
3	C	British	33	14
4	D	French	35	7
5	F	Dutch	13	8
6	G	New Zealander	10	4
7	H	Australian	40	8
8	I	Australian	40	5
9	J	Australian	14	10
10	K	Thai	7	5
11	L	Swiss	21	11
12	M	American	39	20
13	N	Australian	16	3
14	O	Australian	10	5
15	P	American	16	11
16	Q	Canadian	41	19
17	R	Thai	14	8
18	S	American	14	9
19	T	Austrian	17	7
20	U	Thai	14	11

interview we asked each respondent to offer advice to newcomers to teaching in Thailand. (Please see Appendix 1 for a list of our interview questions.)

Criterion sampling (Patton, 2002) was used to set the profiles of the expert informants who could contribute knowledge to the research study. Having framed a profile of the "ideal" set of individuals whose opinions could aid the research exploration, we identified suitable respondents who met the pre-designed profile. We selected foreign (non-Thai) nationals who had taught in their own, as well as in other, countries around the world. All respondents had lengthy experience of teaching at graduate (master's degree) level in Thailand. Later in our research, we decided to include Thai nationals who have taught at master's degree level in countries other than Thailand. Our rationale here was that outstanding Thai teachers with international experience may have experienced the necessity to adapt their teaching styles when returning to their homeland. We believed that these teachers would be able to provide us with insights into the Thai teaching perspective. In this study, selection of respondents was therefore purposive. Table 1 shows the profiles of the 20 respondents. We sought new respondents until we felt we had achieved theoretical saturation; that is "where collecting additional data seems counterproductive" (Strauss & Corbin, 1998, p. 136).

We synthesized our raw data using a content analysis approach. In order to analyse our data, we followed three steps (Rubin & Rubin, 1995, p. 236ff). We cross-compared each interview transcript with each of the other transcripts in an attempt to identify patterns, similarities and differences between each individual data set. Next we shared our opinions on what we identified as the key themes from each interview. We then grouped together relevant statements for each theme from individual interviews. Our aim was to make sense of the raw data by looking for identifiable patterns in teacher behaviour.

Research findings

From our respondents' interview statements we identified five main aspects of Thai culture where teachers felt the need to expand/adapt their existing teaching repertoires.

These aspects are: fun; hierarchy; authority with kindness; group-based activities; and localized class content. In our interviews we asked respondents about adaptations that they had made to their existing teaching styles in order to create a more conducive learning environment in the Thai culture. Thus, each of these attributes relates to specific features of Thai culture. In all of the interviews, the respondents felt that by adapting these aspects their classroom environment would better accommodate the expectations of their students. Our respondents said that they made these decisions on the basis of personal introspection over time.

Fun (sanuk)

All of our respondents agreed that the learning environment in Thailand needs to be fun; that is, an environment that learners perceive as amenable and non-threatening, and which gives an atmosphere conducive to learning. *Sanuk* (Thai for "fun") is a key attribute of Thai culture and involves a light-hearted approach to life. From a Thai perspective, something that is not fun is not worth doing.

Respondent B elaborated how he starts his classes in Thailand:

> I say 'look we got some serious things to achieve in the class, but along the way we are going to have a bit of fun'. And I try to put it in that context. I try to assure the students that we will have a bit of fun.

TEACHERS' PERCEPTIONS, EXPERIENCE AND LEARNING

Respondent L mentioned that he uses humour to convey negative feedback to a student in a one-on-one discussion (not in front of others) and he includes himself in the remark to make it less intimidating:

> You never say 'you have screwed up'; you may say 'oh boy, did we screw up, didn't we? ... maybe I did not show you what I really wanted, therefore you could not really give me what I wanted'. I found them quite responsive to that. You are making a joke but they understand that the joke is actually serious. But you say it with a smile, and you say it softly.

This light-hearted way of giving feedback makes the teacher's behaviour less threatening to Thai students. As Respondent B stated, "humour is used to defuse situations".

Respondent D pointed out that in the beginning of his teaching in Thailand, Thai students perceived him as too challenging and he had to make his classes more light-hearted and fun to create the right balance for Thai students:

> I feel that if it is too easy it is impossible to have the motivation to learn. Fun with no challenge is boring, if there is too much challenge and no fun they give up.

*Hierarchy (*kreng jai*)*

Another attribute of Thai culture which our respondents identified as a cultural area to address in the classroom is the hierarchical nature of Thai society. In Thai culture, concepts of hierarchy are supported by *kreng jai* (an unwillingness to disturb others, especially people more senior). Our respondents found that *kreng jai* inhibits communication in classrooms as learners are extremely reluctant to criticize or even question their teacher which would imply that the teacher has been unclear. Our respondents suggested several ways of handling this issue. Respondent A explained how he generates an informal atmosphere in class with the purpose of breaking down "*kreng jai*" attitudes:

> I want to create an atmosphere of comfort; [to avoid] fear of language ... to empower and engage learners, to get them to speak ... to get them to interact.

Respondent D mentioned that over time he had to learn to read Thai body language because asking students directly did not achieve the expected results:

> I can read on the faces of the students that something is wrong. I see it in their eyes. It is useless to ask them whether they understand because they will always say yes.

Another way to make sure that learners are up to speed and not inhibited by their "*kreng jai*" attitude, is for teachers to make themselves available to students outside of class. Several respondents mentioned that they consciously made a decision to make themselves available to students outside of class times after experiencing a lack of feedback from the students in class. Some respondents said that they formalize such activity as part of the learning environment. For example, respondent N allots specific time for the students to ask questions during the class even if it is also planned during the remainder of the teaching period. Respondent T makes appointments with project groups outside of class-time to encourage them to report on work progress and to ask questions. This strategy proved to be successful in bringing up issues and problems the students may be uncomfortable to mention in class. It also helps the instructor to make sure that students do not fall behind in their work (which is an expected part of the instructor's role in Thai classrooms). Respondent A shared his experience of what happens when you do not monitor Thai students:

> When you wait until the final presentation and you go holy cow! They completely went the wrong way and I did not know or I did not know they did not get it.

TEACHERS' PERCEPTIONS, EXPERIENCE AND LEARNING

This experience alerted him to the need to make sure that he regularly met with groups outside the class over the course of the term.

Authority with a kind heart (**jai dee***)*

Respondent A pointed out the Thai learners' "external locus of control" which has the following implications. On the one hand the teacher is seen as the source of personal discipline for learner behaviour; in essence, the teacher will be the learners' benchmark. He noted: "learners seem to expect the teacher to set the rules". In practice this means that the teacher needs to communicate expectations clearly and set standards from the onset of the course. In a Thai classroom (at all levels of education) there is an innate expectation that the environment will be teacher-directed and that the learners' should comply with the given instructions. Secondly, "external locus of control" also means – to the surprise of Western teachers in this study – that teachers are perceived to be responsible for the learning success of their students. In other words, if students fail the exam, the teacher did not do a good job. To pre-empt this situation, teachers need to proactively monitor their students' progress and take actions to prevent failure.

Our respondents agreed that the way to handle this is by combining discipline with a caring attitude. According to Respondent A, learners appreciate "kind strictness". By this he means that discipline is employed in a manner that is non-threatening and non-confrontational. Thai culture proscribes loud aggressive behaviour (*jai ron*, literally hot heart). This sort of behaviour is regarded as ill-mannered and uncouth. In Thai culture, *jai yen* (cool heart = calm, easy-going) is the social demeanour to be emulated. Therefore teachers desiring smooth social interactions with their students should practise kindness and patience as key virtues (derived from Buddhist teachings). On those occasions when disciplinary action is needed, it becomes necessary to temper the discipline with kindness. Respondent A advised "Be patient – always! Once you 'lash out' at a class, it is difficult to regain confidence."

Respondent B explained his perspective: "You've got to be firm – firm but friendly, set certain expectations" in cases where discipline is required, he explained that his method was to state in clear terms "this is what we agreed, you have not done it, what can we do about this?" Respondent M suggested that for him, the secret of success is to balance discipline with kindness. Thai learners say about his approach that he is "*Jai dee tae kiauw*" (kind-hearted but high standards). And Respondent R, one of our Thai respondents, confirmed that Thai students expect their teacher to be "*jai dee*" and not "*du*" (fierce). Respondent H counselled that foreign teachers need to be quite careful with their feedback in order not to be perceived as "*du*" by the students: "You have to take great care in critiquing their comments in a very constructive way in order not to discourage them".

Collectivistic group-based activities

Another area where our respondents noted a cultural preference is the collectivistic style of Thai learners. Respondent A noticed that Thai learners feel more confident in smaller groups of their peers and are more willing to share their views in a peer-group format. He therefore often creates opportunities to use problem-based learning (PBL) in small groups. While it may be true for most students that they feel more at ease in small groups, this aspect has additional relevance in the Thai cultural context. In a group-oriented society such as Thailand this allows students to choose group members that they already know and with whom they feel socially at ease. Thai students tend to be very shy and reluctant to share their opinion for fear of losing face (*sia naa*) in front of others. Another reason for their reluctance to speak up is that they do not want to be seen as "*aw naa*" (showing off) which has a negative connotation in Thai classrooms.

Respondent M pointed out that it is important to ensure that individual students are not put on the spot. He would therefore typically ask students to write down their answers first and then share their personal answer with their group because this gives them more confidence when they subsequently share the answer with the class.

Respondent L pointed out an important lesson for instructors who use teamwork in Thailand. Over time he realized that if he encourages students to work in teams and then discuss their experiences with the class, he should then summarize the discussion for the students ("put things in a bag and close the zip for them"), otherwise students might feel lost (not know the essence of the lessons learned), since they expect the teacher to be the sole authority in the classroom.

Localized class content for the Thai context

Each of our respondents emphasized the importance of knowing and understanding the local business context of their Thai learners in order to localize the content of class materials. Several respondents mentioned that they spend a considerable amount of time adjusting or adapting their existing content of class activities. That is, these respondents say they spend time and effort familiarizing themselves with the business and commercial background in Thailand in order to provide learners with relevant class content. They use newsworthy items to liven up their teaching. The intention is to make a bridge between learners' local work experiences and the particular lesson point to be covered. Respondent H elaborated: "I got the same class objectives but I realize I have to develop and operationalize them in a different context and use local Thai examples." Respondent U explained: "The more I link the topics to their lives, the more I relate it to things around them, the more questions I receive."

Blending theory and practice: teacher mindfulness and cultural sensitivity in teaching

By way of concluding this paper, we pull together the strands of theory and teaching practice as exemplified by our respondents. Our interviews provide evidence of the efforts made by our respondents to engage with Thai students in their classrooms and to use this experience to develop their teaching styles and strategies. The teachers seemed to maintain a continuous internalized dialogue about their interaction with their students as well as considering their students' perceptions of their teaching. In essence, this relates to the concept of mindfulness as defined by Thomas (2006). According to Thomas, mindfulness includes self-awareness, open-mindedness and empathy among other characteristics. Often, self awareness provided an impetus for our teachers to change, as the following example illustrates: "In 2003 I was like a machine gun. I learned to slow down my speech to allow them to absorb what I am saying" (Respondent O).

A willingness to see a classroom situation from a different perspective helped our respondents to empathize with their learners. As respondent M explained:

> I would often ask students 'write down your answer first' – I want to give them time to think because I am aware that they are all learning in a second language and it is much more difficult for them to think and express themselves immediately.

Mindfulness also means "creating new mental maps" by "seeking out fresh information to confirm or disconfirm" the evolving mental maps (Thomas, 2006, p. 85). Evidence from our research suggests that this process is not invariably straightforward. In seeking strategies to make sense of Thai culture, some of our respondents struggled at first. Respondent D, who had a successful teaching career in several countries before he came to Thailand, shared his feelings:

> When I arrived here, it was my most difficult time in terms of teaching. Every time after teaching I could not sleep during the night. I did not feel any resonance with the students – 80% of the classroom was lost completely. And I asked myself should I stay or should I leave.

Some respondents felt a strong need to seek out fresh information to aid their creation of a new mental map: "I felt I needed to do a course on how to teach Thai students" (Respondent G).

Mindfulness alone is only one component of cultural intelligence. Appropriate actions are needed. As we know from Thomas (2006), culturally appropriate actions emanate from applied mindfulness and knowledge about culture. Our interview data exemplify the efforts taken by the respondents to generate appropriate behaviour in a Thai cultural setting. This included teachers' adjusting their own behaviours to fit in with the Thai context. However, this is not the only way to be culturally intelligent. Some of our respondents reported that they consciously chose to focus on changing their students' expectations in order to set new learning goals. Respondent S, who uses weekly case presentations and critique by his students, said:

> I haven't adjusted to Thai students as much as I expected the students to adjust to my way of teaching. I raise the bar as I feel the capabilities have been increasing – once they know that they can say whatever they think, that nobody is going to criticize them. I do not raise the bar if the students are not ready for it. I decide this on a class by class basis.

This response exemplifies what Thomas et al. (2008) suggest is one of the hallmarks of a culturally intelligent individual who does not solely adjust but actually creates a new environment by facilitating a positive attitude with their interlocutors (which can be seen in this teachers' anonymous feedback evaluation from his students). Kennedy (2002) citing Kegan (1994) reminds us that this type of behavior builds a "consciousness bridge" between the students' previous learning experiences and new teaching approaches.

We offer our empirical data as examples of practice in use. As Thomas (2006, p. 94) suggests, cultural intelligence is gradually developed through "iterations of experiential learning". Thus, it is an ongoing learning process which provides individuals with opportunities to improve over time. Our paper offers insights from experienced practitioners who responded to new cultural stimuli and thereby developed their professional expertise. Our aim is to inspire other teaching practitioners who may find themselves in novel cultural settings.

References

Aguinis, H., & Roth, H. A. (2005). Teaching in China. Culture-based challenges. In I. Alon & J. R. McIntyre (Eds.), *Business and management education in China* (pp. 141–164). River Edge, NJ: World Scientific Publishing.

Apfelthaler, G., Hansen, K., Ong, S. H., & Tapachai, N. (Eds.). (2006). *Intercultural communication competencies in higher education and management.* Singapore: Marshall Cavendish Academic.

Atmiyanandana, V., & Lawler, J. J. (2003). Culture and management in Thailand. In M. Warner (Ed.), *Culture and management in Asia* (pp. 228–248). London: RoutledgeCurzon.

Biggs, J. (1994). Asian learners through Western eyes: An astigmatic paradox. *Australian and New Zealand Journal of Vocational Educational Research, 2*, 40–63.

Bodycott, P., & Walker, A. (2000). Teaching abroad: Lessons learned about inter-cultural understanding for teachers in higher education. *Teaching in Higher Education, 5*, 79–94.

Bondy, E., Ross, D. D., Gallingane, C., & Hambacher, E. (2007). Creating environments of success and resilience: Culturally responsive classroom management and more. *Urban Education, 42*, 326–348.

Boonsathorn, W. (2007). Understanding conflict management styles of Thais and Americans in multinational corporations in Thailand. *International Journal of Conflict Management, 18*, 196–221.

Brown, M. R. (2007). Educating all students: Creating culturally responsive teachers, classrooms, and schools. *Intervention in School and Clinic, 43*, 57–62.

Coleman, H. (1987). Teaching spectacles and learning festivals. *ELT Journal, 41*, 97–103.

Deveney, B. (2005). An investigation into Thai culture and its impact on Thai learners in an international school in Thailand. *Journal of Research in International Education, 4*, 153–171.

Earley, P. C. (2002). Redefining interactions across cultures and organizations: Moving forward with cultural intelligence. *Research in Organizational Behavior, 24*, 271–299.

Earley, P. C., & Ang, S. (2003). *Cultural intelligence: Individual interactions across cultures.* Stanford, CA: Stanford University Press.

Gay, G. (2000). *Culturally responsive teaching: Theory, research and practice.* New York: Teachers College Press.

Gay, G. (2002). Preparing for culturally responsive teaching. *Journal of Teacher Education, 53*, 106–116.

Gay, G. (2010). Acting on beliefs in teacher education for cultural diversity. *Journal of Teacher Education, 61*, 143–152.

Goh, M. (2012). Teaching with cultural intelligence: Developing multiculturally educated and globally engaged citizens. *Asia Pacific Journal of Education, 32*, 395–415.

Hallinger, P., & Kantamara, P. (2001). Exploring the cultural context of school improvement in Thailand. *School Effectiveness and School Improvement, 12*, 385–408.

Hofstede, G. (1991). *Culture and organizations: Software of the mind.* London: McGraw-Hill UK.

Holmes, H., & Tangtongtavy, S. (2003). *Working with the Thais: A guide to managing in Thailand.* Bangkok: White Lotus Books.

Jin, L., & Cortazzi, M. (2006). Changing practices in Chinese cultures of learning. *Language Culture and Curriculum, 19*, 5–20.

Kegan, R. (1994). *In over our heads: The mental demands of modern life.* Harvard, MA: Harvard University Press.

Kennedy, P. (2002). Learning cultures and learning styles: Myth-understandings about adult (Hong Kong) Chinese learners. *International Journal of Lifelong Education, 21*, 430–455.

Knutson, T. J., Komolsevin, R., Chatiketu, P., & Smith, V. R. (2003). A cross-cultural comparison of Thai and US American rhetorical sensitivity: Implications for intercultural communication effectiveness. *International Journal of Intercultural Relations, 27*, 63–78.

Komin, S. (1990). Culture and work-related values in Thai organizations. *International Journal of Psychology, 25*, 681–704.

Komin, S. (1991). *Psychology of the Thai people: Values and behavioural patterns.* Bangkok: National Institute of Development Administration (NIDA).

Ladson-Billings G. (1995). But that's just good teaching! The Case for Culturally Relevant Pedagogy. *Theory into Practice, 34*, 159–165.

Lui, N.-F., & Littlewood, W. (1997). Why do many learners appear reluctant to participate in classroom learning discourse? *System, 25*, 371–384.

McAllister, G., & Irvine, J. J. (2002). The role of empathy in teaching culturally diverse students: A qualitative study of teachers' beliefs. *Journal of Teacher Education, 53*, 433–443.

Montgomery, W. (2001). Creating culturally responsive, inclusive classrooms. *Teaching Exceptional Children, 33*, 4–9.

Monthienvichienchai, C., Bhibulbhanuwat, S., Kasemsuk, C., & Speece, M. (2002). Cultural awareness, communication apprehension and communication competence: A case study of Saint John's International School. *The International Journal of Education Management, 16*, 288–296.

Morrison, K., Robbins, H. H., & Rose, D. G. (2008). Operationalizing culturally relevant pedagogy: A synthesis of classroom-based research. *Equity & Excellence in Education, 41*, 433–452.

Mulder, N. (2000). *Inside Thai society – religion, everyday life, change*. Chiang Mai: Silkworm Books.

Nguyen, P., Terlouw, C., & Pilot, A. (2006). Culturally appropriate pedagogy: The case of group learning in a Confucian heritage culture context. *Intercultural Education, 17*, 1–19.

Patton, M. Q. (2002). *Qualitative research and evaluation methods*. Thousand Oaks, CA: Sage Publications.

Richards, C. (2004). From old to new learning: Global imperatives, exemplary Asian dilemmas and ICT as a key to cultural change in education. *Globalisation, Societies and Education, 2*, 337–353.

Rubin, H. J., & Rubin, I. S. (1995). *Qualitative interviewing – The art of hearing data*. Thousand Oaks, CA: Sage Publications.

Sheets, H. R. (1995). From remedial to gifted: Effects of culturally centered pedagogy. *Theory Into Practice, 34*, 186–193.

Sternberg, R. J. (2007). Who are the bright children? The cultural context of being and acting intelligent. *Educational Researcher, 36*, 148–155.

Strauss, A., & Corbin, J. (1998). *Basics of qualitative research techniques and procedures for developing grounded theory*. London: Sage Publications.

Thomas, D. C. (2006). Domain and development of cultural intelligence: The importance of mindfulness. *Group & Organization Management, 31*, 78–99.

Thomas, D. C., & Inkson, K. (2004). *Cultural intelligence: People skills for global business*. San Francisco, CA: Berrett-Koehler.

Thomas, D. C., Elron, E., Stahl, G., Ekelund, B. Z., Ravlin, E. C., Cerdin, J. L., … Lazarova, M. B. (2008). Cultural intelligence: Domain and assessment. *International Journal of Cross Cultural Management, 8*, 123–143.

Villegas, A. M, & Lucas, T. (2002). Preparing culturally responsive teachers–Rethinking the curriculum. *Journal of Teacher Education, 53*, 20–32.

Villegas, A. M., & Lucas, T. (2007). The culturally responsive teacher. *Educational Leadership, 64*, 28–33.

Wang, V. C. X., & King, K. P. (2008). Transformative learning and ancient Asian educational perspectives. *Journal of Transformative Education, 6*, 136–150.

Weinstein, C. S., Tomlinson-Clarke, S., & Curran, M. (2004). Toward a conception of culturally responsive classroom management. *Journal of Teacher Education, 55*, 25–38.

Young, E. (2010). Challenges to conceptualizing and actualizing culturally relevant pedagogy: How viable is the theory in classroom practice? *Journal of Teacher Education, 61*, 248–260.

Yourn, B. R., Kirkness, A.. (2003). *Adapting to a new culture of education: Not just an issue for students*. Proceedings of the Higher Education Research & Development Society of Australasia (HERDSA) International Conference, Canterbury, New Zealand.

Appendix 1

Interview questions:

Stage 1: biographical details (professional qualifications and teaching experience prior to teaching in Thailand)

Stage 2: Critical incidents (classroom examples from Thailand)

1. What teaching strategies have you identified for your own instructional purposes as successful in Thai classrooms at graduate degree level?
2. What personal development strategies have you followed to put these strategies into practical application?
3. What changes in your prior teaching methodologies have you made for teaching in classrooms in Thailand?
4. With hindsight, how have your teaching practices evolved over time in relation to your novel classroom experiences in Thailand?
5. What do Thai learners say they like about your class?

Stage 3: Advice to newcomers to teaching in Thailand

6. From your experience, what advice and suggestions would you give to a teacher coming to teach in a Thai master's degree programme for the first time?

Teachers' experience with inclusive education in Singapore

Lay See Yeo, Wan Har Chong, Maureen F. Neihart and Vivien S. Huan

Teachers' positive attitude is most critically and consistently associated with successful inclusion. However, little is known about teachers' first-hand encounters with inclusive education in Singapore. We present findings from a qualitative study on inclusion based on focus group interviews with 202 teachers from 41 resourced primary schools. The data were transcribed and coded using Interpretive Phenomenological Analysis and NVIVO software. Two broad clusters identified were teachers' positive and negative experiences in implementing inclusion. More reference was made to negative than positive experiences. The most dominant negative experience was stress from challenging behaviours and instructional difficulties of catering adequately for diverse needs in the same classroom. The most salient positive experience was satisfaction with pupils' progress and new learning for teachers. Classroom practices that facilitated inclusion and the value of training in shaping teachers' attitudes towards inclusion were highlighted.

Introduction

Internationally, a trend towards inclusive educational practices has gained in strength and momentum since the development of the Salamanca Statement in 1994 (UNESCO, 1994), which ignited an ethical imperative for countries to embrace diversity and grant individuals with disability equal opportunities to be educated in regular schools. Inclusion is compelling because it is borne out of values of equality, non-discrimination, and fairness (Avramidis, Bayliss, & Burden, 2000; Thomazet, 2009). The fundamental principle of inclusion is the right of every child to be educated in a general education school. It is not surprising therefore that many countries worldwide have implemented or refined legislation to support educational inclusion. Early starters for inclusive legislation are the US (the Education for All Handicapped Children Act, PL 94-142, 1975; Individuals with Disabilities Education Act, PL 105-17, 1990, revised1997, and amended 2004) and the UK (1981 Education Act) (Norwich, 2008). Since 2000, more countries have instituted legislation for inclusion. For example, Hong Kong introduced the Code of Practice of Education under the Disability Discrimination Act in 2001; Ireland enacted the Education for Persons with Special Educational Needs Act in 2004 (Phadraig, 2007); and Australia established the Disability Standards for Education in 2004 (Forlin, Keen, & Barrett, 2008). However, in Singapore, there is no legislation yet for inclusion although primary schools have adopted inclusive educational practices since 2005.

The literature abounds with copious evidence of the challenges in translating the ideals of inclusion into practice even for countries that are pioneers in inclusion and have the benefit of legislative support. Singapore is an interesting departure given the history of segregated special needs education for children dating from the 1960s, and a sophisticated legal system for which a mandate for inclusion is absent. Arguably, the success of inclusion cannot hope to rest on legislation alone. What is stipulated in legislation is not necessarily translated adequately into practice (Curcic, 2009). In reality, it is teachers who play the most pivotal role in making inclusion work (Sharma, Forlin, Loreman, & Earle, 2006). A study on inclusion in Singapore seems timely given recent developments in special education locally and the limited research on inclusion in Southeast Asia.

History of inclusion in Singapore

A brief history of inclusion in Singapore provides the background for this paper. Details are available in Poon, Musti-Rao, and Wettasinghe (2013) and Yeo, Neihart, Tang, Chong, and Huan (2011). In the early 1960s, children with disabilities attended separate special schools. This practice persisted until 2004 despite calls in the late 1980s for inclusion. In 2004, the government's vision of Singapore becoming an inclusive society spurred phenomenal effort towards providing funding, school infrastructures, and teacher training catering for students with special needs. From 2005 until the present, training in interventions for children with special education needs (SEN) is being provided for Allied Educators for Learning and Behaviour Support (AEDs[LBS]) and Teachers of Students with Special Needs (TSNs) to support children with mild to moderate disabilities in mainstream schools (Lim & Tan, 2004). As of 2012, all primary schools have been staffed with at least one AED(LBS). The Ministry of Education (MOE) plans to recruit additional AEDs(LBS) to extend support for inclusion at the secondary school level (MOE, 2012).

Variations in inclusive educational practices

Inclusion is differentially understood and practised in countries worldwide. In a comprehensive meta-synthesis of inclusive practices in 18 countries from 1996 to 2006, Curcic (2009) concluded that although there is consensus on the philosophy and spirit of inclusion, it is impossible to standardize inclusive practices across countries given the wide ranging diversity of history, levels of economic, social, and educational development, and uniqueness of cultures represented.

Educational inclusion can be broadly defined as the practice of educating students with SEN in mainstream schools (Wilde & Avramidis, 2011). All children are regarded as full-time participants of their school. Built on the premise that all learners have a basic right to being educated in a general education setting, inclusion begs a paradigmatic shift in beliefs about disability. Disability is to be viewed no longer as an abnormality inherent in the individual person, but as the lack of fit between the environment and the individual's needs. Inclusion necessitates a radical transformation of school (Thomazet, 2009) which must assume complete responsibility for all learners irrespective of their disabilities. In practice, this necessitates rethinking the curriculum (Phadraig, 2007), reorganizing curriculum content, and modifying modes of instruction to teach all students. The demands are daunting as these reforms impact every teacher and call for mammoth adjustments.

Levels of educational inclusiveness vary on a continuum in actual practice. Wilde and Avramidis (2011) presented a continuum of approaches to inclusive pedagogies. Integration represents a type of continuum to address learner diversity. The pull-out integration model is applied in some countries, such as Israel and Hong Kong. Children with SEN may receive a modified curriculum but need to fit into existing structures. In Israel, options range from special school attendance to partial or full inclusion in a general education classroom. The general education teacher is supported by a special needs teacher and a teacher aide; the latter works with children who are included either within or outside the classroom (Ronen, 2007). In Hong Kong, students with mild SEN attend mainstream school but are withdrawn for additional support by a resource teacher and/or learning support assistant (Wong, Pearson, & Lo, 2004). Under a School Partnership Scheme which empowers general education schools to support students with SEN, the Hong Kong Education Bureau avails on-site support, training and consultation to 13 Resource Schools that implement a Whole School Approach to cater for diverse educational needs. In addition, short-term attachment programmes in 12 Special Schools cum Resources Centres are available to students with intellectual disability and severe adjustment difficulties on a needs basis (Education Bureau, 2011).

However, according to Ainscow (2000), fitting a student with special needs into a general education classroom with support from a teacher aide, working on separate assignments, and providing individual or group instruction should not be regarded as inclusion. Such practices skirt on the boundaries of exclusion despite good intentions to improve learning for individuals with SEN. Inclusion has a social dimension too. Children cannot be said to be included if they are only "in" (i.e., included) but not "of" (i.e., socially excluded) the classroom. Inclusion goes beyond physical placement to social acceptance and a sense of belonging to a community (Booth & Ainscow, 2002; Warnock, 2005). Conceivably, true inclusion is hard to achieve.

Nonetheless, over time some countries such as Ireland have fine-tuned their educational provisions for children with disabilities and moved closer to the inclusion ideal. Tracing the development of inclusion in Ireland from 1991 to 2004, Phadraig (2007) reported that Irish children with SEN access a continuum of services with full time placement in a general education classroom as priority but with additional support as needed. By 2000, the regular classroom teacher assumes major responsibility for the needs of all children. Teaching is differentiated for children with dyslexia or autism through close collaboration between the class teachers and learning-support teachers and parents. Withdrawing a child for individual or group instruction is ostensibly not considered appropriate inclusive practice.

Another variation in inclusive practices is a separate system of special education tracks within mainstream schools, such as is practised in the Netherlands (Imants, 2002). In an interesting permutation of inclusive practices, Koutrouba, Vamvakari, and Steliou (2006) reported that in Cyprus, a small percentage of children with mild disabilities receive adapted instruction in special classes within general education. Students with severe disabilities attend special schools, strategically built within the compounds of the general education school buildings, whereas the vast majority of students with mild SEN are fully included in general education schools. In these instances, inclusion is a placement concept in which all children are schooled under one roof albeit in different tracks.

In Southeast Asian countries such as Hong Kong, Korea, and Singapore, special educational provisions typify a dual system. Children with severe disabilities are served in separate special schools; children with mild disabilities within general education schools.

Teachers' concerns about inclusion

The extent to which inclusion successfully meets the needs of all children in the classroom is dependent to a very significant degree on the attitudes of the teachers and special educators towards inclusion and their willingness to create optimal learning environments (Avramidis & Norwich, 2002; Sharma, et al., 2006). Internationally, the research strongly suggests that most general education teachers hold favourable attitudes towards inclusion, but have concerns about its implementation (Hwang & Evans, 2011). Forlin et al. (2008) summed up three categories of concerns: administration, classroom-based, and personal.

First, administrative concerns include additional time in preparing and modifying curriculum materials, identifying suitable teaching aides, and collaborating with other staff members and paraprofessionals. Teachers have insufficient time to attend case management meetings, update students' progress on their Individual Education Plans (IEPs), complete paperwork, and meet parents.

Second and probably the greatest concern relates to the minutiae of day-to-day classroom practices (Forlin et al., 2008). Concerns include large class sizes, managing difficult behaviours (e.g., aggression), and insufficient material and manpower resources. A Canadian study showed that 65% of elementary school teachers in the Prince Edward Island Elementary Schools expressed concerns about individualizing instruction for a diverse class of pupils and instructing a wide range of learners all in one class (Horne & Timmons, 2009).

A related classroom-based concern is teaching children with severe SEN (Avramidis & Norwich, 2002; Ferguson, 2008; Wong et al., 2004). Teachers from Canada, Australia, Hong Kong, and Singapore are least positive about including students who are verbally or physically aggressive, or disruptive (Loreman, Forlin, & Sharma, 2007). Students with emotional and behavioural disturbances (Wilde & Avramidis, 2011) are least tolerated. However, teachers are more willing to include students with learning disabilities, physical or sensory disabilities, and those who require little teacher assistance (Ferguson, 2008; Wong, et al., 2004).

Third, teachers have personal concerns about their professional knowledge, competence, and level of training in special needs to successfully include atypical children (Sharma et al., 2006). Teachers in Western Australia reported concerns in identifying children's capabilities and effectively teaching both typically developing children and those with disabilities (Forlin et al., 2008). Teachers tend to be more open towards inclusion when they have stronger perceptions of their competence, training, and experience in teaching students with SEN. Primary and secondary teachers in the UK who have had experience with inclusion held more positive attitudes towards it (Avramidis et al., 2000). The lack of training opportunities is also consistently associated with negative reception of inclusion across different school systems. Teachers in Cyprus experience mistrust towards inclusion largely due to a lack of graduate training in special education (Koutrouba, Vamvakari, & Steliou, 2006).

Singapore is a newcomer to inclusion. Very few research studies on educational inclusion have been published locally. Tan, Nonis, and Chow (2011) conducted a single-subject research study that examined the effects of a Balance Programme on the balance control of a seven-year-old child with hearing impairment and a peer who had no hearing impairment, both of whom attend a mainstream school. Results were mixed with improvement in balance control observed on only some of the static and dynamic balance tasks. In one of the earliest qualitative studies on inclusion in Singapore, Yeo et al. (2011) explored the facilitators of and barriers to inclusion in two childcare centres where young children with mild special needs were supported by a therapy outreach team from a local hospital. Support from specialist teachers and occupational therapists included pull-out individual instruction for children with special needs that eventually transitioned to in-class support, and consultation to the preschool teachers in their respective classrooms.

The outcomes were very encouraging with all the stakeholders recognizing that inclusion was facilitated by communication, collaboration, and the availability of training and resources. The preschool teachers reported a sense of inadequacy and anxiety related to large class sizes, absence of teacher aides, insufficient training and resources in special needs. However, their attitude towards inclusion improved when the outreach team modelled classroom management techniques, provided in-class support, and shared useful skills and teaching tools.

There is currently no published empirical data on inclusion in Singapore primary schools. The purpose of the study is to investigate teachers' experience with inclusion. Qualitative research on inclusion in the literature tended to employ small sample sizes, usually in the range of 10 to 30, and provide little information on coding procedures and data analysis. This is a fairly large qualitative study involving 202 primary school teachers. It hopes to give the teachers a voice in identifying the factors that influence the practice of inclusion and to highlight practices that can strengthen inclusive education irrespective of national boundaries. According to international research, teacher training is often acknowledged as a cornerstone of inclusion and the lack of training as a monumental barrier to inclusion. However, little is known about what truly empowers teachers in inclusive classrooms.

Method

Procedure and participants

Ethics clearance and approval for this study were obtained from the Nanyang Technological University Institutional Review Board and MOE, Singapore. A list of resourced primary schools was obtained from the MOE's Psychological Services Branch. These resourced schools are essentially primary schools with one difference, that is, they have additional funding and trained special needs personnel on staff to provide support for pupils with SEN who attend general education primary schools. At the time of this study, only 108 out of 177 primary schools are resourced schools. Letters describing the study and inviting participation were sent via email to the principals of all resourced primary schools. In each participating school, an AED(LBS), a TSN and three mainstream teachers who teach children with SEN in their classrooms were identified by their principals to be interviewed.

The total sample consisted of 202 teachers from 41 resourced primary schools. They comprised three groups of teachers: (1) 28.6% (n = 42) AEDs(LBS), (2) 32.0% (n = 47) TSNs and (3) 39.4% (n = 58) mainstream teachers. Fifty-five (27.2%) teachers did not indicate their designation.

The AED(LBS) is a special needs personnel who has completed a one-year full time diploma programme in special education. The training, which included a supervised practicum in special needs, encompassed knowledge and skills in identifying special needs, assessing learner strengths and weaknesses, developing, implementing, and evaluating IEPs. The AED(LBS) is a teacher aide who provides in-class or pull-out support for children with SEN, assists teachers, and coordinates transitions. He or she takes responsibility only for children with SEN in the general education classrooms. Most AEDs(LBS) have GCE "A" level qualifications or a polytechnic diploma; a few have a basic university degree. The TSN, on the other hand, is a qualified mainstream teacher who has completed a one-year part time basic certificate programme in special needs support and is knowledgeable about diverse learners and adaptations for classroom instruction. He or she assumes responsibility for all pupils in the class and may have additional duties serving on case management teams and mentoring other teachers on special needs.

In terms of special needs training, the AEDs(LBS) received the most training compared to the other teachers. The one-year diploma in special needs for AEDs(LBS) is a full-time 36-credit training programme which consists of 10 courses and a 10-week practicum. Seventy-four percent of the AEDs(LBS) had attended at least two training programmes. Almost all of the TSNs (93%, n = 50) had received one training programme in special needs. The one year part-time certificate in special needs for TSNs is a nine-credit programme that consists of three courses. The mainstream teachers were the least well trained in special needs, as 91% (n = 95) had no training in it. In terms of years of teaching experience, the TSNs were the most experienced teachers ($M = 14.19$, $SD = 9.16$, range from three to 43 years), followed by mainstream teachers ($M = 11.13$, $SD = 10.03$, range from one to 41 years), and AEDs(LBS) ($M = 5.00$, $SD = 2.39$; range from two to eight years).

Research design

The present study is part of a larger, mixed method research study funded by the Office of Educational Research, National Institute of Education. Owing to the extensive amount of data obtained, this paper focused only on the qualitative data from focus group interviews with teachers on their experiences with inclusion.

Interviews

Focus group interviews were conducted with the teachers of the 41 participating schools in groups of five. Each group generally comprised one AED(LBS), one TSN, and three general education teachers. Forty focus group interviews were conducted. As this was an exploratory study, interview questions were broadly framed to obtain an understanding of the state of inclusive education in the primary schools. The questions were not piloted prior to the study. A semi-structured schedule guided the interviews, which consisted of open-ended questions on the teachers' understanding of inclusion, classroom practices and personal experiences. For this paper, data from the following four interview questions were used to provide information about the teachers' experiences with inclusion:

- How are SEN students included as full participants in your classroom/school?
- How are activities planned and adapted to meet the SEN students' needs?
- What are the ways in which the SEN students' needs are accommodated within the curriculum?
- Can you describe your personal experience of including a student with special needs in your classroom?

Qualitative data collection and analysis

A sheet with a copy of the interview questions was distributed to all participants for reference and collected at the end of the interview. The interviews were conducted by all four members of the research team and two graduate research assistants (RAs). The interviews were audio-recorded with the consent of participants who were assured of confidentiality and anonymity. The participants were requested to identify their teaching role before they spoke. Each interview lasted around 90 minutes and was conducted at the school sites.

The audiotapes were transcribed by two RAs. The data were coded and analysed using Interpretive Phenomenological Analysis (IPA). IPA is widely used in research when there is a need to understand how people perceive, experience, and make sense of events in their lives (Lyons & Coyle, 2007). All the research team members first read through two transcripts individually to obtain an appreciation of the intricacies of inclusion as encountered by the participants. Please refer to Table 1 for the steps to data analysis and examples.

At the first step, data were organized and assembled on the basis of meaning units. A meaning unit was an item in the transcripts that reflected a specific response to inclusion. Altogether 659 meaning units were generated. The following is an example of a meaning unit: "Initially I felt a lot of frustration because I did not know how to reach that particular child. I really did not know how to reach him." At the second step, the team members read each meaning unit to determine its general theme(s) and to assign a code or codes. For the above-mentioned meaning unit, two themes were identified. The first theme was coded as "frustration", the second theme as "insufficient knowledge in special needs". In total, 54 codes were generated and served as guidelines for coding the transcripts.

Team members coded the transcripts in pairs. Where there was disagreement, we worked towards achieving consensus, and when that could not be achieved, we agreed to disagree and identified an existing code that provided the best fit. Reliability was calculated by dividing the number of agreements by the sum total of the number of agreements and disagreements and multiplying the quotient by 100. When coding was completed, 25% of the transcripts were checked by a third member for reliability and accuracy of the previous coding. Overall inter-rater reliability was 92%.

At the third step, codes with similar themes were grouped to construct categories. There were seven categories: practice of inclusion; positive feelings; positive experiences; factors contributing to positive experiences; negative feelings; negative experiences; factors contributing to negative experiences. The categories formed two broad clusters that summed up the teachers' experience of implementing inclusion – positive experiences and negative experiences.

Results

The teachers' approaches to inclusion will first be discussed followed by their positive and negative experiences and the contributing factors. Since teachers spoke of their feelings as an integral facet of their experiences, we discussed feelings and experiences jointly as one phenomenon. Quotations were selected based on how well they represented the common experience of the majority interviewed and how distinctly they illustrated a local inclusive practice. Where quotations were used, teachers' responses in Singlish (Singapore English) were edited to Standard English for greater clarity.

Approaches to teaching children with special needs in the mainstream classroom

The interviews indicated several ways in which teachers created a learning environment to cater for children with SEN. First, the mainstream teacher made adjustments to the lesson (e.g., ensuring physical accessibility to a child with limited mobility, or providing one-on-one time for a child with SEN when the rest of the class is given work to do). An art teacher who wanted to conduct an outdoor lesson described bringing her class to an area accessible to a child who has limited mobility so that he can view and draw the same surroundings. A mainstream teacher described individualizing instruction for a pupil with dyslexia:

TEACHERS' PERCEPTIONS, EXPERIENCE AND LEARNING

Table 1.   Steps to data analysis.

Steps	Description	Number	Examples
Step 1. Assembling Meaning Units	A meaning unit is an interviewee's verbatim description that reflected a specific response to inclusion. Meaning units were gathered from the transcripts.	659 meaning units	1. "It is very, very difficult especially when you have a full class with at least a quarter of them with other needs." 2. "When there's more than one [special needs child] in the class, like the first year when I had two ADHDs and one Down's Syndrome in the class. So it's very, very frustrating, especially when you have the syllabus to complete by a certain period of time."
Step 2. Coding	Each meaning unit was reviewed to determine its general theme(s) and to assign a code(s).	54 codes	1. Managing more than one child with special needs in class 2. Teaching experiencing physical harm 3. Teacher receiving complaints from parents 4. Inappropriate management or support provided for pupils with special needs 5. Teacher feeling bad about negative reactions to pupils in class 6. Teacher having to manage her own feelings 7. Discussing with parents the needs of pupils with special needs These seven codes were subsequently grouped to form one category titled "Negative Experiences".
Step 3. Categorizing	Codes with similar themes were grouped to construct categories.	seven categories	Categories 1. Practice of inclusion 2. Negative Feelings 3. Negative Experiences 4. Factors contributing to negative experiences 5. Positive Feelings 6. Positive Experiences 7. Factors contributing to positive experiences
Step 4: Clustering	Categories were grouped to form clusters.	two clusters	Clusters 1. Negative experiences in implementing inclusion 2. Positive experiences in implementing inclusion

Every time the children are doing their own word cut-outs, and we are working on phonics, I will go letter by letter with this child, and we use task cards to help him pronounce a certain word. After a while, he managed to read.

A TSN mentioned simplifying instructions for a child with autism:

I give him a separate set of instructions. It's the same instruction but I broke it up, so it's easier for him to understand.

Another TSN shared how she abandoned the curriculum for a child with intellectual impairment:

I didn't follow the curriculum because I know it is pointless. When we came back from the museum, she spoke and I wrote it out. What I was trying to do through this interaction was to improve her vocabulary in speaking and listening.

These examples suggested that teachers included children with SEN by deliberately creating space within class time to provide additional coaching, breaking down a task, and departing from the curriculum.

Another approach was to withdraw pupils for learning support by the AEDs(LBS). The child with mild special needs is removed from his or her classroom for one or two class periods and given individual coaching and attention by the AED(LBS). One TSN described the support for a child with dyslexia:

During my lessons, at times he is withdrawn from class where there is specific support given to him. Even spelling is separate for him.

An AED reported,

My experience with special needs pupils has always been pleasant, especially during the withdrawal lessons. The pupils will just be very excited to learn new strategies, new things, because once they are back in class, they know they can apply some of these skills. They will be very proud and tell their classmates, 'Hey, I have a magic (trick) to learn spelling'.

Finally, teachers created within the class an awareness of the needs of classmates with disability to foster an accepting learning environment. A TSN shared:

One day when he [child with special needs] was absent, I explained to the class that he is special. Every one of us is special, but he is a little bit more special because he needs more attention than us. So now it is very pleasant.

Another teacher communicated how the class supported a child with special needs:

Each time he goes to the board to do a sum, they clap for him without being told to do so because they could see it as an achievement, having been with him the previous year.

Teachers and pupils consciously created a classroom that embraced children with special needs.

Positive feelings and experiences

Of the total number of responses coded, 39.6% were on teachers' positive feelings and experiences. The most dominant positive feeling (30%) was a sense of satisfaction. Satisfaction referred to a feeling of gratification, contentment, pride and fulfilment. The feeling of satisfaction stemmed from the progress and success of pupils with SEN. A TSN expressed satisfaction when a child who was extremely shy opened up to her: "The kind of joy you get and satisfaction is really indescribable but it takes a lot, a lot of time." Another TSN was pleased to witness change in the child's aggressive behaviour. A teacher reported satisfaction in observing the support the class gave to her and the child with special needs.

She said, "On many occasions, they helped me when I tried to ask him to do certain things or to behave. They will go up to him and pull him back or guide him along."

The next strongest feeling (28%) was happiness. Happiness referred to expressions of joy, delight, and pleasure. Invariably, happiness was linked to the children's improvement or academic success, new learning gained on the job, and appreciation for the support children render to their atypically developing classmates. One AED said this of her pupils with SEN, "They can really make you smile, make you happy because really every little step they make is big achievement." Another AED echoed the same sentiment, "They made little progress, but this little progress meant a lot to them and their parents."

Other positive experiences included the new learning teachers acquired on account of inclusion. One TSN probably expressed a common sentiment,

> I feel it is very enriching and rewarding but I wouldn't deny that there are lots of challenges along the way and I think we ourselves have not truly been equipped, but it is a job where we really learn. It's really on-the-job training.

Teachers also learned to exercise sensitivity, for example, in the language they used in class. One teacher put it aptly,

> What should we say? What should we not say in front of him to make him feel included in a class? We are not reminding him that he has some disabilities but he is just a bit different from us. So we try to make him feel that actually we are the same.

Factors contributing to positive experiences

The teachers offered insight into factors that contributed to positive experiences with inclusion. First, the most frequently mentioned factor (40%) was having discovered or acquired strategies to make inclusion work in their classrooms. One approach was adapting activities to accommodate the child with SEN. For example, a teacher reported making sure her class did not stomp their feet during Music even though it was an activity the class wanted to do because the girl with autism was "very sensitive to sound". Additionally, teachers encouraged the class in their effort to include their peers with disabilities. One TSN related how she reinforced her class for helping a child with SEN to read:

> One day she read, I turned to the class and I said, 'First term, she was sitting in the Red Group. Thank you Red Group. It's your effort.' And I turned to the Blue Group, 'Term 2, she was with you. It was you people. You all have made it possible.' I credit all of them because I need to build this team up, so that she can learn and they can make a difference.

Thus, teachers demonstrated a positive example of how each child, no matter how different, was valued.

The second factor that contributed to positive experiences was support from school personnel, parents, and the children. Teachers were appreciative of the principal or vice-principal being present during case management meetings, of understanding colleagues, of the AED who was "an extra pair of hands and did a lot of in-class support", and of parents who gave strong home support.

The last supportive factor resided in the nature of the disability for which accommodations were needed. One teacher said, "If the child is high-functioning, it tends to make inclusion a little easier. If the child is low-functioning or unidentified, it makes things a little more challenging." Another teacher alluded to a child with cerebral palsy who "could catch up with all the class work". She added, "The only thing was he was physically handicapped. No problem if the child has the mental capacity."

Negative feelings and experiences

Of all the coded responses, 60.4% referenced negative feelings and experiences about inclusion. The dominant feelings (31%) were stress followed by frustration (20%), fear and anxiety (16%), and exhaustion (14%). These were frequently encountered in the process of teaching and managing behaviour.

The challenge of inclusion seemed to be most intimidating for the general education teachers and the TSNs who were new to their roles. Teachers observed that "no matter what the books tell you, when you meet them, then you know". One teacher said, "I am not trained in special needs. So given children with special needs, of course, I feel apprehensive." A TSN similarly reported,

> My first experience with a special needs child was when I was really clueless. So when I had him, I had a really hard time. It really wasn't the most pleasant experience and it went on for the entire year. So I tried lots of methods. He was just not responding and it was very discouraging.

Thus, insufficient training was a challenge to inclusion.

Teachers also felt daunted by large class sizes and the pressure of meeting curriculum and examination requirements. A TSN said this of a child who has Attention Deficit/ Hyperactivity Disorder (ADHD):

> It was really, really challenging. It was ongoing the whole day. And because I was also dealing with 29 other Primary One children who can be very energetic and in need of my attention all the time, I was very drained at the end of the day.

A very common stressor was reflected in this response:

> There's always concern about the lower ability pupils in our class because they take so much of my time and energy. I find that I can't help the lower ability pupils as much as I want to.

Many teachers mentioned examination pressures, such as this teacher who lamented: "I'm just a normal human being with normal patience. Then at Primary 6, you have a lot to cover, you have to be ready for the exams and it's so difficult." The most frequently cited negative experience is managing more than one child with special needs in a class. One teacher reported: "I have an autistic boy and I have another ADHD, serious ADHD boy. It was really challenging and especially during Science period, you are like working with two time bombs."

Teachers experienced fear and anxiety from working with children with challenging behaviours. One TSN raised concerns for the rest of the children in the class as the child with anger management issues might hurt them. Another TSN shared her anxiety about a child with autism: "Every day I worry about what he is going to do tomorrow." Even AEDs, the best trained teachers in special needs, were apprehensive as evident in this response: "I come to school every day feeling very scared, thinking what is he going to do today. Which time? What period? Any time now the teacher is going to call me [for assistance]."

Factors contributing to negative experiences

The foremost factor contributing to negative experiences with inclusion was managing challenging behaviours in the classroom. Children who had autism or ADHD or violent behaviours disrupted teaching and prevented teachers from completing the syllabus. One TSN recalled an aggressive child who acted up the whole day: "We have to stop the lesson most of the time. It really did affect the marks of the rest of the pupils. So for someone who is that extreme, I would not recommend him for inclusion."

The second factor related to instructional challenges. Teachers were cognizant of having to deliver the "normal curriculum" and struggled when they had to accommodate a child who was different and made no progress. Invariably, almost all the teachers never lost sight of national examinations and "trying to get them [children with special needs] to pass the PSLE". (PSLE refers to the Primary School Leaving Examinations.) In an astute observation, one TSN remarked, "What IEP? It's all about PSLE."

Discussion

Teachers were interviewed about their personal experience of inclusion and approaches to including pupils with mild disabilities as full participants in their classrooms. The teachers felt that only children with mild disabilities should be included in the general education classroom. This is consistent with the prevailing concern schools have about including children with severe disabilities in mainstream education (Loreman et al., 2007; Wilde & Avramidis, 2011). At this point in time, we are not yet able to meet what Ferguson (2008) described as the "newest challenge to make inclusive practices available to everybody, everywhere and all the time" (p.109). However, progress has been made. Never before had mainstream teachers and special education teachers worked together to provide support in the general education classroom for pupils with SEN. The learning curve was very steep.

Teachers experimented with various inclusive practices in the general education classroom. They provided as much one-on-one instruction for the pupil with disabilities when the rest of the class was completing seatwork or they built in time for personalized coaching at the end of the school day. Thus, they employed a range of approaches on the continuum (Wilde & Avramidis, 2011) ranging from withdrawal support to within class one-on-one instruction. Most importantly, they created a socially welcoming classroom environment to foster a sense of belonging (Booth & Ainscow, 2002) by setting an example of acceptance and cultivating in their pupils a willingness to embrace differences.

The experiences of teachers in Singapore were very similar to their counterparts internationally, such as Hong Kong (Wong, et al., 2004), Canada (Horne & Timmons, 2009), and Australia (Forlin et al., 2008). Their greatest concern was classroom-based (Forlin et al., 2008) and revolved around the challenges of engaging all students, juggling teacher attention in order not to compromise the progress of any group of pupils, managing disruptive behaviours, and completing the syllabus to prepare pupils for high stakes examinations.

Using focus group interviews provided first-hand accounts of what teachers thought and felt about inclusion, why they experienced inclusion the way they did, and what they perceived supported their work. Important learning points were distilled from the data about what made inclusion work for them.

First, inclusive practices can be achieved through school-wide collaboration. The teachers shared information about working together as teaching teams. They engaged in one of the best practices in inclusive education (i.e., planning, learning, and working together to transform classroom practices) (Ferguson, 2008). In this partnership, the AEDs (LBS) played a key role in providing consultation and direct assistance. There was an attempt at blending specialist knowledge and skills as teachers shared specific strategies that worked for them.

Second, teachers are willing to support inclusion when they have opportunities to experience success. Positive attitudes arose when they had exposure to teaching pupils with SEN and in the process acquired a variety of strategies they could use to good effect in the inclusive classroom. With a growing sense of competence came greater receptivity to inclusion. This was consistent with Woolfson and Brady's (2009) perception that mastery experiences were instrumental in fostering positive beliefs about inclusion.

Third, children with SEN can be both "in" and "of" the general education classroom when teachers actively teach their pupils how to be supportive of peers who are different from themselves. Horne and Timmons (2009) noted that students were more tolerant and accepting of students with disabilities when they understood the nature of the disability and when teachers communicated this information to them. Similarly, Frederickson, Simmonds, Evans, and Soulsby (2007) attributed social acceptance in the UK for children with SEN to peer preparation workshops which enabled students to perceive strengths of special pupils and develop empathetic support.

The most salient learning point is that training is important but it is not what makes teachers feel adequate. Training in special needs does not necessarily make teachers feel competent about teaching children with disabilities (Woolfson & Brady, 2009). It is not training per se but successful classroom experiences that influence teachers' sense of efficacy and attitude towards inclusion.

One recommendation to enhance the value of training is to provide opportunities for mainstream teachers to co-teach with a colleague trained in special needs and interventions, such as the AEDs(LBS), and to observe effective specialist support in action. Research consistently indicated that teachers learned more and developed self-efficacy when they engaged in deep learning through collaborative learning structures that included guidance by and observation of knowledgeable colleagues who had expertise in a specific content area, feedback from colleagues' observation of their teaching, and reflective discussion (Chong & Kong, 2012; Postholm, 2008).

Another option is to deploy the AED(LBS) as a consulting teacher so that his or her knowledge could filter down to a larger number of teachers. He or she can provide expertise in differentiation of content (what pupils learn), processes (how pupils learn) and product (how pupils show what they have learned) (Ferguson, 2008). Yet another possibility was to make greater use of cooperative teaching. Indeed, Ferguson (2008) found that one of the practices that supported educational inclusion was a new cooperative practice negotiated by special educators and mainstream teachers.

There were limitations to this study. First, data were obtained from less than 40% (41/108) of the resourced primary schools and participating teachers were nominated by their principals. Thus, the findings may not representatively capture the full picture of inclusive education in Singapore. Schools that chose not to participate may have a different experience of inclusion, which cannot be reported in this study. Second, only observational data were collected, which made it difficult to verify the degree to which the interview responses matched the day-to-day activities that took place in the inclusive classrooms. Third, only teachers were interviewed and the status of inclusion was based solely on their perception. At the centre of these discussions were the children with special needs who might have a totally different experience of schooling compared to that of their general education counterparts. Their story would be an interesting area of study for future research.

Future research

For countries such as Singapore which is relatively new to inclusive education, care must be undertaken to build teachers' capacity to accommodate children with special needs in the general education classroom. Our findings suggest that experiences of success in the classroom build capacity, which is vital for sustaining inclusion over the long haul.

A possible area for future research is to explore mentorship or coaching models that will strengthen teachers' practical skills in special education support and enhance their sense of efficacy. Another possible area of research is to examine differentiated support that is being provided for various disabilities in the general education classroom with a view to identifying best practices that will benefit children with special needs.

Conclusion

This study aimed to document teachers' experience of inclusive education in Singapore. As inclusion is new to Singapore schools, it is understandable that the teachers felt greatly challenged. However, there were encouraging accounts of experiences that registered joy and satisfaction from this inclusive learning journey. Whereas they were accustomed to working separately, general education and special education teachers had begun to work collaboratively. Experience will deepen the new connections they have established and make this partnership more commonplace. Needless to say, there is room for ongoing teacher training and collaborative learning that will build teacher-efficacy and further the ideals of inclusion.

Acknowledgment

This work is supported by the Office of Educational Research, National Institute of Education (Singapore), [OER 8/09 YLS].

References

Ainscow, M. (2000). The next step for special education: Support the development of inclusive practices. *British Journal of Special Education, 27*(2), 76–80. doi: 10.1111/1467-8527.00164

Avramidis, E., Bayliss, P., & Burden, R. (2000). A survey into mainstream teachers' attititudes towards the inclusion of children with special educational needs in the ordinary school in one local education authority. *Educational Psychology, 20,* 191–211. doi: 10.1080/713663717

Avramidis, E., & Norwich, B. (2002). Teachers' attitudes towards integration/inclusion: A review of the literature. *European Journal of Special Needs Education, 17,* 129–147. doi: 10.1080/08856250210129056

Booth, T., & Ainscow, M. (2002). *Index for Inclusion: Developing learning and participation in schools.* Bristol: CISE.

Chong, W. H., & Kong, C. A. (2012). Teacher collaborative learning and teacher self-efficacy: The case of lesson study. *The Journal of Experimental Education, 80,* 263–283. doi: 10.1080/00220973.2011.596854

Curcic, S. (2009). Inclusion in PK-12: An international perspective. *International Journal of Inclusive Education, 13,* 517–538. doi: 10.1080/13603110801899585

Education Bureau. (2011). *Information sheet: Special education.* Hong Kong: Author. Retrieved from http://www.edb.gov.hk/index.aspx?nodeID=7389&langno=1

Ferguson, D. L. (2008). International trends in inclusive education: The continuing challenge to teach each one and everyone. *European Journal of Special Needs Education, 23,* 109–120. doi: 10.1080/08856250801946236

Forlin, C., Keen, M., & Barrett, E. (2008). The concerns of mainstream teachers: Coping with inclusivity in an Australian context. *International Journal of Disability, Development and Education, 55,* 251–264. doi: 10.1080/10349120802268396

Frederickson, N., Simmons, E., Evans, L., & Soulsby, C. (2007). Assessing the social and affective outcomes of inclusion. *British Journal of Special Education, 34,* 105–115. doi: 10.1111/j.1467-8578.2007.00463.x

Horne, P. E., & Timmons, V. (2009). Making it work: Teachers' perspectives on inclusion. *International Journal of Inclusive Education, 13,* 273–286. doi: 10.1080/13603110701433964

Hwang, Y. S., & Evans, D. (2011). Attitudes towards inclusion: Gaps between belief and practice. *International Journal of Special Education, 26,* 136–146. Retrieved from http://www. internationaljournalofspecialeducation.com/articles.cfm?y=2011&v=26&n=1

Imants, J. (2002). The counterproductive effects of a national reform initiative: Reflections from organizational theory. *School Effectiveness and School Improvement, 13,* 31–61. doi: 10.1076/ sesi.13.1.31.3440

Koutrouba, K., Vamvakari, M., & Steliou, M. (2006). Factors correlated with teachers' attitudes towards the inclusion of students with special educational needs in Cyprus. *European Journal of Special Needs Education, 21,* 381–394. doi: 10.1080/08856250600956162

Lim, L., & Tan, J. (2004). Learning and diversity. In L. Lim & M. M. Quah (Eds.), *Educating learners with diverse abilities* (pp. 1–28). Singapore: McGraw Hill.

Loreman, T., Forlin, C., & Sharma, U. (2007). An international comparison of pre-service teacher attitudes towards inclusive education. *Disability Studies Quarterly, 27.* doi: http://dsq-sds.org/ article/view/53/53

Lyons, E., & Coyle, A. (2007). *Analysing qualitative data in Psychology.* Los Angeles, CA: Sage Publishing.

Ministry of Education. (2012). *Support for children with special needs.* Retrieved from http://www. moe.gov.sg/education/programmes/support-for-children-special-needs/

Norwich, B. (2008). What future for special schools and inclusion? Conceptual and professional perspectives. *British Journal of Special Education, 35,* 136–143.

Phadraig, B. M. (2007). Towards inclusion: The development of provision for children with special educational needs in Ireland from 1991 to 2004. *Irish Educational Studies, 26,* 289–300. doi: 10. 1080/03323310701491562

Poon, K. K., Musti-Rao, S., & Wettasinghe, M. (2013). Special education in Singapore: History, trends, and future directions. *Intervention in School and Clinic, 49,* 59–64.

Postholm, M. B. (2008). Teachers developing practice: Reflection as key activity. *Teaching and Teacher Education, 24,* 1717–1728. doi: 10.1016/j.tate.2008.02.024

Ronen, C. (2007). Issues and debates concerning mainstreaming and inclusion in educational settings. In S. Reiter, Y. Leyser, & D. Avissar (Eds.), *Inclusiveness learners with disabilities in education* (pp. 27–56). Haifa: "AHVA".

Sharma, U., Forlin, C., Loreman, T., & Earle, C. (2006). Impact of training on pre-service teachers' attitudes about inclusive education, concerns about inclusive education, and sentiments about persons with disabilities. *International Journal of Special Education, 21,* 80–93. doi: 10.1080/ 09687590802469271

Tan, S. Y. J., Nonis, K. P., & Chow, J. Y. (2011). The balance control of children with and without hearing impairment in Singapore: A case study. *The International Journal of Special Education, 26,* 260–275. Retrieved from http://repository.nie.edu.sg/jspui/bitstream/10497/8911/3/IJSE-26-3-260_a.pdf

Thomazet, S. (2009). From integration to inclusive education: Does changing the terms improve practice? *International Journal of Inclusive Education, 13,* 553–563. doi: 10.1080/ 13603110801923476

UNESCO. (1994). *The Salamanca statement and framework for action on special needs education.* Paris: Author.

Warnock, M. (2005). *Special educational needs: A new look.* London: Philosophy of Education Society of Great Britain.

Wilde, A., & Avramidis, E. (2011). Mixed feelings: Towards a continuum of inclusive pedagogies. *Education, 39,* 83–101. doi: 10.1080/03004270903207115

Wong, D. K. P., Pearson, V., & Lo, E. M. K. (2004). Competing philosophies in the classroom: A challenge to Hong Kong teachers. *International Journal of Inclusive Education, 8,* 261–279. doi: 10.1080/1360311032000160599

Woolfson, L. M., & Brady, K. (2009). An investigation of factors impacting on mainstream teachers' beliefs about teaching students with learning difficulties. *Educational Psychology, 29,* 221–238. doi: 10.1080/01443410802708895

Yeo, L. S., Neihart, M., Tang, H. N., Chong, W. H., & Huan, V. S. (2011). An inclusive initiative in Singapore for preschool children with special needs. *Asia Pacific Journal of Education, 31,* 143–158. doi: 10.1080/02188791.2011.566990

Factors associated with staff perceptions towards inclusive education in Singapore

Kenneth K. Poon, Zijia Ng, Meng Ee Wong and Sarinajit Kaur

> In this study, we sought to examine the perceptions of teachers and other school professionals towards the inclusion of secondary school students with special educational needs (SEN), and the associated factors. The Sentiments, Attitudes and Concerns about Inclusive Education Revised scale (SACIE-R) was completed by 131 teachers and school professionals from two mainstream secondary schools in Singapore. The findings revealed an overall neutral attitude towards inclusion. Together, confidence in teaching students with SEN, the level of training SEN support, as well as experience teaching students with SEN account for a large proportion of the variance in ratings of inclusive perceptions. Further analyses revealed that confidence in teaching or supporting students with SEN was found to be a significant predictor of inclusive perceptions. The findings suggest that schools seeking to engage in inclusive practices should focus on ways to develop the confidence of personnel to support students with SEN. Professional development and mentorship were suggested as possible avenues.

The perceptions that teachers and other educational personnel have towards inclusion have been widely studied in other countries. However, limited research has been conducted in Singapore, particularly in secondary schools. Staff attitudes have a considerable bearing on the success of inclusion (Avramidis & Norwich, 2002) and with the inclusive education system in Singapore still in its infancy (Poon, Musti-Rao, & Wettasinghe, 2013), it is important to identify existing attitudes of Singapore mainstream school staff to better address their concerns during initial training or professional development. This study sought to understand the perceptions of mainstream secondary school staff towards the inclusion of students with special educational needs (SEN) in Singapore, and to explore the factors which may be associated with these attitudes.

Importance of staff perceptions toward inclusion

Inclusion when applied to the context of students with SEN refers to the process of educating these students in regular schools with the provision of appropriate support and resources (Winter, 2006). Whilst many educational systems internationally espouse this philosophy, there is considerable heterogeneity within which inclusion is interpreted and implemented. It is well documented that successful implementation of inclusive education policies and practices is largely dependent upon the positive attitudes of mainstream school staff (de Boer, Pijl, & Minnaert, 2011; Forlin, Keen, & Barrett, 2008). The views and perceptions of staff are critical in the endeavour to promote effective inclusion as negative beliefs and attitudes may impinge on their acceptance and commitment to the cause (Avramidis & Norwich, 2002; Ernst & Rogers, 2009).

School leaders play a key role in the initiation and maintenance of support for inclusion. They reform systems, manage and coordinate resources, and supervise and guide educators in the process of change (Angelides, Antoniou, & Charalambous, 2010; Horrocks, White, & Roberts, 2008). As school leadership sets the tone for the entire school community, their attitudes can make or break the movement towards a more inclusive education. Similarly, it is crucial for educators to embrace inclusion as they work directly with students with disabilities on a daily basis (Chong, Forlin, & Au, 2007). Furthermore, transference of positive attitudes from school staff to typically developing students contributes to an inclusive ethos where diversity is valued and students with disabilities are regarded as full members of the school community.

Studies of perspectives towards inclusion, such as this study, are predicated on a few assumptions. First, it is often tacitly assumed that the perceptions of school personnel towards inclusion may be changed. Next, is the assumption that a change in attitudes will lead to a corresponding change in teacher behaviour. The final assumption is that behavioural changes on the part of school personnel will lead to corresponding changes in student outcomes. Whilst the first and third assumptions have some support (e.g., Campbell, Gilmore, & Cuskelly, 2003), the premise that attitudes are associated with teacher practice needs further examination as the link is less often studied. The Bruns and Mogharreban (2007) report that teachers of young children with more inclusive attitudes engage in general strategies but not with more specialized strategies provides some support for this. However, this attitude-behaviour link has been investigated in the broader field of psychology. In their meta-analysis of 41 studies examining the conditions that attitudes predict future behaviour, Glasman and Albarracín (2006) reported that the relationship was strongest when the attitudes were easy to recall and stable over time. Attitude stability was in turn predicted by the participants expressed confidence in their attitudes, when these attitudes were based on experience, and when they had the opportunity to consider the issue from both sides. Together, these studies seem to suggest that there is a link between perceptions and behaviour but the strength of the relationship is influenced by other variables. Glasman and Albarracín's (2006) meta-analysis suggests that some of these variables which are associated with the behaviour appear to also be similar to the variables that impact upon perceptions towards inclusion.

Factors associated with staff perceptions towards inclusion

Negative attitudes often reflect practical concerns rather than ideological dissonance (Abbott, 2006; Avramidis & Norwich, 2002). While most school staff endorsed inclusion from a theoretical and philosophical standpoint of social justice and equal opportunity, many share deep reservations about its practical implementation (Avramidis & Kalyva, 2007; de Boer et al., 2011). They are apprehensive about their capacity to manage and educate students with SEN, and feelings of anxiety and inadequacy may manifest as resistance to inclusion. Due to the large corpus of studies that have been conducted, a comprehensive review is beyond the scope of this paper. However, studies of teachers in Singapore and countries have yielded several findings. Sharma, Forlin, and Loreman (2007) in their comparison of preservice teacher concerns about inclusion across Singapore, Hong Kong, Canada, and Australia indicated that preservice teachers in four countries reported the 'lack of resources' to be the greatest concern followed by the 'lack of skills'. This was followed by 'non-acceptance' and 'increased workload'. Of the individual items among Singaporean pre-service teachers, the lack of knowledge and skills, the lack of special education material, and the lack of resources/special education staff were the top three concerns (mean of 3.3 and 3.25 on a four-point rating scale). Some pertinent factors which may impact upon attitudes towards inclusion are briefly reviewed.

Degree of training and professional development

In supporting students with SEN is essential. The positive impact of teacher preparation and professional development upon staff attitudes toward inclusion has been well documented (Avramidis & Kalyva, 2007; Avramidis & Norwich, 2002; Chong et al., 2007; de Boer et al., 2011; Forlin et al., 2008). For instance, Sosu, Mtika, and Colucci-Gray (2010) attributed positive changes in student teachers' attitudes to initial training inputs such as conceptual knowledge of inclusion, differentiated pedagogy, and practical observations. Similarly, Ernst and Rogers (2009) showed that ongoing professional development had a positive impact upon the attitudes of high school teachers.

Experience in supporting or teaching students with SEN

Is another vital ingredient in shaping staff attitudes toward inclusion (Avramidis & Norwich, 2002; Chong et al., 2007; de Boer et al., 2011; Ernst & Rogers, 2009; Horrocks et al., 2008; Vermeulen, Denessen, & Knoors, 2012). Experience translates training into practice, and enhances the skills of school personnel in managing and educating students with SEN (Villa, Thousand, Meyers, & Nevin, 1996). Avramidis and Kalyva (2007) reported that primary school teachers who had been working with students with SEN were more receptive to inclusion than those with little or no experience. They contended that favourable staff attitudes were a function of experience and the expertise that developed through the process of implementation. In addition, the quality of experiences also seems to play a role. Vermeulen et al. (2012) reported that receptiveness was dependent on whether staff experienced success or problems with the inclusion of students with disabilities.

Confidence and self-efficacy

Factor analyses reveal the construct of teacher efficacy to be bidimensional (Coladarci & Breton, 1997; Ghaith & Shaaban, 1999; Gibson & Dembo, 1984). Personal efficacy is the belief in a personal ability to achieve results, whereas teacher efficacy is the belief in the power of teaching to achieve results in the classroom. Studies have established that accumulation of experience and acquisition of knowledge and skills build teacher efficacy or confidence that one can competently accommodate and support students with SEN, and this in turn produces positive attitudes toward inclusion (Avramidis & Norwich, 2002; de Boer et al., 2011; Sharma et al., 2007; Vermeulen et al., 2012).

Other demographic factors

In addition to the dynamic factors mentioned above, demographic factors also impact upon the degree to which a person expresses positive perceptions towards inclusion. For instance, the role of gender is inconclusive (Avramidis & Norwich, 2002) with some studies suggesting that female teachers may express more positive perceptions (Eichinger, Rizzo, & Sirotnik, 1991), some other studies suggest that male high school teachers were more receptive to inclusion than their female counterparts (Ernst & Rogers, 2009) and others (Horrocks et al., 2008; Sharma et al., 2007) report non-significant results. Other demographic factors which have not received much attention in research literature but may impact upon inclusive perceptions include age and level of education.

Apart from the many factors which may impact upon staff perceptions of inclusion, it is also frequently necessary to understand the impact of the broader context. This is especially important as most of these studies cited are situated in contexts where there is a relatively longer history of inclusive education. This is not necessarily the case in many educational contexts.

Inclusion of students with SEN in Singapore

Singapore is an ideal context for understanding the broader contextual influences on staff perceptions towards inclusion. Like many of the contexts cited in studies such as Australia, Hong Kong, the United Kingdom, and the United States of America, Singapore is a country with a high level of economic development. It has also performed well in international benchmarking studies of mathematics and science achievement (Gonzales et al., 2008). It has been suggested that the educational system plays a role in this achievement (Leung, 2006). Singapore's education system is characterized by a series of high stakes examination with the Ministry of Education (MOE) taking a central role of shaping the curriculum (Tan & Gopinathan, 2000). Teachers within Singapore schools are also well educated with a large proportion of them having at least a bachelor's degree (Lim & Tan, 2001).

It was reported in 2012 that about 2.5% of students in primary and secondary schools were identified as having some form of disabilities in mainstream schools (Enabling Masterplan 2012–2016 Steering Committee, 2012). This figure is reported to be an underestimate as the reported incidence among pre-schoolers for the same period was 3.2%. Another possible reason for this low figure is the presence of a dual education system (c.f., Lim & Sang, 2000) where students with milder forms of SEN are generally included and supported in regular education schools and with those requiring more intense support educated in a special school. Finally, the system of regular examinations makes it hard for many students with SEN to stay within the regular education system. In addition, students with SEN need to pass the examination offered at the end of primary education before they can gain admission into a secondary school. Although Singapore has provided, in some form, organizations supporting students with SEN since the 1940s, Singapore's experience of supporting students with SEN within regular educational settings is less established with formal initiatives introduced only as recently as 2005 (Lim, Wong, & Cohen, 2011; Poon et al., 2013; Yeo, Neihart, Tang, Chong, & Huan, 2011). In response to the growing need to support students with SEN in regular schools, Allied Educators (Learning and Behavioural Support; AED [LBS]) have been introduced to all primary schools and one-third of secondary schools in Singapore (Ministry of Education, 2012). AED (LBS) are professionals with specialized training to provide in-class support, small group intervention, transition support, and case management to support the learning, socio-emotional, and behavioural needs of students with SEN. In addition, all schools are resourced with at least one counsellor (AED [Counselling]) who provides direct counselling intervention to at-risk students with social, emotional and behavioural concerns, some of whom have SEN.

Apart from that, 10% to 20% of the teaching staff in all regular primary and secondary schools received over 100 hours of in-service training to support students with SEN. Although these initiatives represent a milestone in inclusive education, the majority of teachers receive very limited training in the support of students with SEN (Poon et al., 2013). As part of the teacher preparation programme, all trainee teachers receive between 12 and 36 hours of introductory level course work in teaching and managing students with SEN. This could take several forms including an awareness programme, presentations on specific topics, and/or embedded within part of a course on classroom management. The introductory nature of pre-service training on SEN contains mainly generic content that raises awareness.

Methods

Settings and participants

Two mainstream secondary schools were purposefully sampled for our study. Both schools were nominated by professionals (i.e., teachers, psychologists, and psychiatrists) and parents of children with disabilities as exemplary schools that have shown good support for students with disabilities. The first school is a co-educational government school resourced by the MOE to support students with autism spectrum disorder (ASD) since 2007. The school adopted restorative practices as a school-wide approach. Restorative practice within education contexts is defined as an approach seeking to develop a set of school ethos, policies and procedures that reduce the possibilities of conflict and harm, and when it occurs to provide avenues for the restoration of relationships (McCluskey et al., 2008). At the time of the study, the first school had about 1,200 students, of which 17% were eligible for financial assistance. A total of 24 students were identified with SEN (or 2% of the school population), including 11 students diagnosed with ASD. A fifth of the 82 teachers were trained in special needs. The students with SEN in the school were supported by four school counsellors and one AED (LBS). The school leadership was supportive of students with SEN and take an active role in their support. As such, the support for students with SEN is embedded within the school systems (e.g., induction of new teachers, transition between levels) and teachers apply, where possible, class-wide strategies for including students with SEN (e.g., augmenting communication with visual information).

The second school is a government-aided Christian mission all-boys school resourced by the MOE to support students with dyslexia since 2007. This school had about 1,400 students, of which 6% was eligible for financial aid. Ninety-nine students were identified with SEN (or about 7% of the student population). The school was staffed with 94 teachers, of which 12% were trained in special needs. In addition, students in the school were supported by eight school counsellors and one AED (LBS). Like the first school, the values of respect, responsibility, and care are deeply embedded in the school mission and philosophy which was interpreted to impart an acceptance and appreciation for inclusion and inculcate a positive climate of helping students in need. Support for students with SEN is provided via the coordination services of an AED (LBS) who contacts and supports teachers of students with SEN. The AED (LBS) also provides support in the transitioning of students with SEN across levels.

The participants of this study were 131 staff (55% female and 45% male) who are mainly teachers (90%), AEDs (8%), or school leaders (2%). As indicated in Table 1, the majority of the participants are females aged between 26 and 45 years of age with university degrees (68%). Although most participants indicated that they had at least some interaction with persons with SEN (97%) and some experience teaching or supporting students with SEN (90%), many expressed very low to average confidence in teaching or supporting these students (92%). Moreover, more than half of the participants reported receiving no training or less than 10 hours of training in special needs education. Chi square and Mann-Whitney tests indicated no significant differences between the two schools in gender ($\chi^2 = .95$, $df = 1$,

$p = .37$), age ($p = .30$), education ($p = .97$), training ($p = .89$) and interaction ($p = .11$). However, personnel in the first school indicated that they are significantly more confident in supporting students with special needs ($p = 0.26$).

Materials

The Sentiments, Attitudes, and Concerns about Inclusive Education Revised scale (SACIE-R; Forlin, Earle, Loreman, & Sharma, 2011) is a 15-item questionnaire designed to elicit the perceptions of school staff regarding inclusive education. Respondents were invited to indicate their agreement with a list of statements along a four-point rating scale ($1 =$ strongly disagree to $4 =$ strongly agree). These statements load on the three aspects of perceptions regarding inclusive education, namely Sentiments, Attitudes, and Concerns. The Sentiments subscale (5 items; $\alpha = .63$) assesses staff sentiments or comfort when engaging with persons with SEN. The Attitudes subscale (5 items; $\alpha = .65$)

Table 1. Personal and professional characteristics of the sample (percentage in parentheses).

Characteristic	N (%)
School Staff	
Teacher	118 (90)
Allied Educator/School Counsellor	10 (8)
School Leader	3 (2)
Gender	
Male	59 (45)
Female	72 (55)
Age	
25 years or below	9 (7)
26 to 35 years	49 (37)
36 to 45 years	32 (24)
46 to 55 years	29 (22)
56 years or above	12 (9)
Educational Attainment	
Postsecondary Certificate	13 (10)
Bachelor Degree	89 (68)
Postgraduate degree	29 (22)
Training in Special Needs Education	
None	44 (34)
Introductory (less than 10 hours)	56 (43)
Some (10 to 39 hours)	17 (13)
High (at least 40 hours)	14 (11)
Interaction with persons with disabilities	
None	4 (3)
Some	105 (79.5)
A Lot	23 (17.4)
Confidence in teaching or supporting students with disabilities	
Very low	4 (3)
Low	45 (35)
Average	71 (55)
High	9 (7)
Very High	1 (1)
Experience in teaching or supporting students with disabilities	
None	13 (10)
Some	97 (75)
High (at least 30 full days)	21 (16)

measures staff acceptance of students with SEN. The Concerns subscale (5 items; $\alpha = .71$) addresses staff concerns about inclusive education. In addition, a Total score (15 items; $\alpha = .77$) corresponding to fewer concerns and more positive perceptions towards inclusion was computed. Minor adaptations were made to the demographics section based on a pilot administration of this survey to about 15 teachers. These adaptations were made so that the wordings within the categories and items made more sense to educators in the local context (e.g., names of certificates indicating the highest levels of education, "mainstream classrooms" instead of "regular classes" etc.).

In addition to the SACIE-R, the participants were also asked to indicate various characteristics such as gender, age, the highest level of education, the degree of interaction with persons with disabilities, experience teaching or supporting students with disabilities, confidence in teaching or supporting these students, as well as the degree of training in special needs education. The highest level of education was measured with the respondent checking off the category presented on a list (e.g., diploma, bachelor degree, postgraduate degree). The level of interaction and experience of supporting students with SEN was measured along a three-point rating scale (i.e., none, some, high/a lot). The level of training to support students with SEN was measured along a four-point rating scale (i.e., none to high), and the level of confidence in supporting students with SEN was measured along a four-point rating scale (i.e., very high to very low).

Procedure

Ethical clearance was obtained from the Institutional Review Board and permission was obtained from the schools before the study commenced. Participants were approached to participate in this study during a staff meeting where they were provided with written and verbal explanations of the nature and purpose of the study before they were invited to complete the SACIE-R scale. The researchers collated a total of 131 completed questionnaires (response rate of 66%). Due to the anonymous nature of the survey, it was not possible to make an analysis of the non-respondents.

Data preparation and analysis

Once the surveys were collected, the responses on the surveys were transferred to a database for data analysis. First, the accuracy of data entry was established via an examination of the ranges of the scores. Once done, the subscale scores were computed. The Attitudes subscale was computed by averaging individual items in the subscale. Higher attitude scores were indicative of more positive attitudes toward inclusion. The Sentiments and Concerns scores were computed by reverse coding then averaging all items in the respective subscales. As in the case of the Attitudes subscale, higher scores were reflective of more positive sentiments and lower level of concerns. The average of the three subscale scores generated the SACIE Total score.

Likewise, the other variables from the first part of the survey such as gender, age, the highest level of education, the degree of interaction with persons with disabilities, experience teaching or supporting students with disabilities, confidence in teaching or supporting these students, as well as the degree of training in special needs education were included into the analysis. All predictor factors were included as ordinal variables except for gender which was a nominal variable and all outcome factors (i.e., SACIE) were treated as interval variables.

Results

Staff perceptions toward inclusion

As seen in Table 2, the participants responded with a SACIE-R mean total score of 2.45 (SD = .31) which indicated that school staff, on average, held neutral attitudes toward inclusion. The SACIE-R mean Sentiments, Attitudes, and Concerns subscale scores were 2.23 (SD = .40), 2.47 (SD = .41), and 2.89 (SD = .42) respectively.

Factors associated with staff perceptions toward inclusion

The bivariate relationships between the predictor variables were explored using the Spearman's correlation. As indicated in Table 3, there were significant bivariate correlations between various independent variables. In general, there were few significant relationships between the demographic variables of age, gender, and education. There were medium to large relationships found among the SEN exposure variables such as training in supporting students with SEN, interaction with people with SEN, experience of

Table 2. Means and standard deviations for scores on the SACIE-R Scale.

Item	M	SD
Concerns	2.89	0.42
I am concerned that it will be difficult to give appropriate attention to all students in an inclusive classroom.	3.18	0.53
I am concerned that my workload will increase if I have students with disabilities in my class.	2.74	0.70
I am concerned that I will be more stressed if I have students with disabilities in my class.	2.71	0.66
I am concerned that I do not have the knowledge and skills required to teach students with disabilities.	2.91	0.64
I am concerned that students with disabilities will not be accepted by the rest of the class.	2.89	0.54
Attitudes	2.47	0.41
Students who need an individualized academic programme should be educated in mainstream primary and secondary schools.	2.27	0.67
Students who have difficulty expressing their thoughts verbally should be educated in mainstream primary and secondary schools.	2.67	0.68
Students who require communicative technologies (for example Braille and sign language) should be educated in mainstream primary and secondary schools.	2.31	0.61
Students who are inattentive should be educated in mainstream primary and secondary schools.	2.65	0.57
Students who frequently fail exams should be educated in mainstream primary and secondary schools.	2.43	0.60
Sentiments	2.23	0.40
I find it difficult to overcome my initial shock when meeting people with severe physical disabilities.	2.06	0.55
I am afraid to look directly at a person with disability.	1.82	0.59
I tend to make contacts with people with disabilities brief and I finish them as quickly as possible.	2.18	0.57
I dread the thought that I could eventually end up with a disability.	2.35	0.77
I would feel terrible if I had a disability.	2.71	0.67
Total	2.45	0.31

Table 3. Spearman correlations between predictor variables.

	1	2	3	4	5	6	7	8	9	10	
1. Gender	1										
2. Age	−0.10	1									
3. Education	−0.02	0.09	1								
4. Interaction	0.13	0.18*	0.02	1							
5. Training	0.20*	−0.04	−0.04	0.45**	1						
6. Knowledge of policies	0.07	0.13	0.08	0.38**	0.48**	1					
7. Level of confidence	−0.02	0.16	0.06	0.29**	0.24**	0.55**	1				
8. Experience in teaching	0.19*	−0.04	0.04	0.49**	0.39**	0.31**	0.34**	1			
9. Sentiment Score	0.01	−0.06	−0.13	0.29**	0.19*	0.31**	0.44**	0.25**	1		
10. Attitude Score	−0.11	−0.08	0.17	0.16	0.20*	0.22*	0.39**	0.23**	0.29**	1	
11. Concern Score	−0.02	0.11	−0.09	0.15	0.17	0.38**	0.49**	0.09	0.46**	0.28**	1

Note: $*p < .05$, $**p < .01$

TEACHERS' PERCEPTIONS, EXPERIENCE AND LEARNING

teaching students with SEN, and knowledge of policies pertaining to SEN. There were also moderate relationships between the subscales of the SACIE.

Multiple regression analyses were conducted in blocks to determine the degree to which personal and professional factors were associated with an inclusive disposition among school staff (see Table 4). Demographic factors such as gender, age, and education were entered in the first block. Following that, other factors like interaction, training, knowledge, confidence, and experience were added in the second block. Tolerance values for predictors ranged from 0.78 to 0.99, exceeding the recommended value of 0.10 (Tabachnick & Fidell, 2001). The high tolerance values indicated an absence of multicollinearity among the predictors.

In terms of the Sentiments subscale, the combination of gender, age, and educational attainment did not predict sentiments among school staff, $R^2 = .02, F(3,121) = .92, p = .44$. However, the model was statistically significant after factors of interaction, training, knowledge, confidence, and experience were included, $\Delta R^2 = .21$, $F(3,118) = 5.97$, $p < .001$. A total of 21% of the total variance in sentiments toward inclusion can be explained by the second model. Only confidence in teaching students with SEN ($\beta = .41, p < .001$) was a significant predictor of positive sentiments toward inclusion.

In terms of the Attitudes subscale, the combination of gender, age, and educational attainment did not predict attitudes among school staff, $R^2 = .23, F(3,120) = 2.23, p = .09$. However, the model was statistically significant after factors of interaction, knowledge, training, confidence, and experience were included, $\Delta R^2 = .19, F(3,171) = 6.30, p < .001$. A total of 19% of the total variance in attitudes toward inclusion can be explained by the second model. A more detailed analysis of the findings indicate that being male and having higher levels of confidence in teaching SEN were the only variables that were associated with attitudes toward inclusion ($\beta = -.18, p = .04; \beta = .32, p < .001$).

In terms of the Concerns subscale, the combination of gender, age, and educational attainment did not predict concerns among school staff, $R^2 = .15$, $F(3,121) = .95$, $p = .42$. However, the model was statistically significant after factors of interaction, training, knowledge, confidence, and experience were included, $\Delta R^2 = .24$, $F(3,118) = 7.12, p < .001$. A total of 24% of the total variance in concerns toward inclusion can be explained by the second model. Only confidence in teaching SEN ($\beta = .50, p < .001$) was a significant predictor of inclusive disposition Table 4.

Table 4. Predictors of inclusive disposition.

Variable	Model	R^2	F	ΔR^2
Total	1: Gender, age, & education	0.007	0.27	
	2: Gender, age, education, training, confidence, & experience	0.36	10.64***	0.36
Sentiments	1: Gender, age, & education	0.02	0.92	
	2: Gender, age, education, training, confidence, & experience	0.23	5.97***	0.21
Attitude	1: Gender, age, & education	0.23	2.23	
	2: Gender, age, education, training, confidence, & experience	0.49	6.30***	0.19
Concerns	1: Gender, age, & education	0.15	0.95	
	2: Gender, age, education, training, confidence, & experience	0.52	7.12***	0.24

Note: *$p < .05$, **$p < .01$, ***$p < .001$

Discussion

This study is the first to investigate the perceptions held by school personnel towards the inclusion of students with disabilities in Singapore mainstream secondary schools. It also explored the degree to which demographic factors (e.g., gender, age, educational attainment) and factors associated with SEN (e.g., interaction with people with SEN, knowledge of local policies regarding SEN, training in SEN support, and experience and expressed confidence in teaching or supporting students with SEN) were associated with perceptions towards inclusion among school staff.

Staff perceptions of inclusion

Consistent with previous studies (Avramidis & Norwich, 2002), this study revealed that school personnel held generally neutral attitudes toward the inclusion of students with SEN. Although the schools that were sampled in this study were resourced to support students with SEN, both schools had less than four years of experience in the formal support process. Coupled with the relatively new state of SEN support in Singapore (Poon et al., 2013), the relatively neutral attitudes that the staff expressed were understandable.

Factors associated with staff perceptions of inclusion

The positive association between perceptions towards inclusion and, across the board, knowledge of local policies regarding SEN, training in SEN support, experience with persons with SEN and confidence in teaching and supporting students with SEN is consistent with prior research (Abbott, 2006; Avramidis & Norwich, 2002). This set of factors was especially important in determining the attitudes and concerns of school personnel towards inclusion of students with SEN as they together account for about half of the total variance in responses. However, the finding that only self-rated confidence in teaching and supporting students with SEN emerged as singularly important was surprising.

The lack of no significant gender differences in staff attitudes toward inclusion (with the exception of the Attitudes subscale) is not surprising as past studies examining the relationship between gender and staff attitudes had been inconclusive. However, the lack of association between experience with inclusion and staff perceptions is unexpected and is inconsistent with earlier research showing that school staff who had previous experience of teaching or supporting students with SEN held more positive attitudes toward inclusion than those with less or no experience (Chong et al., 2007; de Boer et al., 2011; Ernst & Rogers, 2009). It is possible that the experiences of students with SEN might have been negative (Vermeulen et al., 2012). This is plausible as these secondary schools had only about five years of experience of being resourced to support students with SEN. Future studies need to examine how different types of experience with inclusion (e. g., negative or positive, personal or professional, short or long term) affect staff attitudes.

The lack of an association between training in SEN support and positive perceptions towards inclusion was also contradictory to international research (Avramidis & Norwich, 2002; de Boer et al., 2011; Forlin et al., 2008). One possible reason for this lack of association is that the majority of participants in this study (89%) had less than 40 hours of training in supporting students with SEN. Likewise, Chong et al. (2007) suggested that a 20-hour module was insufficient to prepare student teachers for challenges in an inclusive classroom. Similarly, Avramidis and Kalyva (2007) highlighted that one-shot or brief professional development was inadequate to increase the competence or influence the attitudes of in-service teachers.

This study highlighted the importance of the school personnel's confidence that one can competently accommodate and support students with SEN (Avramidis & Norwich, 2002; de Boer et al., 2011; Vermeulen et al., 2012). Confidence in supporting students with SEN in this study had a positive impact on inclusive disposition despite the absence of significant relationships between staff attitudes and training or experience.

Implications for schools

This study provides some ideas on how schools may better support students with SEN. In terms of *staff selection*, the findings from this study suggest that teachers who express confidence in supporting students with SEN possessed more positive perceptions towards inclusion. It follows that schools seeking to include students with SEN will need a critical mass of teachers with sufficient experience and training to support students with SEN (Abbott, 2006; Avramidis & Norwich, 2002). In terms of *staff deployment*, following from the findings of Villa et al. (1996) who reported more positive views towards inclusion at the end of the implementation cycle, teachers who are new to supporting students with SEN need to do so with sufficient support and mentorship. School personnel with more experience supporting students with SEN in this study did not emerge as being independently associated with inclusive disposition. What seemed to be the most important was the expressed confidence of teachers to support students with SEN. This seems to suggest that teachers need not only experience but a wealth of positive experiences in supporting students with SEN. What these together imply is that in order to cultivate a supportive and inclusive climate within secondary schools, there needs not only to be special training in SEN support but also a mentorship structure to ensure that teachers who are new to supporting students with SEN develop positive experiences. Finally, *professional development* programmes preparing staff to support students with SEN need to focus not only on knowledge and skills, but also on the attitudinal component. In this study, teachers who were more educated were not necessarily the ones with more positive inclusive disposition. In contrast, the teachers who were the most confident in supporting students with SEN rated most positive in perceptions towards inclusion.

Limitations and future directions

Although this study represents a first in the study of perceptions towards inclusive education within Singapore secondary schools, it is important to keep in mind that this study was limited to staff from two secondary schools that were nominated by professionals and parents of children with disabilities as exemplars of an inclusive school. As the sample size was comparatively small, the application of these findings to other contexts warrants careful consideration and caution. In addition, this study examined perceptions but as mentioned earlier, the link between perceptions and behaviour is not always clear. Future research with a large nationally representative sample is needed to capture a broader range of staff attitudes and practices. However, the continuation of this research could be informed through qualitative interviews which will provide a rich and in-depth understanding into school staff's experiences and perceptions of inclusive education in Singapore.

Acknowledgements

This paper makes use of data from the research project "Supporting students with special needs in secondary schools: A study of perspective, practices, and support structures" (OER25/09/KP), funded by the Centre for Research in Pedagogy and Practice, National Institute of Education, Singapore. The views expressed in this paper are the author's and do not necessarily represent the views of the Centre or the Institute. We would like to thank Ruth Koh for her assistance in the preparation of this manuscript as well as all of the youth with HFA, their families, and the school personnel who participated in this study.

References

Abbott, L. (2006). Northern Ireland head teachers' perceptions of inclusion. *International Journal of Inclusive Education, 10,* 627–643. doi: 10.1080/13603110500274379

Angelides, P., Antoniou, E., & Charalambous, C. (2010). Making sense of inclusion for leadership and schooling: A case study from Cyprus. *International Journal of Leadership in Education, 13,* 319–334. doi: 10.1080/13603120902759539

Avramidis, E., & Kalyva, E. (2007). The influence of teaching experience and professional development on Greek teachers' attitudes towards inclusion. *European Journal of Special Needs Education, 22,* 367–389. doi: 10.1080/08856250701649989

Avramidis, E., & Norwich, B. (2002). Teachers' attitudes towards integration/inclusion: A review of the literature. *European Journal of Special Needs Education, 17,* 129–147. doi: 10.1080/08856250210129056

Bruns, D. A., & Mogharreban, C. C. (2007). The gap between beliefs and practices: Early childhood practitioners' perceptions about inclusion. *Journal of Research in Childhood Education, 21,* 229–241.

Campbell, J., Gilmore, L., & Cuskelly, M. (2003). Changing student teachers' attitudes towards disability and inclusion. *Journal of Intellectual and Developmental Disability, 28,* 369–379.

Chong, S., Forlin, C., & Au, M. S. (2007). The influence of an inclusive education course on attitude change of pre-service secondary teachers in Hong Kong. *Asia-Pacific Journal of Teacher Education, 35,* 161–179. doi: 10.1080/13598660701268585

Coladarci, T., & Breton, W. A. (1997). Teacher efficacy, supervision, and the special education resource-room teacher. *The Journal of Educational Research, 90,* 230–239.

de Boer, A., Pijl, S. J., & Minnaert, A. (2011). Regular primary school teachers' attitudes towards inclusive education: A review of the literature. *International Journal of Inclusive Education, 15,* 331–353. doi: 10.1080/13603110903030089

Eichinger, J., Rizzo, T., & Sirotnik, B. (1991). Changing attmitudes toward people with disabilities. *Teacher Education Special Education: The Journal of the Teacher Education Division of the Council for Exceptional Children, 14,* 121–126.

Enabling Masterplan 2012–2016 Steering Committee. (2012). *Enabling Masterplan 2012–2016: Maximising potential, embracing differences.* Singapore: Ministry of Community Development, Youth, and Sports. Retrieved from http://app1.mcys.gov.sg/Policies/DisabilitiesPeoplewith Disabilities/EnablingMasterplan20122016.aspx

Ernst, C., & Rogers, M. R. (2009). Development of the inclusion attitude scale for high school teachers. *Journal of Applied School Psychology, 25,* 305–322. doi: 10.1080/15377900802487235

Forlin, C., Earle, C., Loreman, T., & Sharma, U. (2011). The sentiments, attitudes, and concerns about inclusive education revised (SACIE-R) scale for measuring pre-service teachers' perceptions about inclusion. *Exceptionality Education International, 21,* 50–65.

Forlin, C., Keen, M., & Barrett, E. (2008). The Concerns of mainstream teachers: Coping with inclusivity in an Australian context. *International Journal of Disability, Development and Education, 55,* 251–264. doi: 10.1080/10349120802268396

Ghaith, G., & Shaaban, K. (1999). The relationship between perceptions of teaching concerns, teacher efficacy, and selected teacher characteristics. *Teaching and Teacher Education, 15,* 487–496.

Gibson, S., & Dembo, M. H. (1984). Teacher efficacy: A construct validation. *Journal of Educational Psychology, 76,* 569–582.

Glasman, L. R., & Albarracín, D. (2006). Forming attitudes that predict future behavior: A meta-analysis of the attitude-behavior relation. *Psychological Bulletin, 132,* 778–822.

Gonzales, P., Williams, T., Jocelyn, L., Roey, S., Kastberg, D., & Brenwald, S. (2008). Highlights from TIMSS 2007: Mathematics and science achievement of U.S. fourth- and eighth-grade students in an international context [Monograph]. Retrieved from http://www.eric.ed.gov/

Horrocks, J. L., White, G., & Roberts, L. (2008). Principals' attitudes regarding inclusion of children with autism in Pennsylvania public schools. *Journal of Autism and Developmental Disorders, 38*, 1462–1473. doi: 10.1007/s10803-007-0522-x

Leung, K. S. F. (2006). Mathematics education in East Asia and the West: Does culture matter? In K. S. F. Leung, K-D. Graf, & F. J. Lopez-Real (Eds.), *Mathematics education in different cultural traditions – A comparative study of East Asia and the West* (pp. 21–46). New York, NY: Springer.

Lim, L., & Sang, S. N. (2000). Special education in Singapore. *The Journal of Special Education, 34*, 104–109.

Lim, L., & Tan, J. (2001). Addressing disability in educational reforms: A force for renewing the vision of Singapore 21. In J. Tan, S. Gopinathan, & W. K. Ho (Eds.), *Challenges Facing the Singapore education system today* (pp. 175–188). Singapore: Prentice Hall.

Lim, S. M., Wong, M. E., & Cohen, L. (2011). Exploring the emerging identities of Disabilities Officers in primary and secondary schools. (Research Brief No. 11-003). Retrieved from National Institute of Education website: http://www.nie.edu.sg/files/oer/NIE_research_brief_11-003.pdf

McCluskey, G., Lloyd, G., Kane, J., Riddell, S., Stead, J., & Weedon, E. (2008). Can restorative practices in schools make a difference? *Educational Review, 60*, 405–417.

Ministry of Education. (2012). Support for children with disabilities. Retrieved from http://www.moe.gov.sg/education/programmes/support-for-children-special-needs/

Poon, K. K., Musti-Rao, S., & Wettasinghe, C. M. (2013). Special education in Singapore: History, trends, and future directions. *Intervention in School and Clinic, 49*, 59–64.

Sharma, U., Forlin, C., & Loreman, T. (2007). What concerns pre-service teachers about inclusive education: An international viewpoint. *KEDI Journal of Educational Policy, 4*, 95–114.

Sosu, E. M., Mtika, P., & Colucci-Gray, L. (2010). Does initial teacher education make a difference? The impact of teacher preparation on student teachers' attitudes towards educational inclusion. *Journal of Education for Teaching, 36*, 389–405. doi: 10.1080/02607476.2010.513847

Tabachnick, B. G., & Fidell, L. S. (2001). *Using multivariate statistics*. Boston, MA: Allyn & Bacon.

Tan, J., & Gopinathan, S. (2000). Educational reform in Singapore: Towards greater creativity and innovation? *NIRA Review, 7*, 5–10.

Vermeulen, J. A., Denessen, E., & Knoors, H. (2012). Mainstream teachers about including deaf or hard of hearing students. *Teaching and Teacher Education, 28*, 174–181. doi:10.1016/j.tate.2011.09.007

Villa, R., Thousand, J., Meyers, H., & Nevin, A. (1996). Teacher and administrator perceptions of heterogeneous education. *Exceptional Children, 63*, 29–45.

Winter, E. C. (2006). Preparing new teachers for inclusive schools and classrooms. *Support for Learning, 21*, 85–91.

Yeo, L. S., Neihart, M., Tang, H. N., Chong, W. H., & Huan, V. S. (2011). An inclusion initiative in Singapore for preschool children with special needs. *Asia Pacific Journal of Education, 31*, 143–158. doi:10.1080/02188791.2011.566990

Developing pedagogical practices in Myanmar primary schools: possibilities and constraints

Frank Hardman, Christian Stoff, Wan Aung and Louise Elliott

This paper presents the findings of a baseline study of pedagogic practices used by Myanmar primary teachers in the teaching of mathematics and Myanmar language at Grades 3 and 5. The main purpose of the baseline study was to inform the design of teacher education programmes and allow for subsequent evaluations of interventions designed to improve the quality of primary education. It found that the majority of observed lessons (n = 728) used a transmission model of teaching in which the teacher often used a chalkboard and/or textbook to transmit recipe knowledge for recall and there was little variation across the teaching of mathematics and Myanmar language at Grades 3 and 5. Drawing on evidence from the baseline, the paper explores the training needs of primary teachers in Myanmar in the light of proposed reforms to teacher education at the pre- and in-service stages.

Introduction

Since the first general election in 2010 marking an important step in the transition from military rule to civilian democracy, and a subsequent election in April 2012 that saw the return of Aung San Suu Kyi and her National League for Democracy party to national politics, Myanmar (formerly known as Burma) has been emerging from decades of international isolation and ethnic conflict. At a time when Myanmar is being welcomed back into the global economy and is introducing reforms to expand trade and investment, there is an urgent need to rebuild its capacity for political, administrative and legal reform, and for the delivery of key public services, especially education and health.

While access to data on education in Myanmar is often limited and out of date, official figures show that primary education has a 97% intake rate with gender parity (Ministry of Education, 2012). According to the official data, there are currently some 41,000 schools and about 276,000 school teachers, as well as 23 education colleges and two institutes of education that produce around 10,000 teachers annually. It is estimated that about half of the primary schools are multi-grade with teachers responsible for more than one grade at a time, usually taught in school buildings lacking partitions or walls between classes. It is claimed that 81% of children complete the full cycle of primary education that ends at the fourth grade. However, it is acknowledged that there are disparities in access to education between states and divisions. For example, the net enrolment for primary schools in Kachin State is 94.8% compared to 61.2% in Shan State East, and 59% in Chin State.

Recent international figures suggest the overall completion rate to be much lower with 45% of children initially enrolled in school failing to complete the final primary grade, with the highest rate of dropout (19%) at the end of first grade (Nations United, 2011). In terms of adult literacy rates, official figures state that it is around 95% (UNESCO, 2010a). However, a recent UNICEF study of literacy and numeracy rates found low levels of learning achievement with the majority of pupils completing the primary school cycle having mastered less than 50% of the competencies set out in the curriculum for Myanmar language and mathematics (Vine, 2010a, 2010b).

In addition to the lack of official information on Myanmar primary schools, there has, until recently, been little in the way of published research on classroom pedagogy. A 2010 study of pedagogic practices in 23 Myanmar primary lessons found that teachers relied on a single method made up of teacher-fronted "chalk and talk" promoting the transmission of knowledge and rote learning and low levels of achievement in Myanmar language and mathematics (Vine, 2010a, 2010b). Such findings suggest the need for powerful teacher education programmes to shift such persistent patterns of teacher-pupil interaction (Timperley, 2011).

However, a study of 10 Education Colleges in Myanmar suggests they are not currently equipped to provide such programmes (Redden, 2007). It was found that teacher educators are not able to challenge the strong images that teaching students bring to their training shaped by their earlier educational experiences because many teacher educators generally hold the same beliefs and perpetuate a transmission mode of instruction. It was also found that the centralized education college curriculum, while creating a uniformity in approach, appeared to be too general, overcrowded and in need of radical reform to develop specialism and expertise in the different phases of basic education (early years, primary, middle and secondary school).

A more recent review of four education colleges found little had changed since 2007 (Hardman, Abd-Kadir, & Tibuhinda, 2012; Hardman, Aung, & Mint, 2012). From the observations, interviews and review of curriculum documentation, it was found that the model of teaching the students were being presented with was essentially transmission-based, stressing a hierarchical learning of knowledge and conventional teacher-fronted classroom organization. It was also evident that key areas in teacher preparation, such as multi-grade teaching, the teaching of languages other than Myanmar and inclusive education, were largely absent from the curriculum.

The colleges also lacked specialist teaching areas and resources, and the current ICT infrastructure was in need of a major overhaul to effectively connect staff and students to the global information highway. Partnerships with schools were largely underdeveloped and college staff played little role in the supervision of students on teaching practicum and with curriculum development at school level. Because the links were minimal, student teacher support and supervision was mainly the responsibility of head teachers, with support from township education officers charged with overseeing and supporting schools.

In the face of these challenges, there is a growing recognition by the Government of Myanmar and its donor partners that a focus on pedagogy and its training implications needs to be at the heart of the commitment to improve student retention, progression and learning (Schweisfurth, 2011; Schwille, Dembele, & Schubert, 2007). In its discussion of quality education in the developing world, the 2010 UNESCO EFA Global Monitoring Report calls for a commitment to policies that focus on the creation of an effective learning environment for all children regardless of background, through the provision of adequate facilities, well-trained teachers, and a relevant curriculum and clearly defined learning outcomes (UNESCO, 2010b). Most importantly, the report acknowledges that educational quality is largely obtained through pedagogical processes in the classroom and that what students achieve is heavily influenced by the knowledge, skills, dispositions and commitment of the teachers in whose care students are entrusted. Therefore, provision for meeting the professional development of teachers needs to be focused on the school.

The President of Myanmar has made the improvement of education standards a top priority and teacher education has been identified as a critical area of concern and a key strategy for improving the quality of education[1]. As part of the commitment to develop the quality of education in Myanmar, a comprehensive education sector review (CESR) was approved by the President of Myanmar calling for a review of the whole teacher education and management system to improve the quality of basic education.

As Myanmar embarks on its reforms of the education system, it is recognized that a motivated and well-trained teaching force is a prerequisite for quality education and that this can only be brought about by improving the status, quality, management, policies and training of teachers (Darling-Hammond, Chung Wei, Andree, Richardson, & Orphanos, 2009; OECD, 2011). In line with other countries in the south east Asian region, it is recognized that such a commitment to the development of teacher capacity will require the bringing together of pre-service education and training (PRESET) and in-service education and training (INSET) programmes to create a continuing professional development framework to upgrade the pedagogic knowledge and skills of teachers over a sustained period of time Suzuki and Howe (2010).

There is also a recognition that reforms to teacher education will need to consider the varying social, cultural, linguistic and educational needs of Myanmar because of its ethnically diverse population and that such reforms will need to be delivered through a decentralized education system. It is therefore important to study the way contextual factors interact with teacher beliefs and classroom practices, particularly in poorly resourced contexts like Myanmar (Alexander, 2008; Avalos, 2011). Such studies will also help to ensure there is a better balance and blending of local cultural practices with internationally informed teacher education reforms.

The baseline study was therefore commissioned to study such factors and to feed into the development of a national teacher development strategy as part of the CESR and to allow for subsequent evaluations of interventions designed to improve the quality of teaching and learning in Myanmar primary schools.

Methodology

The present study set out to investigate the types of interactions primary teachers use in whole class, group-based and one-to-one teaching to present, organize and sustain learning tasks and activities in Myanmar language and mathematics classes. It forms part of a larger, quasi-experimental study designed to investigate the impact of the INSET programme on classroom processes and learning achievement over a four year period (2012–2016)[2].

A multi-method research design using both quantitative and qualitative methods was used to study classroom processes and allow for methodological triangulation to achieve greater validity and reliability in the study. As well as informing the design of teacher education programmes, the baseline study was also seen as a capacity building exercise for the Ministry of Education (MOE), UNICEF field officers, and tutors from education colleges. Forty-two staff from the MOE, UNICEF and education colleges from across the different states of Myanmar were therefore selected and trained as data collectors over the course of a week in October 2011, including a day piloting the observation instruments in primary schools in Yangon. The data collection phase was conducted over a four week period in November 2011.

Research instruments

The classroom interaction study made use of two systematic observation schedules completed in the natural setting of the classroom and interactive analysis of a sub-sample of digitally recorded lessons to investigate the time spent on a range of teaching and learning activities. All three instruments were designed to be comprehensive, manageable and as low-inference as possible in capturing current pedagogical practices in Myanmar primary schools. They were informed by international pedagogical research into effective teaching behaviours focusing on what can be observed in the act of teaching (i.e., task, activity, interaction, assessment) so as to ensure the observations of classroom processes were as valid and reliable as is practically possible (Alexander, 2008; Hardman et al., 2009).

Research into effective teaching has identified a number of key teaching behaviours that lead to higher gains in learning outcomes in which the quality of teacher-pupil interaction is central. They include instructional variety, using and incorporating pupil ideas, appropriate and varied questioning, probing for knowledge and frequent feedback in which classroom interaction is central to the act of teaching (Alexander, 2008; Hattie, 2009; Muijs & Reynolds, 2011). Investigating the quality of teacher-pupil interaction in Myanmar primary schools was therefore a central feature of the study.

All three instruments drew upon a three-part teaching exchange structure that is central to teacher-pupil interaction (Sinclair & Coulthard, 1992). In its prototypical form a teaching exchange consists of three moves: an initiation, usually in the form of a teacher question, a response in which a pupil, or group of pupils, attempts to answer the question, and a follow-up move, in which the teacher provides some form of feedback (very often in the form of an evaluation) to the pupil's response (henceforth referred to as IRF). However, research into classroom interaction suggests that the IRF structure can take on a variety of forms and functions leading to different levels of pupil participation and engagement (Hardman, 2008a; Liu, 2008; Nystrand, Gamoran, Kachur, & Prendergast, 1997; Wells, 1999). Such studies suggest that teacher follow up which goes beyond evaluation of answers (i.e., by asking pupils to expand on their thinking, justify or clarify their opinions, or make connections to their own experiences) can extend the answer in order to draw out its significance so as to create a greater equality of participation.

To ensure the instruments were appropriate to the Myanmar primary school context, they were piloted over three days in 19 primary schools in five Townships. One prominent "questioning" move noted in the piloting of the instruments was the use of a mid-sentence rise in voice intonation that acted as a teacher elicit, designed to get a response from the pupils during, or at the end of, an explanation or following a pupil response. Usually, the elicitation was in the form of a repetition or completion of a phrase or word. It was often direct and pupils often knew from the intonation whether it required an individual answer or a choral response. This was categorized as a "cued elicitation". Cued elicitations and teacher checks therefore largely functioned as ritualized participation strategies designed to keep the pupils involved rather than requiring an answer to a question.

Observation Schedule 1 used timeline analysis and required the observer to record the main teaching activities from a list of prompts every five minute interval in the lesson. In the note section, observers were asked to record activities not covered in the checklist and to provide further contextual information on the activities ticked in the checklist. Because it was systematically recording the main teaching and learning activities of the lesson in real time, the timeline analysis was designed to be formative so as to inform the completion of Observation Schedule 2, which was more summative in design. All lessons were observed by a pair of observers and the observation schedule completed independently.

Observation Schedule 2 was designed to capture the frequency of teacher and pupil behaviours that occurred during the course of a lesson and was completed at the end. The schedule asked the two observers to agree the frequencies of 32 teaching and learning activities taken from the effective teaching literature using a 4 point scale: 1 = behaviour never observed; 2 = behaviour rarely observed (i.e., once or twice); 3 = behaviour occasionally observed (i.e., four or five times); 4 = behaviour consistently observed.

Observation Schedule 3 systematically coded a sub-sample of 40 digitally recorded lessons covering the teaching of mathematics and Myanmar language at Grades 3 and 5 using a computer software program to log the duration of the time spent on a range of teaching-pupil interactions within the IRF teaching exchange structure. For each teaching exchange the computerized system logged the actor, the discourse move and who the receiver was. The scheme therefore primarily focused on the three-part, IRF structure and gathered data on teacher questions, whether questions were answered (and by whom), and the types of evaluation given in response to answers. It also recorded pupil initiations in the form of questions and statements.

Within each discourse move a range of modifiers were available. For example, the system recorded whether teacher questions were "open" (i.e., defined in terms of the teacher's reaction to the answer: only if the teacher accepted more than one answer to the question would it be judged as open) or "closed" (i.e., calling for a single response or offering facts). Responses could be coded according to whether a boy or girl answered or whether there was a choral reply. Teacher feedback to a pupil's answer was coded according to whether it was praised, criticized, accepted or probed for further elaboration. The system also recorded teacher explanations, directions, refocusing of the class, and reading and writing activities. In addition to probing, the system also recorded uptake questions (where the teacher incorporates a pupil's answer into a subsequent question).

Reliability of coding

During the data collection training workshop, inter-rater reliability checks were conducted on Observation Schedules 1 and 2 using digitally recorded lessons and the coding checked using descriptive item analysis. By the end of the 5-day training workshop, the 42 observers were achieving an inter-rater correlation of 0.86. We were, therefore, confident that we were getting over 80% agreement in the coding, adding to the reliability of the findings.

Sample

The classroom interaction baseline study consisted of a stratified sample of 200 schools selected from 1,000 government schools in 20 Townships where UNICEF is currently working. The schools were selected to be representative of urban and rural setting, size of school and ethnicity of pupils. In each of the schools, a Myanmar language and mathematics lesson was to be observed at Grades 3 and 5, giving a total figure of four observations per school. However, due to security risks in some of the border regions, only 182 schools could be visited giving a total sample of 728 lesson observations.

The overall means for the number of pupils in the 728 lessons observed is given in Table 1.

Table 1. Class size.

	Mean	Std. Deviation	Minimum	Maximum
Grade 3	32.35	24.32	1.00	124.00
Grade 5	28.70	22.07	1.00	109.00
All classes	30.89	23.74	1.00	124.00

Observers recorded the language of instruction used in the 728 lessons observed. It can be seen in Table 2 that in nearly 80% of lessons Myanmar was used as the medium of instruction and that code switching between Myanmar and a local language was common in 13% of the lessons observed, with 8% of lessons being taught in an ethnic language other than Myanmar.

In the piloting phase of the study, it was found that teachers follow nationally prescribed textbooks for Myanmar language and mathematics. In terms of the pupil totextbook ratio, it was found that in 76% of the classes observed all the pupils had their own textbook for Myanmar language and mathematics and in 23% of classes they had to share a textbook. Observers also recorded the number of lessons that had a lesson plan. Overall, it was found that 39% of the lessons observed had a plan and that teachers working in rural schools were less likely to plan lessons (i.e., 73% of teachers in rural schools had no lesson plan compared to 38% in urban schools).

Findings

This section presents the main findings of the study. Firstly, an analysis of the timeline data is presented. This is followed by a detailed analysis of the frequency of the 32 teaching and learning behaviours. Finally, an interactive analysis of the time spent on a range of

Table 2. Languages of instruction.

	Frequency	Percent
Chin	6	0.8
Dawei	34	4.7
Karen	4	0.5
Kayan	2	0.3
Myanmar	577	79.3
Myanmar/Chin	28	3.8
Myanmar/Dawei	8	1.1
Myanmar/Dawei/Karen	1	0.1
Myanmar/Kachin	3	0.4
Myanmar/Karen	7	1.0
Myanmar/Kayan	24	3.3
Myanmar/Lahu	4	0.5
Myanmar/Mon	2	0.3
Myanmar/Palaung	4	0.5
Myanmar/Pao	4	0.5
Myanmar/Rakhine	3	0.4
Myanmar/Shan	2	0.3
Rakhine	12	1.6
Total	**725**	**99.6**
Unknown	**3**	**0.4**
Total	**728**	**100.0**

TEACHERS' PERCEPTIONS, EXPERIENCE AND LEARNING

teaching and learning activities in the sub-sample of 40 digitally recorded lessons covering the teaching of mathematics and Myanmar language at Grades 3 and 5 is presented and comparisons drawn across all three observation instruments.

Timeline analysis

Working independently, the two observers completed the timeline analysis schedule during the course of the lesson. The schedule required the observers to record the main teaching activities from a list of prompts every five minute interval in the lesson. Observers could record more than one activity in each of the five minute sections of the lesson. A check on the level of agreement between the two observers showed it was above 90%. The 1,456 lesson observations were subsequently merged and analysed. Table 3 gives a breakdown of the lesson length.

In analysing the data a count of the number of times an activity occurred within a five-minute interval was conducted and divided by the total number of activities in the interval to arrive at a percentage of the time spent on the activity. Officially, Grade 3 lessons are meant to last 30 minutes and Grade 5 lessons 35 minutes so the timeline schedules were completed within these time frames. If the lesson ended before the official designated time, observers coded the behaviour as "off-task". Table 4 and Figure 1 show a breakdown of the most common teaching and learning activities in Grade 3 lessons as a percentage of the lesson time.

Similarly, Table 5 and Figure 2 show a breakdown of the most common teaching and learning activities in Grade 5 lessons as a percentage of the lesson time

The findings suggest that teacher-led explanation, question and answer, rote and chorusing of answers by pupils, and use of the chalkboard by the teacher, were the most common teaching and learning activities in the lessons observed at Grades 3 and 5. There also appeared to be little variation in the underlying pedagogy across grades. Overall, teacher directed activities accounted for over 80% of the lesson time at Grades 3 and 5, with individual seat work, where the pupils work from the chalkboard or a textbook, taking up nearly 9% of the lesson. Paired or group work and pupils demonstrating to the class appeared to be the least used of the teaching and learning activities at both grades accounting for just over 2% of the lesson time. For nearly 5% of the lesson time at Grade 3 and 4% at Grade 5, pupils were observed as being off-task, particularly in the later stages of the lesson. This suggested that lessons were ending early and teachers were not using a plenary session to draw the whole class together at the end of the lesson to summarize, consolidate and extend what has been covered and direct pupils to the next stage of learning.

Further investigation of the timeline data using regression analysis found that class size was the most important factor in determining whether teachers made use of paired/group work and pupil demonstration: their use was significantly higher in classes ranging between 30 and 50 pupils ($p = 0.008$). Such pupil-centred approaches were also more likely to occur in the teaching of mathematics ($p = 0.1$). While teachers in mono-grade classes were more likely to use paired/group work and pupil demonstration, the difference

Table 3.   Lesson length in minutes.

	N	Mean	Minimum	Maximum
All	728	32.71	5	94
Grade 3	362	30.67	5	90
Grade 5	362	34.74	15	94

Table 4. Percentage of time spent on teaching and learning activities at Grade 3.

Teaching activity	1–5 minutes	6–10 minutes	11–15 minutes	16–20 minutes	21–25 minutes	26–30 minutes	Over all
1. Explanation/Question/Answer	25.4	23.6	22.1	20.0	18.9	18.1	21.4
2. Rote/recitation	22.7	21.6	20.1	18.0	16.8	16.8	19.3
3. Chalkboard	19.8	16.5	14.9	13.3	12.6	12.0	14.9
4. Pupils working from chalkboard	2.1	3.8	5.1	6.7	6.5	5.9	5.0
5. Teacher reading	7.2	8.0	6.4	6.6	5.7	4.3	6.4
6. Pupil reading	4.1	5.3	5.9	6.2	5.9	4.6	5.3
7. Pupils working from textbook	1.5	2.4	3.3	4.0	5.5	5.5	3.7
8. Paired/group work	1.5	2.0	1.7	1.8	1.8	1.7	1.7
9. Pupil demonstrating	0.2	0.2	0.6	0.8	0.9	0.4	0.5
10. Teacher reviews topic	2.1	2.6	3.5	4.1	5.0	5.1	3.7
11. Teacher marking	0.1	0.7	1.1	2.1	3.6	3.9	1.9
12. Class management	5.4	5.7	5.8	5.8	5.2	5.5	5.6
13. Class admin.	5.5	4.1	4.0	4.7	4.1	3.9	4.4
14. Interruption	0.8	1.0	1.8	1.6	1.3	1.5	1.3
15. Pupils off-task	1.6	2.6	3.6	4.4	6.1	10.6	4.8

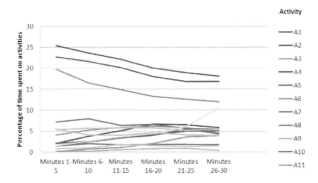

Figure 1. Grade 3 timeline analysis. Note: **Key**: A1, Teacher explanation/question and answer; A2, Teacher rote/chorus responses; A3, Teachers writing on chalkboard; A4, Pupils working from chalkboard; A5, Teacher reading to whole class; A6, Pupil reading to whole class; A7, Pupils working from textbooks; A8, Pupils working in pairs/groups; A9, Pupil demonstrating to class; A10, Teacher reviews lesson topic; A11, Teacher marking work; A12, Class management; A13, Class administration; A14, Interruption to lesson; A15, Pupils off-task.

was not statistically significant. However, the interaction effect between non-Myanmar speaking and multi-grade lessons meant there was significantly less time spent on paired/group work and pupil demonstration in such lessons ($p = 0.06$).

Overall, the timeline analysis suggests Myanmar primary teachers were using a very narrow range of teaching and learning approaches made up of teacher-fronted "chalk and talk" promoting the transmission of knowledge and rote learning. The guided co-construction of knowledge, in which a teacher talks with pupils in whole class, group and individual situations to guide their thinking, together with opportunities for collaborative learning to promote critical thinking and problem solving was rarely observed (Hardman, 2008b).

Frequency of teaching and learning behaviours

Seven hundred and twenty-eight live lessons were analysed using the observation schedule designed to capture the frequency of teacher and student behaviours. A breakdown of the lesson observations by subject and year group is given in Table 6.

The 32 observable practices were categorized into four sections on the observation schedule. In Section 1 there were 15 teaching and learning behaviours covering lesson clarity, the setting of learning objectives, instructional variety (i.e., use of whole class, paired/group-based and individual teaching) and the general climate of the classroom. Six behaviours were captured in Section 2 covering teacher approaches to questioning, and six behaviours were captured in Section 3 covering teacher feedback and follow-up to the questions. Section 4 was made up of three behaviours exploring teacher management of the class.

Of the 32 observable practices whose frequencies were rated on a 4-point scale (1 = never observed; 2 = rarely observed (i.e., once or twice); 3 = occasionally observed (i.e., 4 or 5 times); 4 = consistently observed), it can be seen as shown in Figure 3 that:

- 16 were found to be never or rarely observed in over 90% of the lessons
- a further nine were never or rarely observed in over 80% of the lessons observed

As in the timeline analysis, the data suggest that teacher-fronted activities in the form of closed questions (17), cued elicitations (16) and use of the chalkboard (6) were the most

Table 5. Percentage of lesson time spent on teaching and learning activities at Grade 5.

Teaching activity	1−5 minutes	6−10 minutes	11−15 minutes	16−20 minutes	21−25 minutes	26−30 minutes	31−35 minutes	Overall
1. Explanation/Question/Answer	25.8	25.6	23.9	22.1	21.0	20.9	17.6	22.4
2. Rote/recitation	23.8	22.4	19.9	19.2	17.8	16.9	14.4	19.2
3. Chalkboard	20.0	17.4	15.5	14.2	14.3	13.3	12.5	15.3
4. Pupils working from chalkboard	1.5	3.1	4.0	4.6	5.3	4.9	4.7	4.0
5. Teacher reading	7.3	7.3	6.8	5.7	4.9	4.7	3.7	5.8
6. Pupil reading	4.5	6.3	6.3	6.1	6.4	5.7	5.6	5.8
7. Pupils working from textbook	1.2	1.6	3.1	5.3	5.4	6.4	7.5	4.4
8. Paired/group work	1.1	1.4	1.4	1.7	1.7	1.2	1.6	1.4
9. Pupil demonstrating	0.3	0.3	1.3	1.3	0.8	1.0	0.9	0.8
10. Teacher reviews topic	2.2	3.4	4.0	3.7	4.5	5.9	5.3	4.2
11. Teacher marking	0.1	0.5	0.8	1.7	2.7	3.8	4.2	2.0
12. Class management	5.3	4.5	5.3	5.0	5.2	5.2	4.6	5.0
13. Class admin.	5.0	3.9	4.8	5.7	4.1	4.2	4.6	4.6
14. Interruption	0.8	0.9	1.1	1.4	1.6	1.0	1.1	1.1
15. Pupils off-task	1.2	1.3	1.7	2.3	4.1	5.1	11.7	3.9

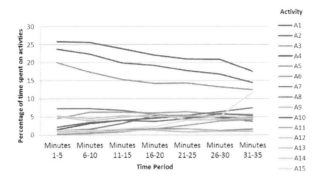

Figure 2. Grade 5 timeline analysis. Note: **Key**: A1, Teacher explanation/question and answer; A2, Teacher rote/chorus responses; A3, Teachers writing on chalkboard; A4, Pupils working from chalkboard; A5, Teacher reading to whole class; A6, Pupil reading to whole class; A7, Pupils working from textbooks; A8, Pupils working in pairs/groups; A9, Pupil demonstrating to class; A10, Teacher reviews lesson topic; A11, Teacher marking work; A12, Class management; A13, Class administration; A14, Interruption to lesson; A15, Pupils off-task.

common teacher behaviours. More dialogic approaches in the form of open questions (18), probing of pupil answers (24) and building their answers into subsequent questions (26) to create greater pupil participation in the talk were the least used. Similarly, pupil questions (27), peer tutoring (12), paired/group work (11) and pupil demonstration (21) were largely absent. The data also suggest that teaching behaviours designed to promote clarity through clear lesson structures, instructional variety and a positive classroom climate were not part of the teaching repertoire. For example, teachers rarely stated the learning objectives (1) of the lesson, checked for prior knowledge (2) or used a plenary to summarize and extend pupil learning (15). They also rarely displayed a positive to tone (8), knew pupil names (9), interacted with individual pupils (14), or encourage the equal participation of both girl and boy pupils (9).

Table 7 shows a ranking of the behaviours according to whether they were "never" or "rarely" observed. The table suggests that teacher use of the IRF to open up space in the whole class talk to allow for the co-construction of ideas between teachers and pupils through the use of open questions, probes and comments on pupil answers, and the building of answers into subsequent questions, was rarely practised, as was the use of peer tutoring, group work and pupil demonstration to encourage teacher-pupil and pupil-to-pupil discussion.

In comparison, Table 8 gives a breakdown of the most commonly observed behaviours in the 728 lessons. It emphasizes how teacher-fronted activities, through the use of closed questions, cued elicitations, writing on the chalkboard and teacher explanation, were the most regularly occurring activities.

Overall, the frequency data analysis suggests many of the teaching behaviours identified in the international literature as being effective in raising attainment are rarely practised by Myanmar primary schools, particularly teaching strategies that promote dialogue and discussion.

Table 6. Breakdown of observed lessons by subject and year group.

	Mathematics	Myanmar Language
Grade 3	128	128
Grade 5	128	128

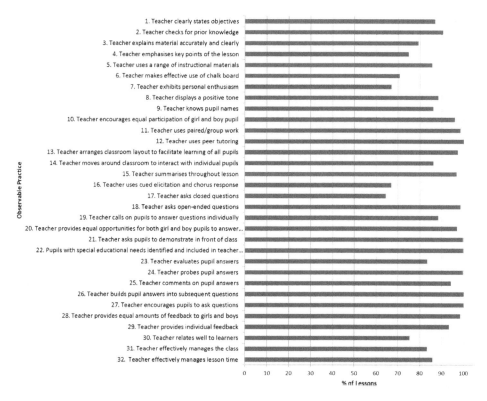

Figure 3. Percentage of lessons where the practice was "never" or "rarely" observed.

The data were further explored using the Mann-Whitney U test to compare whether there were any statistically significant differences in the observations across subjects and grades, and across mono-grade and multi-grade schools. While the following analysis of the ranking of the scores showed there were some significant differences across the subjects, grades and type of school, it should be noted that most of the observable practices were "never" or "rarely" observed in majority of the lessons.

Table 7. Teaching and learning behaviours "never" or "rarely" observed.

Teacher uses peer tutoring	0.0%
Teacher builds pupil answers into subsequent questions	0.0%
Teacher encourages pupils to ask questions	0.1%
Pupils with special needs identified/included in questioning	0.2%
Teacher probes pupil answers	0.4%
Teacher asks pupils to demonstrate in front of class	0.4%
Teacher uses paired/group work	1.4%
Teacher asks open-ended questions	1.4%
Teacher provides equal amounts of feedback to girls and boys	1.6%
Teacher arranges classroom layout to facilitate learning of all pupils	2.6%
Teacher provides equal opportunities for girls and boys to answer questions	3.0%
Teacher summarizes throughout lesson	3.2%
Teacher encourages equal participation of girls and boys	4.0%
Teacher comments on pupil answers	5.9%
Teacher moves around to interact with pupils	6.6%
Teacher checks prior knowledge	9.5%

TEACHERS' PERCEPTIONS, EXPERIENCE AND LEARNING

Table 8.   Summary of most common teaching and learning behaviours.

Teacher asks close-ended questions	35.6%
Teacher uses cued elicitation	33.1%
Teacher exhibits personal enthusiasm	33.1%
Teacher makes effective use of chalkboard	29.3%
Teacher emphasizes key points of the lesson	25.1%
Teacher relates well to learners	24.6%
Teacher explains material accurately and clearly	20.7%

Grade differences

The Grade 3 lesson observations were compared to the Grade 5 lessons for each of the 32 behaviours. It was found that in 29 out of the 32 teaching and learning behaviours there was no significant difference between the grades ($p < 0.05$). This suggests there was little difference in the underlying pedagogic approach used to teach across the two grades. Of the three behaviours that were significantly different (i.e., checking for prior knowledge, open questions and building pupil answers into subsequent questions) they were more likely to be observed in the Grade 5 lessons. In Myanmar language lessons, teachers were more likely to ask open questions and build pupil answers into subsequent questions.

Subject differences

When the Myanmar and mathematics lessons across both grades were compared there were statistically significant differences in 10 of the 32 teaching and learning behaviours ($p < 0.05$). In mathematics, teachers tended to use more explanation and make greater use of the chalkboard and other teaching and learning resources. They were also more likely to show enthusiasm and interact with individual pupils and encourage individual rather than choral responses to their questions, and to comment on individual answers and provide more feedback during individual seatwork in mathematics lessons.

When the grades were examined separately it was noted that there was less likely to be a difference between the frequency of the observable practices in Grade 5 subjects (Myanmar language and mathematics) (6 out of 32 behaviours showing significant differences) compared to the Grade 3 subjects (13 out of 32 behaviours showing significant differences). Where differences did occur it was found that the behaviours were more likely to have been observed in mathematics lessons. At Grade 5, teachers of mathematics were more likely to make use of the chalkboard, interact with individual pupils, evaluate their answers and provide feedback during individual seatwork. In the teaching of Myanmar at Grade 5, teachers were more likely to use open questions and build pupil answers into subsequent questions. At Grade 3, teachers of Myanmar language were more likely to ask open questions, whereas teachers of mathematics were more likely to make greater use of explanation, the chalkboard and other learning resources. Teachers of mathematics at Grade 3 were also more likely to emphasize key points, show enthusiasm in their teaching, interact with individual pupils to provide feedback on their answers and to use paired/group work.

Type of school

Table 9 shows a breakdown of the schools in the sample according to whether the children were taught in mono-grade or multi-grade classes and whether the school was located in an urban or rural area.

TEACHERS' PERCEPTIONS, EXPERIENCE AND LEARNING

Table 9. Type of school and location.

	Mono-grade	Multi-grade	Unknown	Total
Rural	34	71	38	143
Urban	30	2	4	36
Unknown	0	1	2	3
Total	64	74	44	182

As most of the urban schools were mono-grade an analysis was carried out for just the mono-grade schools to see if there were any differences between rural and urban schools. The analysis showed that urban schools were significantly more likely to display the observable behaviours (15 out of 32) ($p < 0.05$). Urban teachers were more likely to state the lesson objectives and check for prior knowledge, and to use the chalkboard and other learning resources. They also showed a greater tendency to interact with pupils, including pupils with special educational needs, by calling on individual pupils by name to answer questions and by using more open and closed questions and to demonstrate in front of the class. There was also more follow up, through teacher evaluation, probing and commentary, to pupil answers. Urban teachers were also more likely to effectively manage the class and the lesson time.

When lessons in the rural mono-grade schools were compared to those in the rural multi-grade schools there were statistically significant differences in 10 out of the 32 teacher practices ($p < 0.05$). Where differences did occur, it was found that the behaviours were more likely to have been observed in the lessons in the mono-grade schools. Teachers in mono-grade schools showed a greater tendency to explain material clearly and accurately, to check for prior knowledge and emphasize key points throughout the lesson. They also showed more personal enthusiasm in their teaching and were more likely to encourage the equal participation of girls and boys, and to have a good rapport with the class. They also appeared to use more closed questions and cued elicitations.

Class size

The data were analysed to investigate whether there were any statistically significant differences in the frequency of use of the 32 teaching and learning behaviours due to class size. Three groupings were created: classes below 30 pupils; classes between 30 and 60 pupils; classes above 60 pupils. No significant differences were found in the teaching and learning behaviours in classes lower than 30; however, 23 behaviours were significantly different in classes above 30 (15 were significantly different in classes of 30–60). While it is difficult to draw any firm conclusions from the analysis as to the optimum class size for promoting the effective teaching behaviours, the use of group work and pupil demonstration was significantly different in classes of 30–60 pupils.

Overall, the frequency analysis suggests Myanmar primary teachers are using a limited repertoire of teaching and learning approaches based on teacher explanation, rote and recitation, with little attention being paid to securing pupil understanding through a blend of whole class, group-based and one-to-one interaction in which pupils play can an active role in the classroom talk.

Analysis of digitally recorded lessons

A sub-sample of 40 digitally recorded lessons from eight townships covering urban and rural settings was analysed to investigate the proportion of time spent on 13 teaching and

TEACHERS' PERCEPTIONS, EXPERIENCE AND LEARNING

learning activities. The average lesson at Grade 3 lasted for 28 minutes and at Grade 5 it was 31 minutes. A breakdown of the lesson observations by subject and year group is given in Table 10.

A continuous sampling method was used to record the amount of time spent on a range of teaching and learning activities in the sub-sample of 40 digitally recorded lessons. This allowed for the lessons to be observed in real-time and for the duration of each of the teaching and learning activities to be calculated as a percentage of the lesson time. It also allowed for more intensive qualitative analysis of the patterning of the teacher-pupil interactions uncovered in the frequency and timeline data. Table 11 presents a breakdown of the percentage of time spent on each of the 13 teaching and learning activities across the two subjects and grades[3].

Overall, the analysis shows a similar distribution of time on the 13 teaching and learning activities across both subjects and year groups to the timeline analysis and they triangulate well with the frequency analysis. When the data were aggregated, they show that teacher directed activities (explaining, question and answer, writing on the chalkboard, reading to the class, asking pupils to read, lesson summary, class management and administration) took up 80% of the lesson time (Figure 4). Individual seat work, where the pupils were working from the chalkboard or textbook took up nearly 12% of the lesson and non-curricular activities (i.e., interruptions, pupils are off-task) took up a further 5% of the time. More pupil-centred forms of learning (i.e., paired or group work, pupil demonstration) accounted for just nearly 4% of the lesson time. The analysis also suggests there was little variation in teaching approaches across the two subjects at both stages of the primary curriculum. In other words, teachers were using the same underlying pedagogy regardless of the subject and grade they were teaching, and there were few opportunities for pupils to contribute their own ideas through dialogic engagement with the teacher in questioning and answer exchanges, and in paired or group work or pupil demonstration.

More in-depth analysis of the teacher-pupil interactions in the 40 lessons found that it was common for the teacher to ask closed questions or to use cued elicitations usually signalled by a mid-sentence rise in voice intonation that was designed to get a response from the pupils during, or at the end of, an explanation or following a pupil response. Usually, the elicitation was in the form of a repetition or completion of a phrase or word and answered in chorus. Choral responses were therefore the dominant method of responding to teacher initiations, making up nearly 80% of the response moves.

It was also common for choral answers to receive no follow-up. When follow-up did occur, teachers usually affirmed an answer or praised it often by asking the class to clap. Teacher comments on pupil answers, whereby they would rephrase, build or elaborate upon an answer, were rare, as were teacher probes (i.e., when the teacher continues to focus on a pupil who has answered and asks for further elaboration upon their answer). The findings also show that when an individual answer was called for a boy was twice more likely to be asked to answer a question by the teacher than girls. Pupil questions were also extremely rare: in all 40 digitally recorded lessons only 12 pupils asked questions, eight of which were boys. Where textbooks were used, the observations suggested that their use

Table 10. Breakdown of digitally recorded lessons by subject and year group.

	Mathematics	Myanmar Language
Grade 3	10	10
Grade 5	10	10

Table 11. Percentage duration of teaching and learning activities.

Teaching/Learning Activity	Grade 3: Maths	Grade 5: Maths	Grade 3: Myanmar	Grade 5: Myanmar	Overall
1. Teacher explanation/question and answer	45.2	47.4	45.6	46.5	46.2
2. Teacher writing on chalkboard	14.8	13.2	11.8	11.2	12.7
3. Pupils working from chalkboard	6.6	5.6	4.8	5.2	5.6
4. Teacher reading to whole class	4.6	4.4	3.7	6.2	4.7
5. Pupil reading to whole class	2.3	3.2	4.8	5.3	3.9
6. Pupils working from textbooks	5.2	5.8	6.2	6.3	5.9
7. Pupils working in pairs/groups	1.6	1.8	1.4	2.1	1.7
8. Pupil demonstrating to class	0.9	2.1	1.8	1.6	1.6
9. Teacher reviews lesson topic	4.2	4.1	3.8	3.4	3.9
10. Class management	4.8	4.4	5.3	4.5	4.8
11. Class administration	4.1	3.4	4.8	3.6	3.9
12. Interruption to lesson	1.5	0.8	1.2	0.9	1.1
13. Pupils off-task	4.2	3.8	4.8	3.2	4.0

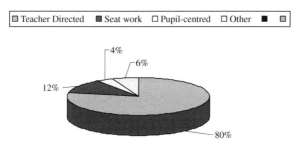

Figure 4. Percentage breakdown of lesson activity.

was often limited to the teacher reading to the class, interspersed with question and answer, individual pupil exercises, and pupils reading to the class, thereby adding to the directive nature of the teaching.

Overall findings

The overall findings from the three observation instruments suggest Myanmar primary teachers are mainly using a transmission model of teaching in which the teacher often used a chalkboard and/or textbook to transmit recipe knowledge for recall. The findings also suggest there was little difference in the way mathematics and Myanmar language were being taught across Grades 3 and 5. Pupils spent a great deal of time listening to the teacher explaining, asking questions, cuing choral responses, writing on the chalkboard, reading and managing the class. The closed nature of the questioning and direction by the teacher meant that pupils were rarely given the opportunity to ask questions or contribute their ideas. It therefore limited the extent to which pupils could develop their oral skills and critical thinking, and take responsibility for their own learning. Because of the high use of closed questions, cued elicitations and choral responses, teacher feedback on individual pupil responses was rare, offering very few opportunities for ideas to be developed or examined from other angles through the use of teacher probes, comments or questions that build on pupil answers.

In addition to the lack of dialogic engagement between teachers and pupils in whole class teaching, there was very little paired or group work to promote problem solving activities. Breaks in this pattern occurred when children were called to the front of the classroom to work at the blackboard or recite. Where textbooks were present in the classroom, they were often not well used by the teachers to promote active learning through paired or group activities or individual research. Teachers appeared to largely work through the textbook exercises and set tests at the end of a chapter, thereby adding to the emphasis on rote and memorization and passivity of the learning.

Many of the teachers observed were working in an environment of genuine constraints caused by a lack of adequate investment in school environments. Schools buildings lacked electricity, learning resources and other facilities and many were in a poor state of repair, particularly in rural areas. Many classrooms were also overcrowded, poorly lit and ventilated with insufficient desks and chairs available, and because many of the schools were multi-grade there was a lack of walls or partitions between classes often resulting in a high volume of noise.

Discussion and conclusions

Overall, the baseline study of Myanmar primary schools suggests improving the quality of primary education in such a poorly resourced context presents a considerable challenge.

Where teachers lack training in multi-grade teaching and material conditions are poor, there are clearly limits on what teachers can do to change their teaching practice. However, research from low income countries suggests it is possible to change pedagogical practices and raise learning achievement through well designed and supported PRESET and school-based INSET system and programme that takes into consideration the contextual reality in which teachers work (Hardman, Ackers, O'Sullivan, & Abrishamian, 2011; Moon, 2007; O'Sullivan, 2010; Schwille et al., 2007).

Helping Myanmar teacher educators and teachers transform classroom talk from the familiar rote, recitation and exposition found in the current study to include a wider repertoire of dialogue and discussion will require professional development programmes that upgrade pedagogic knowledge and skills over a sustained period of time (Mulkeen, 2010; Timperley, 2008). By focusing on the classroom, school-based training at the PRESET and INSET stages can help teachers broaden the repertoire of whole class teaching currently found in Myanmar classrooms. Such an approach builds on the traditional model of whole class teaching but avoids the simplistic polarization of pedagogy into "teacher-centred" versus "child-centred" that has characterized much of the educational discourse in the international donor community (Alexander, 2008; Barrett, 2007; Ginsburg, 2010; Hardman & Abd-Kadir, 2010; O'Sullivan, 2006). It will also help to ensure there is a better balance and blending of local cultural practices in the different regions of Myanmar with internationally informed teacher education reforms (Avalos, 2011; Nguyen-Phuong-Mai, Terlouw, & Pilot, 2012).

In order to bring about such changes, school-based teacher development programmes need to start by helping teachers to explore their own beliefs by getting them to reflect on their classroom practices to bridge the gap between theories and actual classroom practice (Courtney, 2007; Hardman, Abd-Kadir, & Tibuhinda, 2012; Hardman, Aung, & Myint, 2012; Mattson, 2006; O'Sullivan, 2006). Therefore, in the context of Myanmar, a model of professional development which builds on existing systems and structures at the education college, school and cluster level is being proposed as a way of effectively supporting and developing teachers. Working at the school and cluster level will help to ensure teacher education is part of a broader capacity development strategy that supports all actors in the education system at national regional and state level, including, for example, township education officers who supervise schools, head teachers and teacher trainers, and that it is cost effective against all the other competing demands in a resource-poor environment like Myanmar.

While there are many good pedagogic and professional development reasons why teacher education and professional learning should be largely located in the school environment, it should also be recognized that such provision requires a significant investment of time and money in building partnerships, collaboration and delegation (Hardman et al., 2011). The capacity and training needs of those charged with organizing and providing the training, mentoring and coaching, such as township education officers and college tutors, will be central to the success of school-based training, as will the creation of incentives and accreditation for teacher educators who will be working with teachers in school. It also requires a clear division of roles and responsibilities at the national and sub-national level and between district officers, head teachers, schools and teacher educators.

The policy of teaching the primary curriculum through the Myanmar language is exerting a powerful influence on the quality of teaching and learning in some of the Townships visited by presenting communication difficulties for both teachers and pupils. Recent studies point to the advantages of using mother tongue as the medium of teaching and learning in the early stages of education (Pinnock & Vijayakumar, 2009). For the

TEACHERS' PERCEPTIONS, EXPERIENCE AND LEARNING

preschool and primary years in particular, teaching in a language which is not familiar to a child is often too demanding for them to cope with – particularly when they face other barriers to education, such as poverty, hunger and poor learning conditions. Not having access to primary schooling in a familiar language is leading to the exclusion of large numbers of children from education.

It also requires the appropriate training of teachers in the use of both the mother tongue and second language teaching to make the curriculum more relevant by connecting the learning to the pupil's experience, environment and culture. However, the linguistic complexity and financial implications of providing for mother tongue teaching in contexts like Myanmar where there are more than 100 languages spoken has to be recognized. Such an approach therefore requires an analysis of how the country's Myanmar language policy is affecting pupil participation and success in education and to determine which languages would be most likely to increase enrolment, retention and pupil learning.

In addition to the effects that a monolingual policy has on classroom interaction and learning achievement in Myanmar primary classrooms, the end-of-unit teacher tests continue to exert a powerful influence on instruction and the patterning of classroom interaction because of the focus on memorization and factual recall from the textbooks. It is important that other approaches supplement the current normative evaluation and that teachers have a thorough understanding of formative and competency-based assessment (Somerset, 2011; Wiliam, 2010).

Acknowledgements

The baseline study discussed in this paper was funded by UNICEF, Myanmar. We are grateful to UNICEF for their support but the views expressed are those of the authors

Notes

1. Third Planning Commission Meeting, 27 December 2012, Presidential Palace, Nay-Pyi-Taw; and Ministry of Education (2012). Access to and Quality of Education: Education for All in Myanmar. Naypitaw: The Government of the Republic of the Union of Myanmar
2. For the main INSET study, a stratified sample of 1,000 schools from 20 Townships covering a range of urban/rural, multi-grade/mono-grade settings and schools of different size and ethnicity was selected. Sixty schools from three of the 20 Townships were selected to act as a control group to the study. Learning outcome data for Myanmar language and mathematics for all 1,000 schools has been collected as part of the baseline to allow for post testing following the INSET intervention.
3. For the computerized observation analysis cued elicitations were merged under teacher explanation/question and answer and teacher marking was merged with pupils working from the chalkboard and textbooks as they often occurred together.

References

Alexander, R. (2008). *Education for all, the quality imperative and the problem of pedagogy.* London: Department for International Development.

Avalos, B. (2011). Teacher professional development in Teaching and Teacher Education over ten years. *Teaching and Teacher Education, 27*, 10–20.

Barrett, A. M. (2007). Beyond the polarization of pedagogy: Models of classroom practice in Tanzanian primary schools. *Comparative Education, 43*, 273–294.

Courtney, J. (2007). What are effective components of in-service teacher training? A study examining teacher trainers' perceptions of the components of a training programme in mathematics education in Cambodia. *Journal of In-Service Education, 33*, 321–339.

Darling-Hammond, L., Chung Wei, R., Andree, A., Richardson, N., & Orphanos, S. (2009). *Professional learning: A report on teacher development in the United States and abroad.* California: Stanford University/National Development Council.

Ginsburg, M. (2010). Improving educational quality through active-learning pedagogies: A comparison of five case studies. *Educational Research, 1,* 62–74.

Hardman, F. (2008a). Opening-up classroom discourse: The importance of teacher feedback. In N. Mercer & S. Hodgkinson (Eds.), *Exploring talk in school* (pp. 131–150). London: Sage.

Hardman, F. (2008b). The guided co-construction of knowledge. In M. Martin-Jones, A. de Mejia, & N. Hornberger (Eds.), *Encyclopaedia of language and education* (pp. 253–264). New York: Springer Publishing.

Hardman, F., & Abd-Kadir, J. (2010). Classroom discourse: Towards a dialogic pedagogy. In D. Wyse, R. Andrews, & J. Hoffman (Eds.), *The international handbook of English, language and literacy* (pp. 254–264). London: Routledge, Taylor and Francis.

Hardman, F., Abd-Kadir, J., Agg, C., Migwi, J., Ndambuku, J., & Smith, F. (2009). Changing pedagogical practice in Kenyan primary schools: The impact of school-based training. *Comparative Education, 45,* 65–86.

Hardman, F., Abd-Kadir, J., & Tibuhinda, A. (2012). Reforming teacher education in Tanzania. *International Journal of Educational Development, 32,* 826–834.

Hardman, F., Ackers, J., O'Sullivan, M., & Abrishamian, N. (2011). Developing a systematic approach to teacher education in sub-Saharan Africa: Emerging lessons from Kenya, Tanzania and Uganda. *Compare: A Journal of Comparative and International Education, 41*(4), 1–17.

Hardman, F., Aung, W., & Myint, A. A. (2012). *Development of a teacher education strategy framework linked to pre- and in-service teacher training in Myanmar.* Myannmar: UNICEF.

Hattie, J. (2009). *Visible Learning: A synthesis of over 800 meta-analyses relating to achievement.* London: Routledge.

Liu, Y. (2008). Teacher-student talk in Singapore Chinese language classrooms: A case study of initiation/response/follow-up (IRF). *Asia Pacific Journal of Education, 28,* 87–102.

Mattson, E. (2006). *Field-based models of primary teacher training: Case studies of student support systems from Sub-Saharan Africa.* London: Department for International Development.

Ministry of Education. (2012). *Access to and quality of education: Education for all in Myanmar.* Myanmar: The Government of the Republic of the Union of Myanmar.

Moon, B. (2007). *Research analysis: Attracting, developing and retaining effective teachers: A global overview of current policies and practices.* Paris: UNESCO.

Muijs, D., & Reynolds, D. (2011). *Effective teaching: Evidence and practice* (3rd ed.). London: Sage.

Mulkeen, A. (2010). *Teachers in Anglophone Africa: Issues in teacher supply, training and management.* Washington DC: The World Bank.

Nations United. (2011). *Progress report of the Special Rapporteur on the situation of human rights in Myanmar, Tomas Ojea Quintana.* New York: United Nations General Assembly.

Nguyen-Phuong-Mai, M., Terlouw, C., & Pilot, A. (2012). Cooperative Learning in Vietnam and the West-East educational transfer. *Asia Pacific Journal of Education, 32,* 137–152.

Nystrand, M., Gamoran, A., Kachur, R., & Prendergast, C. (1997). *Opening Dialogue: Understanding the dynamics of language and learning in the English classroom.* New York: Teachers College, Columbia University.

O'Sullivan, M. C. (2010). Educating the teacher educator—a Ugandan case study. *International Journal of Educational Development, 30,* 377–387.

OECD. (2011). *Building a High Quality Teaching Profession: Lessons from around the world.* Paris: Organisation of Economic and Co-operation and Development.

O'Sullivan, M. C. (2006). Lesson observation and quality in primary education as contextual teaching and learning processes. *International Journal of Educational Development, 26,* 246–260.

Pinnock, H., & Vijayakumar, G. (2009). *Language and education: The missing link – How the language used in schools threatens the achievement of Education For All.* London: CfBT and Save the Children.

Redden, E. (2007). *Myanmar teacher education review.* Myanmar: UNICEF.

Schweisfurth, M. (2011). Learner-centred education in developing country contexts: From solution to problem? *International Journal of Educational Development, 31,* 425–432.

Schwille, J., Dembele, M., & Schubert, J. (2007). *Global perspectives on teacher learning: Improving policy and practice.* Paris: UNESCO – International Institute for Education Planning.

TEACHERS' PERCEPTIONS, EXPERIENCE AND LEARNING

Sinclair, J., & Coulthard, M. (1992). Towards an analysis of discourse. In M. Coulthard (Ed.), *Advances in spoken discourse analysis* (pp. 1–34). London: Routledge.

Somerset, A. (2011). Strengthening educational quality in developing countries: The role of national examinations and international assessment systems. *Compare: A Journal of Comparative and International Education, 41*, 141–144.

Suzuki, S., & Howe, E. R. (2010). *Asian perspectives on teacher education*. London: Routledge.

Timperley, H. (2008). *Teacher professional learning and development*. Brussels: The International Academy of Education.

Timperley, H. (2011). *Realising the power of professional learning*. London: Open University Press.

UNESCO. (2010a). *UIS statistics in brief: Education profile – Myanmar*. Paris: UNESCO Institute of Statistics.

UNESCO. (2010b). *EFA global monitoring report 2010: Education for all: Reaching the marginalised*. Paris: UNESCO.

Vine, K. (2010a). *Progress in implementation of the child friendly schools programme in Myanmar over the period 2007 to 2009*. Myanmar: UNICEF.

Vine, K. (2010b). *Qualitative study of child friendly school implementation in Myanmar*. Myanmar: UNICEF.

Wells, G. (1999). *Dialogic inquiry: Towards a sociocultural practice and theory of education*. Cambridge: Cambridge University Press.

Wiliam, D. (2010). The role of formative assessment in effective learning environments. In H. Dumont, D. Istance, & F. Benavides (Eds.), *The nature of learning: Using research to inspire practice* (pp. 135–155). Paris: OECD.

Pre-service education for primary school English teachers in Indonesia: policy implications

Subhan Zein

Although English is only an extra-curricular subject at primary level in Indonesia, expectations over the improved quality of the teachers are exceptionally high . This is the case in the past few years in which the low proficiency of primary English teachers and their lack of teaching competencies have repeatedly been pointed out as major constraints. Unfortunately, it remains unclear whether this problem is attributed to the delivery of pre-service education in preparing primary school English teachers. This paper gathered data from teachers, language teacher educators, primary school principals, members of educational boards, and educational consultants. The data were analysed using Grounded Theory in order to examine the adequacy of pre-service education in Indonesia to prepare primary school English teachers as well as factors that contribute to its efficacy or lack thereof. The findings of the study demonstrate the need for specific preparation for primary school English teachers as well as further training for teacher educators. This present study is highly relevant to Indonesia and other Asian countries where teacher efficacy is a major concern.

Introduction

Recent curricular development in Indonesia stipulates a status alteration for English language at primary level from a local content subject to an extra-curricular one. This means the teaching of English under the new Curriculum 2013 is given outside school hours and the subject is not part of schools' final year exam (Sahiruddin, 2013). This status alteration however does not demote the requirements related to teacher qualification. Section 1.b of The Decree of Minister of National Education Republic of Indonesia No. 16/2007 on Standards of Teachers' Academic Qualification and Competence and Chapter 29 of The Government Law of Republic Indonesia No. 20/2005 On National Standard on Education (Departemen Pendidikan Nasional, 2006, 2007) are retained. As a consequence, teachers of English at primary level are required to possess an undergraduate degree from a pre-service institution in order to fully implement the curriculum at primary level.

Efforts to increase the qualifications of English teachers to meet the minimum requirements are evident, and the proliferation of English departments that offer English for Young Learners as an elective unit within their curriculum is indicative of such aspiration (Saukah, 2009). Nevertheless, expectations over the enhanced quality of English teachers at primary level remain exceptionally high over the past few years especially because of the low proficiency of teachers and their lack of teaching competencies (Asriyanti, Sikki,

Rahman, Hamra, & Noni, 2013; Chodidjah, 2008b; Suyanto, 2010). One thing that is unclear however is whether this overwhelming issue is attributed to the delivery of pre-service education in preparing primary school English teachers.

This paper investigates the efficacy of pre-service education in the professional preparation of primary school English teachers. It also examines the factors that contribute to such efficacy or lack thereof. The structure of the paper is as follows. First, it reviews relevant literature on teachers and pre-service education for English teachers at primary level in Indonesia. Second, the methodological tenets employed for collecting and analysing data are discussed. A section on the findings of the research appears after that, followed by a discussion section. Finally, implications arising from the present study are presented.

Literature review

Unlike secondary level in which English is a compulsory subject and is better established in terms of teacher preparation and material provision, English is currently an extra-curricular subject at primary level. The inclusion of English in the primary school timetable in 1993 resulted from the societal pressure demanding stronger foundation of English instruction at primary level in keeping with the demands of globalization. Sadtono (2007) stated that proponents of early English instruction in Indonesia argued that the teaching of English in secondary schools had been considered a failure; therefore, it is expected that early English instruction would contribute to advancing students' overall language competence. English at primary level is expected to improve the overall input of students' quality entering secondary schools.

To carry out English pedagogy in these primary schools, there are 47,577 primary school English teachers appointed, of whom 41,304 teach in the public primary schools, whereas 6,271 teach in the private ones. These teachers teach English only, as opposed to the 1,012,427 classroom teachers, the majority of which are assigned by their school principals to teach English in addition to the compulsory subjects such as Indonesian Language and Science (Kementrian Pendidikan Nasional, 2009). Zein (2011) categorized the teachers who teach English at primary level into two major categories on the basis of their prior educational background at pre-service level.

Teachers without English background

English teachers who have no prior English background are those who did not undertake a major in English during their pre-service teacher education. They come from three pools of the education system: (1) SPG (*Sekolah Pendidikan Guru*/ School for Teacher Education); (2) PGSD (*Pendidikan Guru Sekolah Dasar*/ Primary School Teacher Education); and (3) general undergraduate programmes such as Physics, Mathematics, Biology, among others.

A few of the currently in service primary school teachers are those graduating from SPG, which is equivalent to a high school level of education. The largest bulk of primary school teachers, on the other hand, comprise those who graduate from PGSD. PGSD is a four-year bachelor degree aiming to produce qualified and competitive primary school classroom teachers; to conduct research that involves lecturers, students, and primary school teachers in order to further improve the quality of learning and teaching at primary level; and to conduct community services and become part of the solution of the national education. Graduates of PGSD are conferred with a Bachelor degree in Primary Education, which is the minimum qualification to teach in Sekolah Dasar (SD) as stipulated by Section 1.b of The Decree of Minister of National Education Republic of Indonesia

No. 16/2007 on Standards of Teachers' Academic Qualification and Competence and Chapter 29 of The Government Law of Republic Indonesia No. 20/2005 On National Standard on Education (Departemen Pendidikan Nasional, 2006, 2007).

Although they might have acquired knowledge and skills related to young learner pedagogy, classroom pedagogy, theories of teaching, educational philosophies, teaching practicum, and learning assessment, PGSD graduates' exposure to English is limited. The reason is because they only learn a unit called *English for University Students*, which is taught for 2–4 credit points (100–200 minutes/week) in order to provide them with some general English preparation (Suyanto, 2010). Similarly, most graduates of other non-English programmes such as Biology, Mathematics, Indonesian Language, would have learned the unit at their undergraduate level. This group of teachers might have also obtained a certificate in English language of any kind from a private English course but have no specific preparation in English education during their pre-service education (Author, 2011).

The appointment of teachers who have no English background is prominent in many areas throughout the country such as Bandung, DKI Jakarta, Medan, Malang, Sidoarjo, and Blitar (Damayanti, Muslim, & Nurlaelawati, 2008; Ernidawati, 2002; Lestari, 2003; Nizar, 2004; Suyanto & Chodidjah, 2002). The fact that English occupies an important space in Indonesia, as it is encouraged by stakeholders at various levels: government, employers, and parents (Lamb & Coleman, 2008), seems to have resulted in a widely held belief amongst the community which associates English with beneficial intellectual capital. A school's reputation in the community may also be lifted as long as it offers English in their curriculum timetable. As Suyanto (2010) pointed out, this explains why many school principals put value in offering English instruction in their school. While in most cases classroom teachers are appointed to teach English to the students in their class, in some cases teachers with slightly higher English proficiency despite lack of qualifications are appointed to teach.

Teachers with English background

Teachers of English at primary level with English background are those who undertook a major in an English-related field during their pre-service education. Saukah (2009) stated that the establishment of the consecutive system within higher education in Indonesia allows student teachers to plan their study in two modes.

First, students may attend the English Language Education Programme, in which they decide to become English teachers right from the beginning. In other words, prospective student teachers have already decided to become English teachers by the time they enrolled in the English Language Education Programme. The programme is generally offered in The Institution of Education and Teacher Education (*Lembaga Pendidikan Tenaga Keguruan* – henceforth LPTK). The LPTK is the main form of pre-service teacher education for English teachers in Indonesia, consisting of both public and private higher education institutions whose main role is providing education and pedagogical training for those who are interested in teaching in junior and senior high schools (Cahyono, 2006). According to Saukah (2009), those who graduate from this programme are conferred with a Bachelor of Education in English Language. Teachers graduating from the English Language Education Programme will have acquired English language proficiency knowledge, and knowledge and skills related to curriculum, syllabus, language testing and assessment, teaching methodologies, teaching skills, and materials development. Depending on the emphasis of their curriculum, some English Language Education Programmes offer EYL (English for Young Learners) while others do not.

The second mode is the one that allows students to attend the English Study Programme. The programme is a four-year undergraduate degree consisting of 146 credit points, and offers its graduates a Bachelor of Arts in English. Concentrations in the English Study Programme vary between one university and another, but the most prominent ones are: (1) Linguistics; (2) English Literature; and (3) Translation. Students graduating from the English Study Programme will have acquired a strong foundation in areas of English linguistics (e.g., phonology, syntax, morphology, and semantics), English literature (prose, poem, and drama), or translation studies. EYL (English for Young Learners) is not offered to students of this programme, but English pedagogy is covered in general from units such as Teaching English as a Foreign Language (TEFL).

What can pre-service education do?

The main issue with primary school English teaching, like it has ever been, is the huge shortage of competent and qualified English teachers (Luciana, 2006; Sadtono, 2007; Suyanto, 2010). It has been demonstrated that the quality of English education at primary level is not particularly satisfying (Chodidjah, 2008a; Sadtono, 2007). Many teachers are employed by the schools, even though they are not qualified in English and have limited English proficiency (Chodidjah, 2008a, 2008b; Karani, 2006; Suyanto, 2009, 2010). Chodidjah (2008b) pointed out that some parents are so dissatisfied with the quality of English education at primary level that they send their children to private English courses as well.

But the extent to which such a grim picture is attributed to the delivery of either in-service or pre-service education or both remains unknown. As a consequence, calls for studies on language teacher education for primary school English teachers have been made (Chodidjah, 2007, 2008a; Sadtono, 2007). While Zein (2012b) responded to the calls by conducting a study on policy recommendations for language teacher education for English teachers at primary level, no studies however have been specifically focused on pre-service education.

The examination of the efficacy of pre-service education in the professional development of English teachers at primary level remains a relatively underexplored area. It is largely unknown whether the pre-service teacher education has been effective in enhancing the professionalism of primary school English teachers. Furthermore, it remains to be seen what factors contributed to its efficacy or lack thereof.

This study was carried out in order to fill in the gap. It is the aim of this paper to investigate whether or not the pre-service education system in Indonesia has been adequate to prepare the teachers to teach English at primary level. It also examines factors that contribute to the delivery of pre-service education. Such examination is a vital starting point to frame the reference for a language policy proposal on teacher education for primary school English teachers. As Zein (2012a, pp. 85–86) argued, "the continuously increasing advocacy for a policy on educating primary school English teachers cannot be fully understood without an adequate framework of the various contexts in which the policy is situated".

Research methodology

A total of 24 respondents participated in this study; they spread across five groups, namely teachers, language teacher educators, members of an educational board, primary school principals, and educational consultants.

The 13 teachers participating in this study were from seven provinces in Indonesia, namely Banten, DKI Jakarta, Central Java, East Java, Bali, West Nusa Tenggara, and North Sulawesi. They were selected based on the type of schools and location in order to ensure reasonable representation. Five teachers were from private schools, five were from public schools, and three were from national-standard public schools. Previous research relevant to primary school English teachers was conducted involving teachers in areas such as Bandung (Sary, 2010), Medan (Ernidawati, 2002), and Palangkaraya (Karani, 2006). It was decided to conduct research involving teachers in other areas such as Tomohon, North Sulawesi; Denpasar, Bali; Lombok, West Nusa Tenggara; Rempoa, Banten; and Tegal, Central Java, primarily to cover areas which had not been included in previous research. Furthermore, previous research in Malang (Rachmajanti, 2008) and DKI Jakarta (Suyanto & Chodidjah, 2002) may need to be followed up, and so it was decided to also involve teachers in these two areas.

Other groups of participants were four language teacher educators (LTEs), two members of the educational board (MEBs), two primary school principals (PSPs), and two educational consultants (ECs). These groups of participants were selected in order to match the purpose of the study, to generate rich and insightful data, and to corroborate information as gathered from the other group of participants (teachers), as suggested by scholars including Boije (2010) and Marshall and Rossman (2010).

Boije (2010) suggested the recruitment of participants through networking and formal invitation, and so these were implemented in this study. First, the researcher contacted his acquaintances to help find teachers who might be willing to participate in the study. After the teachers confirmed their willingness, they were contacted by the researcher who described the nature of the study. A formal letter was then sent to the school principals requesting to conduct an interview session with the teachers. Upon receiving the approval letter from the principal, the teachers were then contacted again to set up the interview schedule. The list of the teachers is provided in Appendix 1.

In sessions of semi-structured interviews, participants were asked the following questions:

(1) Do you find pre-service education adequate to prepare teachers to teach English at primary level?
(2) What factors contribute to the efficacy of pre-service education or lack thereof?

While most participants chose to be interviewed in Indonesian, some chose to code-switch from Indonesian to English or vice versa. Only two participants decided to be interviewed in English. These interviews were digitally recorded and transcribed. Interview quotations occurring in Indonesian were initially translated into English. In this paper, these quotations are typed in normal font, whereas quoted interview responses that took place in English are typed in *italic*.

The data collected from these participants were analysed by using Grounded Theory. Meticulous reading of the interview transcriptions was undertaken. In doing so, initial codes were identified by selecting appropriate key words and associates to "open up data" (Birks & Mills, 2011, p. 95). These key words were then entered into a Computer-Assisted Qualitative Data Analysis Software (CAQDAS) package, NViVo9, in order to help facilitate data management and analysis. Data from NViVo9 resulted in initial codes, which were then classified in a process called focused coding. When certain sub-categories became identifiable within the data, they were then put under scrutiny during the process of theoretical coding in order to identify core categories (Dey, 2004), and these were triangulated with the memos that were written during the process of data analysis (Birks & Mills, 2011).

The categories and focused codes are presented in the tables. The frequency of references is provided in the tables to indicate the degree of importance that the participants attached to a particular code.

Findings

Findings are presented under the following sub-categories: (1) The inadequacy of pre-service education; (2) The lack of specificity of English departments; (3) The lack of specificity of PGSD; (4) The lack of quality of teacher educators in English departments; (5) Overhaul of pre-service education.

The inadequacy of pre-service education

According to EC1, there are two approaches currently in use in pre-service education to produce English teachers at primary level. The first approach is "English department which focuses on English" and the second approach is "PGSD which focuses on several different subjects" (EC1). The data in Table 1 shows that most participants were dissatisfied with pre-service education in preparing the teachers to teach in primary schools, from both approaches. The teacher who graduated from PGSD (PSET8) did not give a positive response, a stance shared by the teacher who graduated from the SPG (PSET7). Both PSET7 and PSET8 stated that in their pre-service education they were "prepared to become a classroom teacher", and not an English teacher (PSET8). Similarly, PSET3 stated that he had "just graduated to become a Physics teacher" (PSET3), PSET2 had graduated from an undergraduate degree "since 1996 to become a French teacher" (PSET2). Furthermore, seven out of these nine teachers who had a prior background in English expressed dissatisfaction with their pre-service education. These include PSET1, PSET4, PSET5, PSET6, PSET9, PSET10, and PSET13. They pointed out that their pre-service education did not well-prepare them to successfully teach English at primary level. PSET9 stated that "the knowledge for teaching English in primary school is difficult" but what he "obtained from pre-service education was not sufficient" (PSET9).

Other groups of participants also showed their agreement with this, namely LTE1, LTE4, LTE2, MEB2, MEB1, PSP1, PSP3, EC1 and EC2. PSP3, for example, pointed out that "little of what graduates receive from pre-service education can be applied" in their vocation (PSP3).

Only two teachers (PSET11 and PSET12) expressed their satisfaction with their pre-service education. Both teachers graduated from the same university and stated that their pre-service education was "very useful" (PSET11) and "was very helpful for developing the lessons, especially classroom management" (PSET12). Their opinion was supported

Table 1. Codes relating to the inadequacy of pre-service education.

Codes	Frequency of references
Pre-service unsatisfactory	11
Pre-service inadequate	7
Pre-service satisfactory	2
Pre-service adequate	1
Quality gap between pre-service institutions	1

by LTE3 who stated that the course EYL offered in the university in four credit points was "adequate" to help prepare student teachers with the challenges of teaching English at primary level (LTE3). Such gap between pre-service institutions was shrewdly observed by PSP3 who stated:

> If we see some English departments, they have good English departments. They are adequate in terms of preparing teachers to teach English at primary level, so when the graduates teach in schools they are good already. But I could tell you that there are many English departments that have not been able to do so.

Specific issues contributing to this gap of quality between one teacher education programme and another are further specified in the subsequent sections.

The lack of specificity of English departments

Table 2 shows that the inadequacy of pre-service education to help prepare English teachers at primary level was distinctively characterized by lack of specificity of English departments. The majority of the participants referred to English departments as being "not specific", "not practical", "generic", and "too theoretical". Seven out of nine teachers who graduated from English major programmes expressed dissatisfaction with their pre-service education in English departments. These include PSET1, PSET4, PSET5, PSET6, PSET9, PSET10, and PSET13. They pointed out that their pre-service education was not adequate as it did not specifically prepare them to successfully teach English at primary level. The lack of specificity of English departments here is not exclusive to the English Language Education Programme but also includes the English Study Programme, because the teachers who stated their dissatisfaction above graduated from these two streams of English departments.

PSET9 and PSET13 who graduated from the English Education Programme revealed the presently occurring gap between the theory they had received in their pre-service education and the classroom realities, while PSET13 highlighted that during college he was "not prepared to teach English to children" (PSET13). PSET6 found it confusing when he had to apply his experience of "teaching practice in a senior high school that" he conducted "during his pre-service teacher education" in the primary school he was teaching (PSET6).

The findings also show that English programmes place a large emphasis on the theoretical aspect of teaching. Teachers such as PSET6, PSET9, and PSET10 believed that English programmes neglect the practicality of English pedagogy in pre-service education. PSET6 stated that English programmes "ignore the practical components such as teaching experience and classroom management". PSET10 stated that her pre-service teacher education "did not provide her with opportunities to prepare lessons and topics and to design materials that are appropriate for young learners" (PSET10). In a quite reasonably similar fashion, PSET9 pointed out that "the knowledge we received during pre-service

Table 2. Codes relating to the lack of specificity of English departments.

Codes	Frequency of references
English departments not practical	8
English departments not specific	5
English departments insufficient	5
Limited curriculum in English departments	2
2 credit points EYL insufficient	1
English departments old-fashioned	1
EYL varies in quality	1

was limited. It was useful yes, but in terms of techniques and methods, it's very limited, very limited" (PSET9). Data from PSETs were consistent with that of participants from other groups (LTE, PSP, MEB, and EC) who identified English departments as being "not specific", "not practical", and "lack of update".

Participants stated that both the English Study Programme and the English Education Programme without EYL are not specifically designed to prepare student teachers to successfully teach English in primary schools. The student teachers in the English Education Programme in particular are trained to become teachers of English at junior and senior high school levels. Two participants confirmed it in the following:

> So the curriculum of English for Young Learners is very limited, still limited. Because those who graduate from Manado State University, the undergraduate students, are projected to become English teachers in senior and junior high schools. (MEB2)

> Yes, in my view, in universities, as far as I am concerned, those teaching colleges prepare their students to become English teachers in junior and senior high schools, not to teach English in primary schools. (EC2)

Participants further suggested that not all graduates of English Language Education Programmes that offer EYL are reliable because the programmes are varied in terms of quality; not all programmes are of exceptional quality. This was confirmed by participants such as PSET11, PSET12, and LTE1 who asserted the quality of an English department in a pre-service education institution in East Java, while PSET10 highlighted the inadequacy of two credit points of EYL in a pre-service education in West Java. She stated that "within two credit points there are so many things we didn't cover" because "most of these two credit points are theories, very raw" (PSET10).

LTE1 stated that teaching English to primary school children is considered *"just as complicated and as complex as teaching older children, if not more so, more difficult, more challenging"* than teaching in high schools (LTE1), but practical components that prepare student teachers with hands on experience have not been given strong emphasis in the curriculum of English departments. The departments provide methodology units such as *"how to teach (.) speaking, how to teach reading, how to teach writing"* but provide no specific reference to prepare students teachers with young learner pedagogy (LTE2). Components such as "teaching methods, learning strategies, as well as using learning facilities, and most importantly the contents in language teaching" are the ones that have often been missing (MEB1) in many English departments.

LTE1 made a remark that during the early years of pre-service teacher education *"there's too much time wasted and not enough time spent on the practical skills of teaching"* (LTE1). During the first year of their pre-service teacher education student teachers *"have got to do citizenship", "religion"* and other units that were deemed as irrelevant to language pedagogy (LTE1). This explains that even when practical components do exist they are usually provided near to completion of the teacher education programme or in LTE3's words *"it is not until later in their course that they do teaching practice"* (LTE1). LTE4 agreed with LTE1 as she stated that many English major programmes *"are very much focusing on"* topics or units *"which are not related to the teaching itself"* (LTE4).

For this reason, EC2 stated that graduates of English departments are not ready to teach English successfully at primary level because "they are lacking of practical training during their pre-service education" (EC2). This explains why EC1 made the following cautionary remark:

> Do not assume that those who graduate from Education University of Indonesia or other teaching colleges are capable of teaching English at primary level proportionately. (EC1)

TEACHERS' PERCEPTIONS, EXPERIENCE AND LEARNING

The lack of specificity of PGSD

Table 3 shows that PGSD is not specific to prepare teachers of English to teach in primary schools. Participants argued that PGSD is not adequately specific in preparing student teachers to successfully teach English in primary schools because "graduates of PGSD are prepared to become classroom teachers" (LTE3) to teach various subjects and "not a particular subject (English)" (EC2). Relying on PGSD to produce English teachers has been reproached by three groups of participants: PSET, LTE, and EC because it does "not provide sufficient input on English", is "not aimed to teach English", and is actually aimed "to teach other subjects".

Table 3. Codes relating to the lack of specificity of PGSD.

Codes	Frequency of references
No sufficient English in PGSD	4
PGSD graduates to teach other subjects	3
PGSD graduates not to teach English	2
Teachers from English departments preferred	1
Employing PGSD graduates imprudent	1

Although PGSD students are required to enrol in *English for University Students*, no significant amount of provision on English language proficiency is given to them. As a consequence of such limited provision on English, LTE4 pointed out that:

> *Graduates of PGSD have almost no proficiency in using English, but they have some knowledge of English. But they have been teaching English in primary schools for some time, so they understand how to handle children, and, and how they actually talk with children in the first language, but they have no English to deliver the message.* (LTE4)

For PSET11, this results in the occurrence of a phenomenon in which "the right person is not in the right place. Teachers have to teach English, but their background is not English". Furthermore, PSET9 pointed out that the fact that PSET graduates "have not been prepared to teach English" makes the employment of teachers with no English background "not a prudent decision".

The lack of quality of teacher educators in English departments

Table 4 demonstrates that the inadequacy of pre-service training is distinctively marked by the lack of quality of teacher educators.

The reason for this, LTE1 argued, is because there are many *"old-fashioned lecturers"* whose teaching practices are in contradiction to what they prescribe. LTE3 further asserted that "the lecturers should become a model" but unfortunately "many lecturers teach but do not give examples" to the student teachers. They are incapable of giving *"inspiration"* and *"ideas to the teachers, to the candidate teachers on how to actually handle the learners"* (LTE4). Student teachers are given preparation on general pedagogy but are left without sufficient theoretical knowledge and practical ideas on how to deal with young learners.

LTE4 further pointed out that often teacher educators do not have sufficient exposure to classroom practice. This is evident in the following:

> *So many lecturers in English departments in Indonesia have no exposure to the classroom practice and therefore it's very hard for them to give inspiration, to give ides to the teachers, to the candidate teachers on how to actually handle the class. So I guess, eh, the failure of teacher training in our context is because the lecturers, which, you know, which they have to call themselves trainers instead of showing. While in primary schools teachers are demanded to be very practical and become a strong model.* (LTE4)

126

TEACHERS' PERCEPTIONS, EXPERIENCE AND LEARNING

Table 4. Codes relating to the lack of quality of teacher educators.

Codes	Frequency of references
Teacher educators not a good model	3
Teacher educators lacking exposure to classroom practice	2
Teacher educators old fashioned	1
Teacher educators do not give examples	1
Teacher educators qualified	1

It is worth noting that findings relating to lack of quality of teacher educators were generated almost exclusively from language teacher educators. None of the school principals, members of the educational board, and educational consultants raised their concern on the quality of teacher educators. Most teachers also did not express any views in regard to the quality of teacher educators. The only commentary gathered from teachers came from PSET11 who stated, "all teacher educators" in the university where they graduated from "are qualified" (PSET11).

PSET11's statement above should not be seen contradictory to the evidence generated from teacher educators. It instead indicates that there is a gap of quality between teacher educators in various English departments across universities in Indonesia, which reiterated the previous finding on the inadequacy of pre-service education. EC2 provided a similar view:

> In big universities, so far, we have good human resources. Some teaching colleges like Education University of Indonesia and other universities, they have good human resources, in my opinion, but others no. (EC2)

Overhaul of pre-service education

Table 5 includes codes relating to the necessity to develop an overhaul of pre-service teacher education to prepare teachers of English at primary level. For PSET1, an overhaul is vital for the presence of a pre-service education that caters for "the needs of the teachers" and takes into account "the situation of primary schools in Indonesia" (PSET1). Similarly, LTE1 stated that

> *If we're looking at the needs of, if we're looking what the needs of the teachers a:re, it all has to start back at the teacher training colleges, and it it's u::hm, that needs an overhaul, that that needs a complete change of direction. (LTE1)*

Participants stated that reform on the pre-service teacher education is necessary to help prepare student teachers with the demands of their vocation. However it is not something that can be done sporadically because *"the whole thing needs rethinking"*, *"money"*, and *"careful setting up"* (LTE1). Both LTE2 and EC2 confirmed their agreement. They highlighted the importance of having a master plan for redesigning the pre-service teacher education to provide adequate preparation for teachers of English at primary level. This is evident in the following:

Table 5. Codes relating to overhaul of pre-service education.

Codes	Frequency of references
Overhaul necessary	4
Overhaul needs setting-up	3
Overhaul needs master plan	1
Overhaul focuses on practice	1
Overhaul contextual	1

Yes, so the first thing is we need a master plan, it's something like a grand design of teaching English at pre-service level. (LTE2)

At the moment we need designing, eh what is it, redesigning teacher education in Indonesia. (EC2)

It has been suggested in the previous section that the inclusion of practical components in English departments is necessary to help prepare student teachers to teach English at primary level. Evidence drawn in this section however suggests that practical components are not exclusive to English departments. The curriculum at the whole pre-service education (including PGSD) needs to be redesigned by placing large emphasis on the practicality of teaching. This was highlighted by LTE1 in the following:

The whole pre-service teacher training, syllabus, is in need of overhauling with so much focus on the practical side of teaching and what teachers are gonna be facing in the real classrooms in the future. (LTE1)

Discussion

The findings generated from this study have demonstrated that three factors contribute to the inadequacy of pre-service education in preparing English teachers at primary level, namely: (1) the lack of specificity of English departments; (2) the lack of specificity of PGSD; and (3) the lack of quality of teacher educators.

The lack of specificity at pre-service level occurring in both English departments and PGSD reflects a similar situation in other Asian countries such as Vietnam (Hoa & Tuan, 2007), China (Hu, 2005; Li, 2007), Japan (Honna & Takeshita, 2005), Bangladesh (Hamid, 2010), and South Korea (Shiga, 2008) where no specific in-service preparation for English teachers at primary level is officially stipulated. Taiwan is the only country that obligates its teaching colleges to establish a specific programme within English departments to prepare English teachers at primary level (Tsao, 2008). The fact that educational policymakers in many Asian countries do not seem to have considered specific preparation for English teachers at primary level as necessary reflects their naïve conception of the professional qualities of foreign language teachers at primary level (Hu, 2005). It is in fact one of the factors contributing to the failure of primary school English teaching (Baldauf, Kaplan, Kamwangamalu, & Bryant, 2011).

Considering the fact that primary school English teaching in Indonesia has not been considered exceptionally successful (Chodidjah, 2008a; Sadtono, 2007; Suyanto, 2010), it is reasonable to argue that such situation is primarily attributed to the minimum preparation that is given to the prospective teachers.

The findings therefore are critical to the current pre-service system for English teachers at primary level. The current two approaches of pre-service (PGSD and English departments) seem to only produce a majority of teachers who found it difficult to make a linkage between theoretical references they had studied with the particular situation of teaching English to young learners.

This means the findings of this study challenge the employment of PGSD graduates. PGSD may enable student teachers to acquire knowledge and skills related to young learner pedagogy, classroom pedagogy, theories of teaching, educational philosophies, teaching practicum, and learning assessment but it does not prepare them with sufficient English skills. The irony is providing student teachers with knowledge and skills on young learner pedagogy, classroom pedagogy, and theories of teaching without particular reference of how they are useful to teach English is groundless. Without adequate provision on both the language skill and relevant references of knowledge and young learner pedagogy, teacher cognition is incomplete (Borg, 2006). This clearly suggests that the current PGSD is not an ideal avenue for those undergraduate students intending to teach English in primary schools.

Second, the findings of the study also challenge the current consecutive and concurrent systems that only allow those interested in primary school English teaching to come from either one of the three majors in English departments: English Language and Literature, English Language Education without EYL, and English Language Education with EYL. Relying on the current systems, which provide no specific preparation to teachers of English at primary level, may only maintain the present situations but provide no long-term solutions. The present pre-service English departments are inadequate to cater for the particular needs of teaching English at primary level. Even in English Language Education Departments that offer EYL, it is no guarantee that the allocation of 2–4 credit points of EYL will be able to tackle the increasing demand of primary school English teaching.

Another major finding of the study is the presently occurring gap of quality between pre-service institutions. This particular finding is consistent with Luciana (2006) who maintained that there is a lack of uniformity between various English departments throughout the country; the majority of English departments are inadequate in preparing English teachers at primary level. The culprit is argued to be the bulk of teacher educators who are not satisfactorily competent and have limited exposure to classroom practice, much less to young learner pedagogy. When teacher educators fail to give examples as well as to become models for their student teachers, it indicates a gap between theory and practice. Teacher educators have been old-fashioned in their practice that they may have made a call for a constructivist approach, which puts large emphasis on reflection, but employ knowledge-transmission approach of teacher education. They argue for an active teaching-learning process but actually implement a passive teaching-learning process. This is not exclusive to Indonesia, however. As demonstrated by Morais, Neves, and Alfonso (2005), such issue is one of the most frequently occurring problems in pre-service education.

Conclusion and implications

The inadequacy of pre-service education in preparing student teachers to teach English at primary level has been argued in this paper. Several policy implications arising from such inadequacy are as follows.

First, the fact that PGSD has been argued not an ideal avenue for those who are interested in primary school English teaching, is however not an excuse to exclude it from the equation. The statistics show that there are only 47,577 primary school English teachers but there 144,228 primary schools throughout the country (Departemen Pendidikan Nasional, 2009). This means there are more primary schools that need English teachers than those who currently have them. PGSD may possibly help to fill in the large gap by producing English teachers, but this is only viable through adequate provision of English skills and relevant practical teaching components. PGSD curriculum therefore needs to be restructured, and an overhaul on the system needs to be made.

Furthermore, the provision of practical components in English departments to attend to the needs of the student teachers to teach English at primary level is vital. This is in line with the contention that the view on teacher education, which does not put large emphasis on practice, has been increasingly challenged for its limitations and inadequacies. A growing pressure to rethink both the structure and practices of teacher education requires that consistent conceptual framework of reference that prepares student teachers with specific knowledge and skills pertaining to their occupational needs is made available within the pre-service system. This provides an answer to Lengkanawati's (2005) assertion for the setting up of standards within teacher education institutions.

Overhaul in English departments needs to allow more practical provision and techniques in teaching English to Young Learners, and this implies the current curriculum at English Language Education Programmes may need to be reformulated. What this means is that English Language Education Programmes may need to introduce innovations that allow specific preparation for students to teach English at primary level in conjunction with English at secondary level. This is of high importance because provision in English for Young Learners needs to be in perfect alignment with the currently established English teaching at secondary level. It has been argued that "with the introduction of English at the primary school level, teachers need special training in the needs of younger learners" (Nunan, 2003, p. 609), and so such innovation is expected to provide the answer to the need for a specific preparation (Raja, 2011) as well as to provide more robust foundation in English language to students prior to their secondary level education enrolment.

The overhaul that includes both PGSD and English departments needs to be contextually and carefully set up. Such an overhaul is expected to produce prospective teachers with relevant educational qualifications to conform to the Decree of Minister of National Education Republic of Indonesia No. 16/2007 on Standards of Teachers' Academic Qualification and Competence and Chapter 29 of The Government Law of Republic Indonesia No. 20/2005 On National Standard on Education.

Second, teacher educators at pre-service level must be given considerable provision in exposure to young learner pedagogy. The reason is because it is difficult for them to inspire their students who train to become teachers, if they have insufficient exposure to EYL. Preparation for student teachers to teach English at primary level is groundless without adequate preparation given to teacher educators who have no specific knowledge and skills relevant to teaching EYL. This is parallel to Korthagen, Loguhran, and Russell's (2006, p. 1034) contention that "learning about teaching is enhanced when the teaching and learning approaches advocated in the program are modeled by teacher educators in their own practice". Only when teacher educators are familiar with the daily challenges in primary school English teaching can they inspire their student teachers. The congruency of action of teacher educators with what they teach means teacher educators have the ability to become role models and to explain the pedagogical and didactical choices they employ in the classroom (Lunenberg & Korthagen, 2003).

While in the Indonesian case these two implications need to feature in the overhaul as recommended in this study, such implications are also relevant to other Asian countries where English is taught at primary level. In countries where a specific professional programme for English teachers at primary level is absent, such a programme needs to be made available within the pre-service education system. This is necessary in order to provide systematic, theoretical, and practical preparation to those intending to teach English at primary level. Moreover, teacher educators who teach in the pre-service system also need to be professionally certified, so they can better equip their students with both knowledge and skills that correspond to the occupational demands of their profession. Such a training scheme for teacher educators seems to go along with the policy alteration that needs to take place within the pre-service education system.

It is however important to note that the scope of the study was particularly limited to the identification of trends in the certain groups of participants in this study. This implies that the relatively small subjects participating in this study makes generalizations from this study undesirable. Further research that involves larger numbers of participants and other

TEACHERS' PERCEPTIONS, EXPERIENCE AND LEARNING

research instruments such as observations is highly necessary. Such research needs to display how other contextual factors such as the teaching of English at secondary level and the provision of materials, among others, are taken into account.

References

Asriyanti, E., Sikki, A., Rahman, A., Hamra, A., & Noni, N. (2013). The competence of primary school English teachers in Indonesia. *Journal of Education and Practice, 4*(11), 139–146.

Baldauf, R. B. Jr., Kaplan, R. B., Kamwangamalu, N., & Bryant, P. (2011). Success or failure of primary second/foreign language programmes in Asia: What do the data tell us? *Current Issues in Language Planning, 12*(2), 309–323.

Birks, M., & Mills, J. (2011). *Grounded theory: A practical guide*. London: Sage.

Boije, H. (2010). *Analysis in qualitative research*. Los Angeles, CA: SAGE.

Borg, Simon (2006). *Teacher cognition and language education*. London: Continuum.

Cahyono, B. Y. (2006, December). *The continuous improvement learning program for English teachers: A case study of a local government policy*. Paper presented at the 54th International TEFLIN Conference, Salatiga.

Chodidjah, I. (2007). Teacher training for low proficiency level primary English language teachers: How it is working in Indonesia. In British Council (Ed.), *Primary Innovations: A collection of papers* (pp. 87–94). Hanoi: British Council.

Chodidjah, I. (2008a, August). *Scrutinizing the teaching of English in primary schools in East Asian countries*. Paper presented at the ASIA TEFL International Conference 2008, Bali.

Chodidjah, I. (2008b, January). *English in primary school: Gem in the mud in Indonesia*. Paper presented at the International Conference on Teaching English to Your Learners, Bangalore, India.

Damayanti, I. L., Muslim, A. B., & Nurlaelawati, I. (2008). *Analisis relevansi mata kuliah English for Young Learners dengan kebutuhan pembelajaran Bahasa Inggris di Sekolah Dasar* [An Analysis on the Relevance of English for Young Learners with the Needs of Teaching English in Primary Schools]. Bandung: UPI Penelitian Hibah Pembinaan.

Departemen Pendidikan Nasional (Department of National Education). (2006). *Peraturan Menteri Pendidikan Nasional Republik Indonesia No. 20 Tentang Standar Isi Pendidikan* [The Government Law of Republic Indonesia No. 20/2005 on National Standard on Education]. Jakarta: Kementrian Pendidikan Nasional.

Departemen Pendidikan Nasional (Department of National Education). (2007). *Peraturan Menteri Pendidikan Nasional Republik Indonesia No. 16 Tahun 2007 Tentang Standar Kualifikasi Akademik dan Kompetensi Guru* [The Decree of Minister of National Education Republic of Indonesia No. 16/2007 on Standards of Teachers' Academic Qualification and Competence]. Jakarta: Kementrian Pendidikan Nasional.

Departemen Pendidikan Nasional (Department of National Education). (2009). *Data Pendidikan Sekolah Dasar Tahun Ajaran 2008/2009*. Jakarta: Kementrian Pendidikan Nasional.

Dey, I. (2004). Grounded theory. In C. Seale, G. Gobo, J. F. Gubrium, & D. Silverman (Eds.), *Qualitative Research Practice* (pp. 80–93). London: Sage.

Ernidawati, T. (2002). *The teaching and learning English at the elementary schools at SDNP Malang and SDNP Sei Petani Medan* (Unpublished master's thesis). Graduate programme in English Department at State University of Malang.

Hamid, M. O. (2010). Globalisation, English for everyone and English teacher capacity: Language policy discourses and realities in Bangladesh. *Current Issues in Language Planning, 11*(4), 289–310.

Hoa, N. T. M., & Tuan, N. Q. (2007). Teaching English in primary schools in Vietnam: An overview. *Current Issues in Language Planning, 8*(2), 162–173.

Honna, N., & Takeshita, Y. (2005). ELT in Japan: Policy plans and their implementations. *RELC Journal, 36*(3), 363–383.

Hu, G. (2005). English language education in China: Policies, progress, and problems. *Language Policy, 4*, 5–24.

Karani, E. (2006). *The implementation of the teaching of English at elementary schools in Palangkaraya, Central Kalimantan* (Unpublished master's thesis). Graduate programme in English Language Education, State University of Malang.

Kementrian Pendidikan Nasional (Ministry of National Education). (2009). *Data Pendidikan Sekolah Dasar Tahun Ajaran 2008/2009* [Educational Statistics for 2008/2009 Academic Year]. Jakarta: Author.

Korthagen, F. A., Loguhran, J., & Russell, T. (2006). Developing fundamental principles for teacher education programs and practices. *Teaching and Teacher Education, 22,* 1020–1041.

Lamb, M., & Coleman, H. (2008). Literacy in English and the transformation of self and society in Post-Soeharto Indonesia. *International Journal of Bilingual Education and Bilingualism, 11*(2), 189–205.

Lengkanawati, N. S. (2005). EFL teachers' competence in the context of English curriculum 2004: Implications for EFL teacher education. *TEFLIN Journal, 16*(1), 21–31.

Lestari, L. A. (2003). Should English be a compulsory subject in the primary schools? *Jurnal Bahasa dan Seni, 31*(2), 197–213.

Li, M. (2007). Foreign language education in primary schools in the People's Republic of China. *Current Issues in Language Planning, 8*(2), 148–161.

Luciana. (2006). Developing standards for language teacher education programs in Indonesia: Professionalizing or losing in complexity? *TEFLIN Journal, 7*(1), 19–28.

Lunenberg, M., & Korthagen, F. A. J. (2003). Teacher educators and student-directed learning. *Teaching and Teacher Education, 19,* 24–44.

Marshall, C., & Rossman, G. B. (2010). *Designing qualitative research* (5th ed.). Thousand Oaks, CA: Sage.

Morais, A. M., Neves, I. P., & Alfonso, M. (2005). Teacher training processes and teachers' competence: A sociological study in the primary school. *Teaching and Teacher Education, 21,* 415–437.

Nizar, H. (2004). *EFL teachers' performance at the elementary schools: A case study of three elementary schools in the city of Bandung* (Unpublished MA thesis). English Education Department Graduate School Indonesian University of Education Bandung.

Nunan, D. (2003). The impact of English as a global language on educational policies and practices in the Asia-pacific region. *TESOL Quarterly, 37*(4), 589–613.

Rachmajanti, S. (2008). Impact of English instruction at the elementary school on the students' achievement of English at the lower secondary school. *TEFLIN Journal, 19*(2), 160–185.

Raja, P. (2011). Should we teach English early? (Some considerations). *TEFLIN Journal, 12*(1), 12–21.

Saukah, A. (2009). Language teacher education in Indonesia. In B. Spolsky (Ed.), *English language teacher education in Asia* (pp. 1–28). Seoul: ASIA TEFL.

Sadtono, E. (2007). *A concise history of TEFL in Indonesia.* Busan: Asia TEFL.

Sahiruddin. (2013, April). *The implementation of the 2013 Curriculum and the issues of English language teaching and learning in Indonesia.* Paper presented at the Asian Conference on Language Learning, Osaka, Japan.

Sary, F. P. (2010, October). *A practice in teaching EFL for Young Learners: A case study in one primary school in Bandung.* Paper presented at the TEFLIN International Conference, Bandung.

Shiga, M. (2008). Development of primary English education and teacher training in Korea. *Journal of Education for Teaching: International Research and Pedagogy, 34*(4), 383–396.

Suyanto, K. K. E., & Chodidjah, I. (2002, October). *The teaching of English in primary schools: The policy, implementation, and future direction.* Paper presented at the 50th TEFLIN International Conference, Surabaya.

Suyanto, K. K. E. (2009). *English for young learners: Melejitkan potensi anak melalui English class yang fun, asyik, dan menarik.* Jakarta: Bumi Aksara.

Suyanto, K. K. E. (2010). *Teaching English as foreign language to young learners.* Jakarta: State University of Malang.

Tsao, F. (2008). The language planning situation in Taiwan: An update. In R. B. Kaplan & R. B. Baldauf (Eds.), *Language planning and policy in Asia, Vol. 1: Japan, Nepal, and Taiwan, and Chinese characters* (pp. 285–300). Toronto: Multilingual Matters.

Zein, M. (2011). One size does not fit all: Unravelling the needs of English teachers in primary schools in Indonesia. In *Proceedings of International Conference of Language, Linguistics, and Literature.* Dubai: Conference Committee.

Zein, M. (2012a). The contexts of English language teaching at primary level in Indonesia. *Journal of Teaching and Education, 1*(3), 85–90.

Zein, M. (2012b). *Language teacher education for primary school English teachers in Indonesia: Policy recommendations* (Unpublished doctoral thesis, PhD in Linguistics). The Australian National University, Canberra.

Appendix 1. Teachers' demography

	Teachers' Demography				
			Pre-Service Education		Length of
Types of Teachers	Teachers	Sex	Degree	EYL	Experience
Teachers without	PSET2	Female	B.A. in French	No	2 years
English Background	PSET3	Male	B.A. in Physics	No	1 year
	PSET7	Female	SPG	No	38 years
	PSET8	Female	PGSD	No	22 years
Teachers with English	PSET1	Male	Diploma 3 in English	Yes	1 year
Background	PSET4	Female	B.A. in English Language & Literature and Certificate IV in Education.	No	2 years
	PSET5	Female	B.Ed. in English Education	No	10 years
	PSET6	Male	B.Ed. in English Education	No	11 years
	PSET9	Male	B.Ed. in English Education	No	18 years
	PSET10	Female	B.Ed. in English Education	Yes	2 years
	PSET11	Female	B.Ed. in English Education	Yes	7 years
	PSET12	Female	Diploma 3 in Business English and B.Ed. in English education	Yes	5 years
	PSET13	Male	B.Ed. in English Education	Yes	8 years

Index

Notes: Page numbers in *italics* refer to figures
Page numbers in **bold** refer to tables

aggressive behaviour 63
Aguinis, H. 56
Ainscow, M. 70
Ajarn (teachers) 60
Albarracín, D. 84
Alfonso, M. 129
Allied Educators for Learning and Behaviour
    Support (AEDs[LBS]) 69, 72, 79, 86
Anderson, N. 7, 9
Argyris, C. 5
The Art of Innovation 5
Attention Deficit/Hyperactivity Disorder
    (ADHD) 78
Attitudes subscale 89
Au, M. S. 93
Aung San Suu Kyi 97
Aung, Wan 97
Australia: teacher concerns about inclusion
    84–5
authority: deference towards 59; with kind
    heart 63
autonomy, gap between desired and granted
    24–5
Avramidis, E. 69, 85, 93–4

balance charts, MPI *43*, 48
Balance Programme 71
Barrett, E. 71
Barseghian, E. 7
Becker, T. E. 34
behaviour: aggressive 63; as component of
    cultural intelligence 58; frequency of
    teaching and learning 105, 107–9, **108–9**,
    108; perceptions and 84
Bodycott, P. 56
Boije, H. 122
Brady, K. 80
Brown, T. 11
Bruns, D. A. 84
Buddhism 58
bunkhun (indebtedness) 59

Canada: teacher concerns about inclusion
    84–5
career development, reminders about 50
challenge scale scores: for Chinese cohort *44*;
    comparisons with corresponding countries
    47, **48**
Chia, Liu Woon 1
children with disabilities, in special schools
    69–70; *see also* students with SEN
China: educational reforms in 33–4; School
    Curriculum Reform (2001) 33–4, 48; school
    teachers 50; Teacher Education Reform
    (2007) 33–4, 48; UGS teachers 40, 51
Chong, S. 93
Chong, Wan Har 68, 69, 71
Chow, J. Y. 71
Clarke, Anthony 33
closed questions 101
Code of Practice of Education: under Disability
    Discrimination Act (2001), Hong Kong 68
cognitive competencies 1
Coleman, H. 58
Collins, John 33
Colucci-Gray, L. 85
commitment: to being cooperating teacher
    33–52; concept of 34, 49; moral 45; to self
    50
comparative pedagogy 45
competencies 1
comprehensive education sector review (CESR)
    99
Computer-Assisted Qualitative Data Analysis
    Software (CAQDAS) package 122
confidence, teacher 85
Constas, M. A. 8
cooperating teachers 34–5, 40; challenges
    facing student teachers 43; commitment to
    pupils 49; feedback and communication
    practices 51–2; guidelines for 50;
    opportunity to share experience with other
    teachers 44–5; qualifications **41**; supervision

INDEX

experience **42**; 2-week residential programme for 40, 48; unclear policies and procedures 51; years of experience **42**

cued elicitations 100

cultural integrity 56

cultural intelligence (CQ): behaviour 58; defined 57; knowledge 57; lens of 56–8; mindfulness 57–8, 65

cultural norms, in education 58–60

cultural sensitivity, in teaching 56, 64–5

culturally relevant pedagogy 56

culturally responsive teaching 56–8; inner work of 58

Curcic, S. 69

Curran, M. 58

curricular autonomy 20–1, 24–5, 29

curriculum development: significance and effects 20–1; teacher autonomy in 19–30

Cyprus 70, 71

Denessen, E. 85

design thinking 4–16; application in non-design organizations 5–6; challenges perceived by teachers 13–15; defining 6; educators' interpretation of 9–10; empathy phase 9; features 12–13; integration with course content 11–13; introduction 4–5; literature overview on 5–6; practice of 7; in schools 6–13; skills 7; teachers' perceptions of 7, 8; in teaching and learning 11; traditional approach of teaching and learning 13; versus traditional thinking 10–11

Dewey, John 7

disabilities 69; inclusion of students with 85; intellectual 70; *see also* students with SEN

Disability Discrimination Act (2001) 68

Disability Standards for Education (2004), Australia 68

disparities, in education access 97

education: society/values/cultural norms in 58–60; system, in Singapore 86; *see also* inclusive educational practices; pre-service education, for English teachers

Education Act (1981), UK 68

Education for All Handicapped Children Act 68

Education for Persons with Special Educational Needs Act (2004), Ireland 68

educational consultants (ECs) 122

educational inclusion 69, 71, 80

Eisenhardt, K. M. 8

Elliott, Louise 97

empathy 9

English for University Students 120, 126

English for Young Learners (EYL) 120, 125, 129

English language: certificate in 120; lack of quality, teacher educators 126–7, **127**; lack of

department specificity 124–5, **124**; at primary level 118; at secondary level 119

English Language Education Programme 120, 124, 130

English Study Programme 121, 124

Ernst, C. 85

Evans, L. 80

experiences: negative feelings and 78–9; positive feelings and 76–7; of teachers 4–16; teaching or supporting students 85

external locus of control 63

EYL *see* English for Young Learners (EYL)

feedback and communication practices, uncertain 51–2

Ferguson, D. L. 79, 80

field notes 39–40

focused coding process 122

forced autonomy 25–6

foreign teachers: efforts in Thailand 55–65

Forlin, C. 71, 84, 93

Frederickson, N. 80

fun (*sanuk*) 59, 61–2

Games-Howell procedure 38

Gay, G. 56–8

Glasman, L. R. 84

Goh, Christine C.M. 1

Grounded Theory 122

group-based activities, collectivistic 63–4

Hallinger, P. 59

happiness 77

Hardman, Frank 97

hierarchy (*kreng jai*) 59, 62–3

Hofstede, G. 59

Hong Kong: teacher concerns about inclusion 84–5

Hong Kong Education Bureau 70

Hong, Won-Pyo 19

Horne, P. E. 80

Howe, E. R. 99

Huan, Vivien S. 68, 69, 71

Hunt, Brian 55

in-service education and training (INSET) programme 99

inclusion: educational 69, 71, 80; perceptions towards 83–94; teacher concerns about 84–5; *see also* staff perceptions towards inclusion

inclusive educational practices: history, in Singapore 69; students with SEN 86–7; teachers' concerns about 70–2; teachers' experience with 68–81; teachers' perceptions towards 83–94; variations in 69–70; *see also* staff perceptions towards inclusion

Individuals with Disabilities Education Act 68

INDEX

Indonesia: pre-service education for primary school English teachers 118–31
The Institution of Education and Teacher Education 120
intellectual disability 70
interpersonal competencies 1
Interpretive Phenomenological Analysis (IPA) 74
intrapersonal competencies 1
Ireland 68, 70
Irvine, J. J. 58
Israel 70

jai dee (authority with kind heart) 63
jai ron (hot heart) 63
jai yen (cool heart) 63

Kainzbauer, Astrid 55
Kalyva, E. 85, 93–4
Kantamara, P. 59
Kaur, Sarinajit 83
Keen, M. 71
Kegan, R. 65
Kelly, David 5
Kennedy, K. 21
Kennedy, P. 65
Knoors, H. 85
knowledge: as component of cultural intelligence 57; content 19, 20, 29; of design thinking 9; guided co-construction of 105; of policies 92, 93; practical 45; prior, checking for 109, 110; and skills 72, 79, 85, 114, 120, 128, 130
Korthagen, F. A. 130
Koutrouba, K. 70
kreng jai (hierarchy) 59, 62–3
Krieger, M. 7

Ladson-Billings G. 56
language teacher educators (LTEs) 122
learning: cultural 58; design thinking in 11, 13; environment, in Thailand 61; mutual 45; reduction of students' burdens of 21–2, 26, 27; time out to monitor pupil 49
Lembaga Pendidikan Tenaga Keguruan (LPTK): pre-service teacher education, for Indonesian English teachers 120
Lengkanawati, N. S. 130
Liedtka, J. 6
Lijie, Lu 33
localized class content, for Thai context 64
Lockwood, T. 6
Loguhran, J. 130
Loreman, T. 84
Lucas, T. 58

Ma, Yunpeng 33
Marshall, C. 122
Martin, R. 6

McAllister, G. 58
members of the educational board (MEBs) 122
Mentoring Profile Inventory (MPI) 34; aggregate reports 38–9; balance charts, for Chinese cohort *43*, 48; challenges for different countries *47*, **48**; challenge scale scores, for Chinese cohort *44*; comparative analysis 38–9; individual analysis 35–8; items/scales/balance charts **37**; macro-level analysis 42–3; micro-level analysis 43–4; motivators for different countries *46*, **46**; motivator scale scores for Chinese cohort *44*; sample report *36*; teachers' responses to open-ended questions 44–5, 48
Meyer, J. P. 34
Meyers, H. 94
mindfulness 57–8, 64–5
Ministry of Education (MOE) 99; plans 69
Ministry of Education, Science and Technology (MEST) 22
Mogharreban, C. C. 84
Montessori, Maria 7
Montgomery, W. 57, 58
Morais, A. M. 129
moral commitments 45
motivator scale scores, MPI: for Chinese cohort *44*; comparisons with corresponding countries *46*, **46**
Mtika, P. 85
Musti-Rao, S. 69
mutual learning 45
Myanmar: improving quality of education 99; pedagogical practices, in primary schools 97–115

National Curriculum (2009), South Korea 19, 22–3, 25
negative feelings and experiences: factors contributing to 78–9; teachers' 78
Neihart, Maureen F. 68, 69, 71
the Netherlands 70
Neves, I. P. 129
Nevin, A. 94
Ng, Zijia 83
Nonis, K. P. 71
North East Normal University (NENU): University-Government-School (UGS) initiative 33
NViVo9 122

open questions 101; teachers' responses to 44–5, 48

Patton, M. Q. 23
pedagogical practices, in Myanmar primary schools 97–115; breakdown of lesson observations **107**; class size **102**, 110; digitally recorded lessons analysis 110–13;

INDEX

findings 102–13; grade differences 109; languages of instruction **102**; lesson length, in minutes **103**; methodology 99–102; overall findings 113; reliability of coding 101; research instruments 100–1; sample 101–2; school type and location 109–10; subject differences 109; teaching and learning behaviours, frequency 105, 107–9, **108–9**, *108*; time spent on teaching and learning activities **104**, *105*, **106**, *107*, **112**; timeline analysis 103–5

perceptions: and behaviour 84; towards inclusion 83–94; and understanding of design thinking 7, 8

PGSD (*Pendidikan Guru Sekolah Dasar/ Primary School Teacher Education*) 119, 123, 128; lack of specificity 126, **126**

Phadraig, B. M. 70

Pink, D. H. 6

Poon, Kenneth K. 69, 83

positive feelings and experiences: factors contributing to 77; teachers' 76–7

power-distance, awareness of 59

practical knowledge 45

practice teaching 45

pre-service education, for English teachers: examination 121; findings 123–8; inadequacy of 123–4, **123**; issue 121; lack of quality, of teacher educators 126–7, **127**; lack of specificity, of English departments 124–5, **124**; lack of specificity, of PGSD 126, **126**; literature review 119; overhaul of 127–8, **127**; at primary level, in Indonesia 118–31; research methodology 121–3; teachers with/ without English background 119–21, 133

pre-service education and training (PRESET) programme 99

predictor variables: of inclusive disposition **92**; Spearman correlations between 90, **91**

Prideaux, D. 21

primary school English teachers: pre-service education in preparing 118–31

primary school principals (PSPs) 122

Primary School Teacher Education, PGSD 119, 123, 126, 128

Prince Edward Island Elementary Schools 71

problem-based learning (PBL) 63

problem-solving approach 7

professional development: model 114; staff attitudes toward inclusion 85

prototyping 12–13

questions: open and closed 101; open-ended 44–5, 48

research assistants (RAs) 73

restorative practice, within education contexts 87

Retna, Kala S. 4

Richards, C. 56

Rogers, M. R. 85

Rossman, G. B. 122

Roth, H. A. 56

Russell, T. 130

Sadtono, E. 119

sanuk (fun) 59, 61–2

satisfaction 76–7

Saukah, A. 120

Schon, D. 5

school-based curriculum development (SBCD) 21

School Curriculum Reform (2001), China 33–4, 48

School for Teacher Education, SPG 119

School Partnership Scheme 70

schools: children with disabilities 69–70; content standards in Korea 29; design thinking in 6–13; imbalanced curriculum 27–8; instructional hours, modifying 22, 25–6; pedagogical practices, in Myanmar 97–115; in Singapore 8; supporting students with SEN 94; type and location 109–10

self-awareness 64

self-efficacy, teacher 85

Sentiments, Attitudes and Concerns about Inclusive Education Revised scale (SACIE-R) 88–92; scores, means and standard deviations for **90**

Sharma, U. 84

Shulman, L. 21

Simmons, E. 80

Simon, H. A. 6

Singapore: design thinking implementation, in schools 8; education system in 86; inclusive education in 68–81, 83–94; teacher concerns about inclusion 84–5; teachers in 86

site visits 39–40

Skott, J. 25

social hierarchy 59

social pressure, on Korean secondary schools 27–8

Sosu, E. M. 85

Soulsby, C. 80

South Korea: constraints of regulated autonomy 25–6; features of 2009 National Curriculum 19, 22–3, 25; gap between desired and granted autonomy 24–5; inflexibility, in restructuring existing teaching staff 26–7; new national curriculum in 19–30; plan for enhancing school autonomy 22; reducing students' burdens of learning 21–2, 26, 27; social pressure on secondary schools 27–8; teachers' curricular autonomy 20–1

special education needs (SEN) *see* students with SEN

INDEX

SPG (*Sekolah Pendidikan Guru*/School for Teacher Education) 119

staff perceptions towards inclusion 83–94; confidence and self-efficacy 85; degree of training and professional development 85; factors associated with 84–6, 93–4; importance of 83–4; other demographic factors 85–6; supporting/teaching students with SEN 85

Stake, R. E. 8

Steliou, M. 70

Stoff, Christian 97

student teachers: in English Language Education Programme 120, 125; forms and guidelines, for assessing 51; promoting pupil engagement 49; reminders about career development 50; supervising, on practicum 33–4, 40, 42, 45; "time-out" to monitor pupil learning 49; *see also* pre-service education, for English teachers

students: burdens of learning, reducing 21–2, 26, 27; cultural codes 57; and teachers, learning partners 58

students with SEN 69–70; approaches to teaching 74, 76; confidence in teaching 89, 93–4; examinations 86; experience in supporting 85; inclusion 86–7; school leadership and 87; schools supporting 94; social acceptance for 80; training 71, 80, 85

Suyanto, K. K. E. 120

Suzuki, S. 99

Taiwan: preparation for English teachers, at primary level 128

Tan, S. Y. J. 71

Tang, H. N. 69, 71

Teacher Education Reform (2007), China 33–4, 48

teachers: adaptation of teaching and classroom management 58, 61; administrative concerns 71; teaching children with SEN 74, 76; autonomy, in curriculum development 19–30; challenges perceived by 13–15; classroom-based concerns 71; cooperating teacher, commitment to being 33–52; cooperative learning environment 58; concerns about inclusion 70–2; cultural learning 58; demography 133; duty of care 60; efficacy 85; efforts in Thai graduate schools 55–65; of English, at primary level 118–19; without English background 119–20, 133; with English background 120–1, 133; experiences 4–16; mindfulness 64–5; negative feelings and experiences

78–9; perceptions towards inclusion 83–94; personal concerns 71; positive feelings and experiences 76–7; in Singapore 86, 68–81; *see also* design thinking; pre-service education, for English teachers; staff perceptions towards inclusion; student teachers

Teachers of Students with Special Needs (TSNs) 69, 72–3, 76

teaching: in different cultural environment 55–65; cultural sensitivity in 56, 64–5; and learning behaviours, frequency of 105, 107–9; practice 45; students with SEN 85

Teaching English as a Foreign Language (TEFL) 121

Thailand: cultural context of teaching in 55–65; foreign teachers' efforts in 55–65; learning environment in 61; localized class content 64

Thomas, D. C. 57, 58, 64, 65

Thousand, J. 94

"time-out" to monitor pupil learning 49

Timmons, V. 80

The Tipping Point 5

Tomlinson-Clarke, S. 58

traditional thinking, design thinking versus 10–11

training, in special needs education 71, 80, 85

University-Government-School (UGS) initiative 1–2; for rural practicum placements 33–52; *see also* Mentoring Profile Inventory (MPI)

Urban Montessori Charter School 7

Vamvakari, M. 70

Vandenberghe, C. 34

Vermeulen, J. A. 85

Villa, R. 94

Villegas, A. M 58

Walker, A. 56

Wang, Fang 33

Weinstein, C. S. 58

Wettasinghe, M. 69

A Whole New Mind and Creative Confidence 5

Wilde, A. 69

Wong, Meng Ee 83

Woolfson, L. M. 80

Yeo, Lay See 68, 69, 71

Youngs, Peter 19

Zein, M. 121

Zein, Subhan 118